RESIDENSITY

A CARBON ANALYSIS OF RESIDENTIAL TYPOLOGIES

A|S ADRIAN SMITH + GORDON GILL
G|G ARCHITECTURE

ORO Editions
Publishers of Architecture, Art, and Design
Gordon Goff: Publisher

www.oroeditions.com
info@oroeditions.com

Published by ORO Editions

FOLLOW ONLINE
smithgill.com
smithgill.blog
Facebook @smithgillarch
Instagram @asggarch
Twitter @smithgillarch
WeChat: ASGG_Architecture

10 9 8 7 6 5 4 3 2 1 First Edition

ISBN: 978-1-954081-39-0

Color Separations and Printing: ORO Group Ltd.

Printed in China.

ORO Editions makes a continuous effort to minimize the overall carbon footprint of its publications. As part of this goal, ORO Editions, in association with Global ReLeaf, arranges to plant trees to replace those used in the manufacturing of the paper produced for its books. Global ReLeaf is an international campaign run by American Forests, one of the world's oldest nonprofit conservation organizations. Global ReLeaf is American Forests' education and action program that helps individuals, organizations, agencies, and corporations improve the local and global environment by planting and caring for trees.

CONTENTS

FOREWORD

What if we could build a mile high?

What if we could build a mile high? How would we experience traveling to the highest floors? What would it be like to live there? How much energy would it take and where would the energy come from? Why would we want to do this? What drives people to think about building higher and most importantly, is it even the right thing to do? Alternatively, why do some people live in houses in the suburbs, surrounded by land for miles? The question is, how do our choices of habitat affect the environment?

It is certain that we are all interconnected. We rely on each other for those things we cannot provide for ourselves, and with an increasing population comes increasing interdependency on others. We are urbanizing at an exponential rate and this movement toward concentration is posing fundamental questions about how we should build one of our most basic life necessities of how we shelter ourselves.

This book is an analytical study of residential building typologies. Its goal is to develop an understanding of the relationships between different building densities, with respect to the amount of land and infrastructure required to support them, and to discover how much energy, both embodied and consumed, is used in each typology. The study also investigates the relationship between density and open space from the viewpoint of sustainability, carbon emissions, and carbon sequestration, factoring in each to determine what building typology is the most sustainable on a comparative basis. As much as possible, real issues of construction and lifestyle have been taken into account in a balanced and objective manner with insights that are based on fact, not hyperbole.

This study documents one aspect of the ongoing research that we are advancing at Adrian Smith + Gordon Gill Architecture (AS+GG). It does not, however, consider the potential of clean-energy generating devices that can be applied to each building type. Its conclusions suggest that certain typologies that emit more carbon should be required to self-generate more energy from their site to be on par with the typologies that are low emitters. Our hope is that this study adds to the body of knowledge about the built environment and how we are affecting it with each building type.

INTRODUCTION

In the 21st Century a greater proportion of people live in urban areas than ever before. Currently over half the world's population live in cit es. Given current growth trends, urban population is on the path to reach two-thirds of earth's inhabitants by 2025 (***United Nations, 2014***). The choice of where to live defines and enriches our lives in a variety of ways. It also has an integral connection to the footprint we leave on the planet, including our carbon footprint, the spaces we occupy, the embodied energy of the buildings and possessions we have, and our ability to affect our communities by interacting with others.

In ancient cities, people lived in mixed-use environments out of necessity. It was not possible to get into a car and drive several miles to buy a loaf of bread, go to school, go to work, or conduct a business transaction. Instead, everything that satisfied basic needs and services had to be within a walking distance. Although these communities were modest, they offered everything that was needed for day-to-day life within a relatively small geographic radius. Business was conducted face-to-face and often the most convenient or dense areas of the city were those closest to regional supply chains. Some cities became more concentrated out of a practical need to protect occupants against outside threats. Historically, mixed-use, medium density, often fortified cities had greater advantages due to the necessities of survival.

As technology advanced and the world changed, the density of major cities became overcrowded and uncomfortable. Urban density was associated with disease, pollution, and poverty. In the 20th Century, people gained greater mobility and with it a choice to move away from such close quarters. The concept of the "suburbs" was developed partly because residents no longer had to live close to their place of work. People felt the benefits of having their own space.

In the last half of the 20th Century, and as the 21st Century has dawned, cities are once again evolving. More people work in service industries, manufacturing is cleaner, and in some countries, large cities have significantly reduced their pollution and industrial infrastructure, giving way to more vibrant urban cores that consist of business centers, government corridors, open public spaces, and culture facilities.

(Left) La Sagrada Familia, Barcelona, Spain

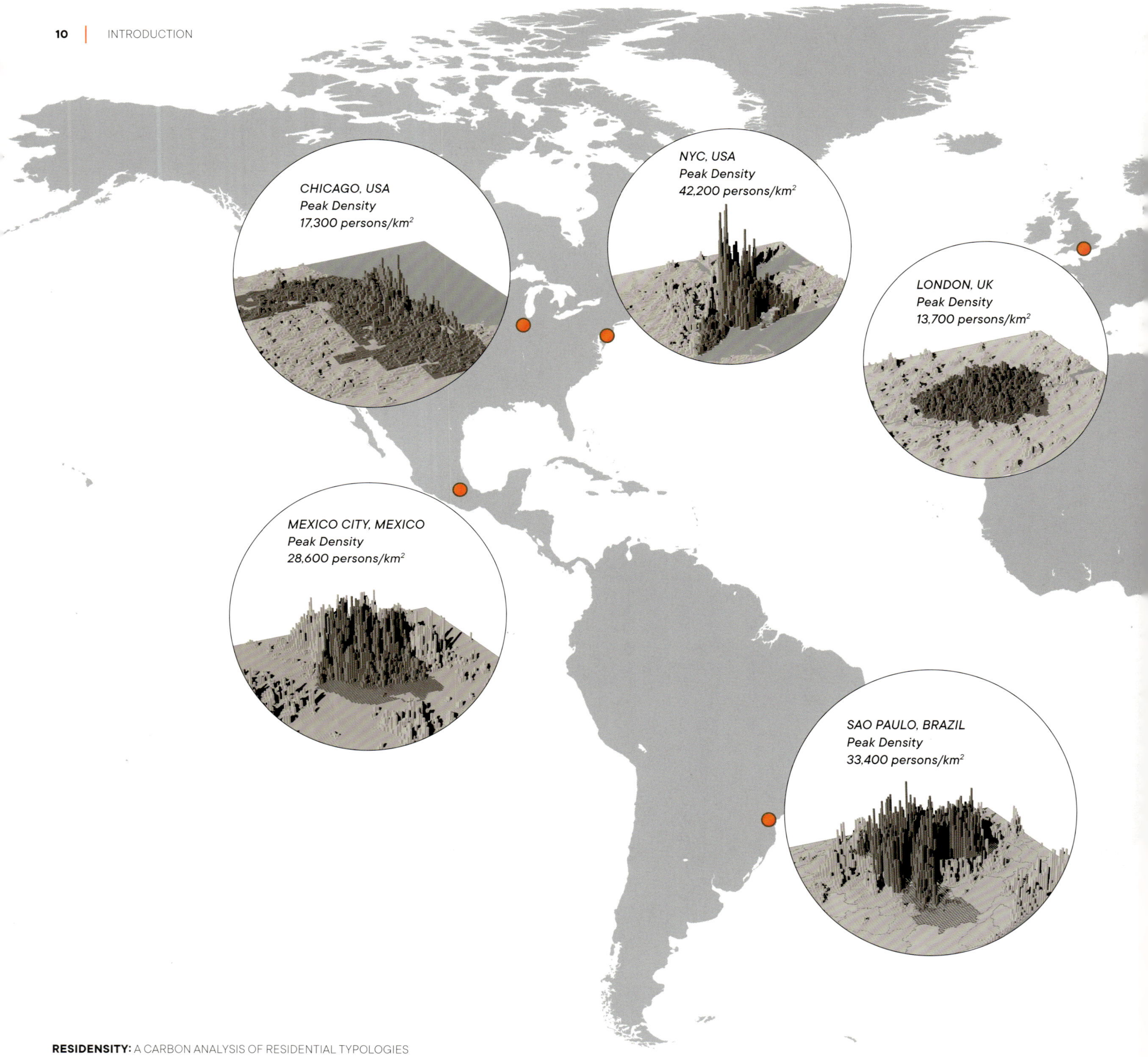
CHICAGO, USA
Peak Density
17,300 persons/km^2
NYC, USA
Peak Density
42,200 persons/km^2
LONDON, UK
Peak Density
13,700 persons/km^2
MEXICO CITY, MEXICO
Peak Density
28,600 persons/km^2
SAO PAULO, BRAZIL
Peak Density
33,400 persons/km^2

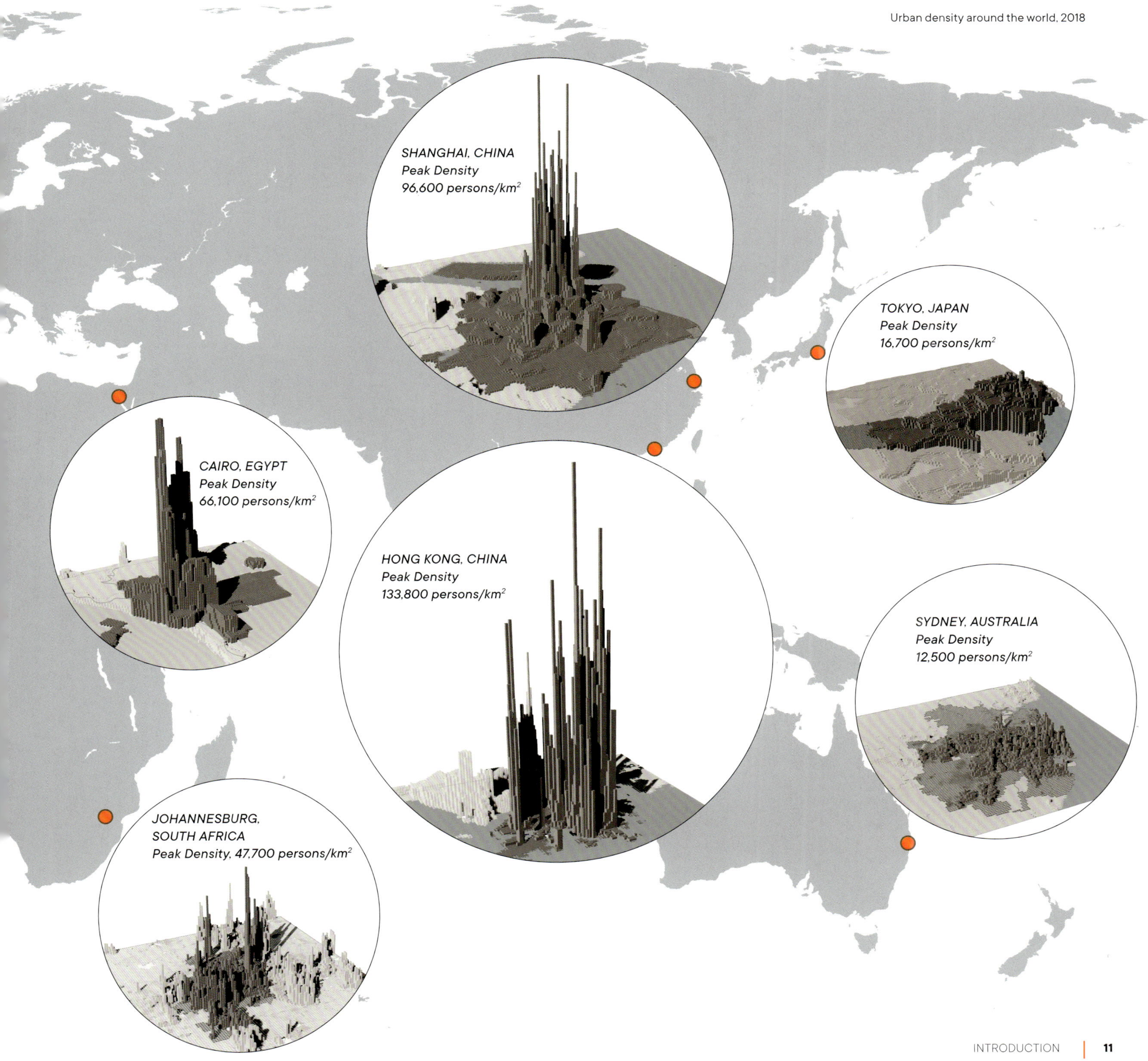
Urban density around the world, 2018
SHANGHAI, CHINA
Peak Density
96,600 persons/km²
TOKYO, JAPAN
Peak Density
16,700 persons/km²
CAIRO, EGYPT
Peak Density
66,100 persons/km²
HONG KONG, CHINA
Peak Density
133,800 persons/km²
SYDNEY, AUSTRALIA
Peak Density
12,500 persons/km²
JOHANNESBURG,
SOUTH AFRICA
Peak Density, 47,700 persons/km²

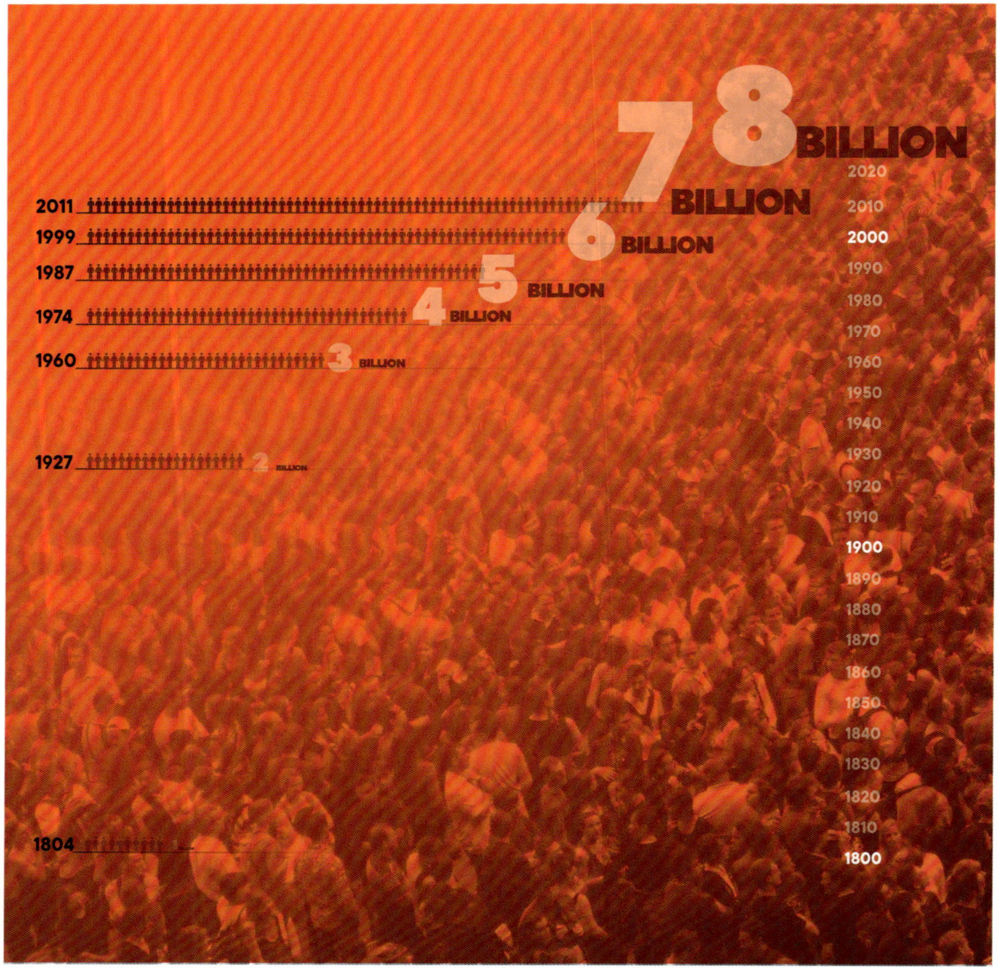

Figure 1 Global Population

What is the ideal density? How can we promote and balance the best quality of life at the lowest carbon footprint? Is there a limit to how much density is appropriate, and what determines that? Just because we can build a building that is a mile high, what is it that informs us whether we should?

Due to the expansion of the suburbs in the late 20th-Century, low-density developments have taken over many United States metropolitan areas. However, as people are rediscovering the benefits of a mixed-use, vibrant, dense environment with a lifestyle of culture, museums, parks, and restaurants, many people are choosing to remain in, or return to, the city. As the city core evolves from a daytime-only environment, and more housing choices are developed, cities are increasingly becoming live-work environments again.

A growing number of millennials—the newest adult generation who came of age at the turn of the 21st Century—are choosing to live in the city because of better career opportunities, lessened commute times, and better access to a wider range of goods and services, among other reasons. Convenient transportation—walking, bicycling, ride-sharing, and public transit—is also a major factor. Density and mass transit are mutually reinforced. Transit systems promote and benefit from higher density around stations, just as higher density requires access to transit systems for inter-district mobility.

Much of the world's population has rediscovered how density can cater to a variety of people, promote a sense of community, and facilitate human interaction with diverse groups in a way that enriches our existence. They have found that a walkable neighborhood, that has access to goods and services—without getting in a car—can be enjoyable, healthy, and convenient. They have also discovered that the character of urban neighborhoods can offer unique access to local culture. In our society, populations are often still separated by their social demographics and cities and neighborhoods are changing with the definition of luxury and convenience. It should be noted, however, that high-density building typologies are not a low-cost solution.

This study explores the ideal built environment using a data-driven analysis to evaluate several building prototypes through a standard lens, creating a detailed matrix that can be used by developers, builders, architects, and planners as a guideline to design and develop low-carbon environments that will work to meet people's needs now and in the future.

BACKGROUND: URBAN DENSITY

In 2018, the global population reached over 7.6 billion people and is expected to exceed 8 billion by 2025 (Figure 1). According to a 2014 United Nations study, the population is expected to reach approximately 11 billion by the end the century (Figure 2). This unprecedented growth will prompt an increase in overall average population density, from 53.3 people/km^2 in 2010, to 62.6 in 2025, reaching 86.2 people/km^2 by 2100 ***(United Nations, 2015).*** Looking at density alone can be misleading however. For reference, the current population densities of the United States and China are 32 and 142 people/km^2 respectively. These projections conservatively assume that as populations increase, fertility rates decrease, meaning that figures could potentially exceed these predictions. but do not reflect that much of the land area included in the calculation is polar, desert, or mountainous regions, which have very few inhabitants.

Figure 2 Population density, 1950-2100 (United Nations, 2015 estimate).

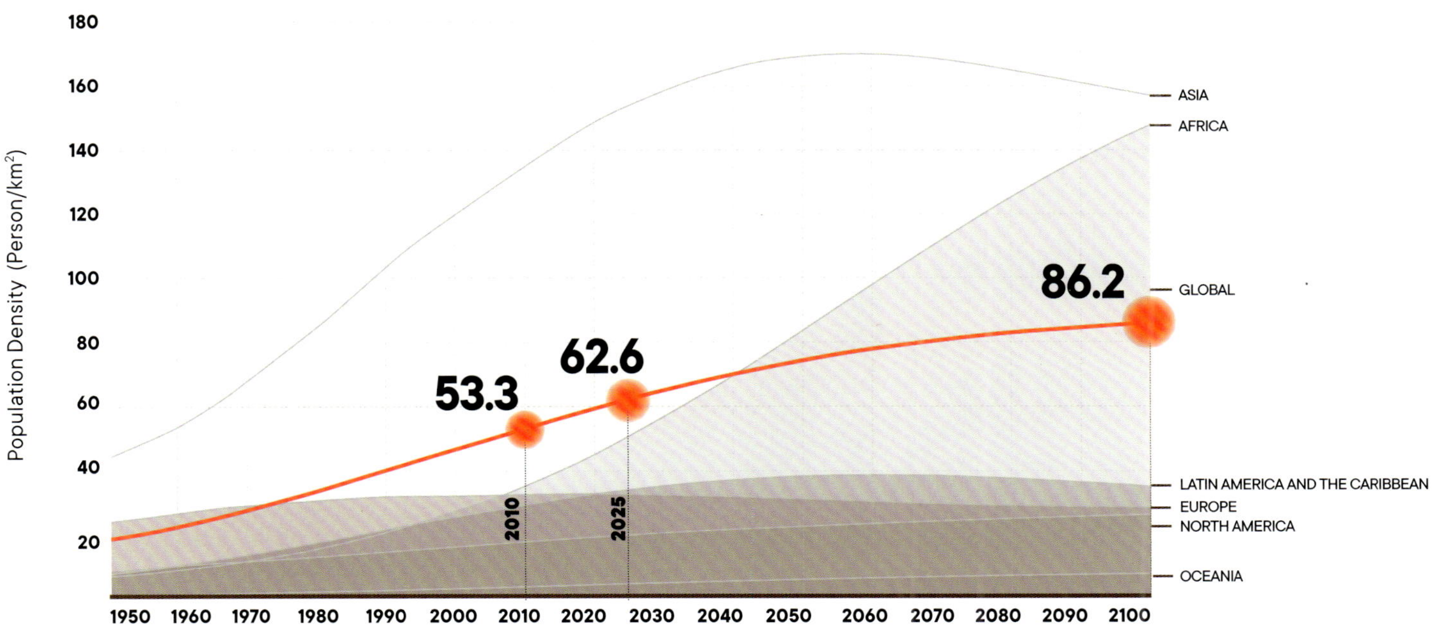

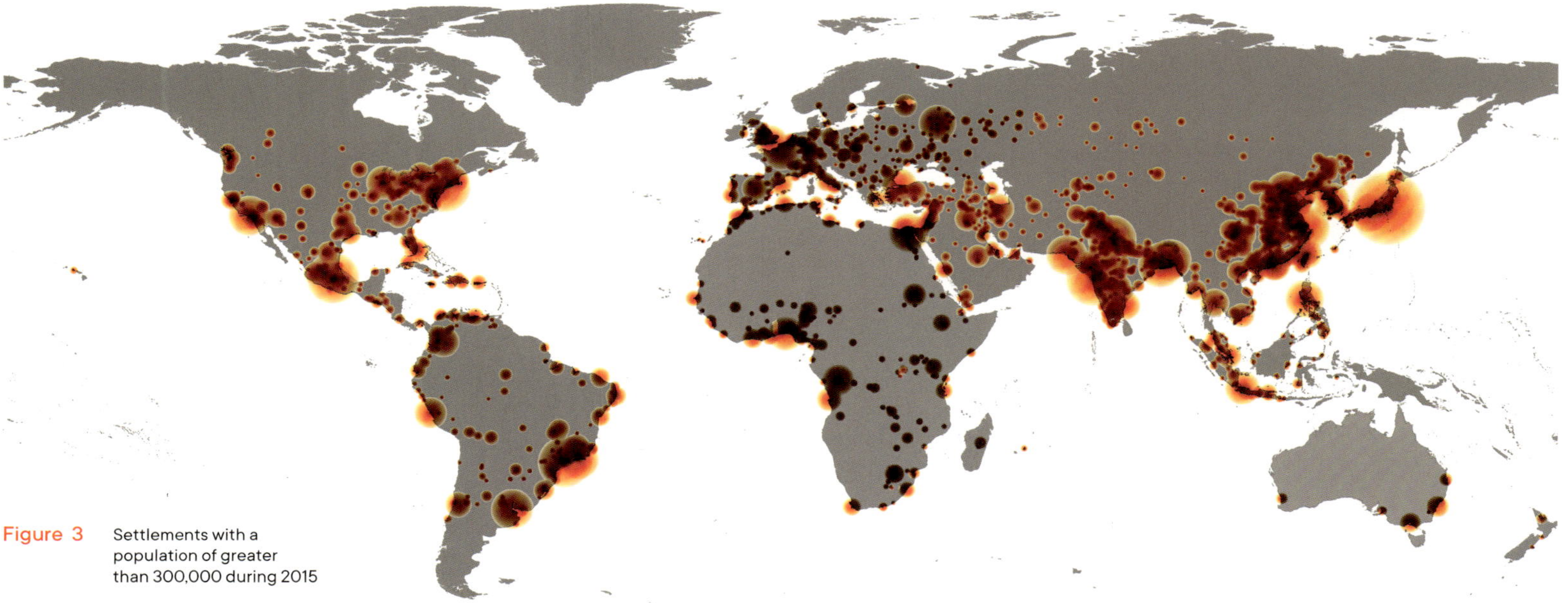

Figure 3 Settlements with a population of greater than 300,000 during 2015

Figure 4 Settlements with population over 1,000,000 during 1900, 1950, 2015

SETTLEMENTS WITH POPULATION OVER ONE MILLION, 1900

A more effective way to examine population density is to consider the number of people living in urban areas and the size and frequency of those areas. A milestone in global development was reached in 2010, when for the first time in history, more than half of the world's population lived in cities. The United Nations World Urbanization Prospects report predicts that this number will exceed 66% by 2050 ***(United Nations, 2014)***. In 1900, when the global population was estimated to be 1.6 billion, there were only 12 cities with a population of greater than one million people.

The number of settlements with a population of greater than 300,000 people is currently recorded at 1,692 ***(United Nations, 2015)*** and the distribution of these is shown in Figure 3. This growth in the number of cities has been accompanied by a rise in their density.

By the 1950s, when the United Nations began studying trends in urban growth, the world population had grown to 2.5 billion with 83 cities over one million people. By 2015, the population rose to 7.3 billion, with over 500 cities of at least one million inhabitants, including 29 megacities containing more than ten million people, and eight with populations exceeding 20 million, as illustrated in Figure 4 ***(United Nations, 2015).***

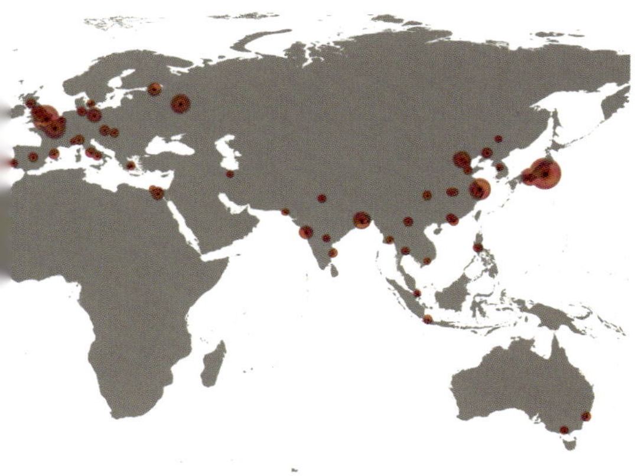

SETTLEMENTS WITH POPULATION OVER ONE MILLION, 1950

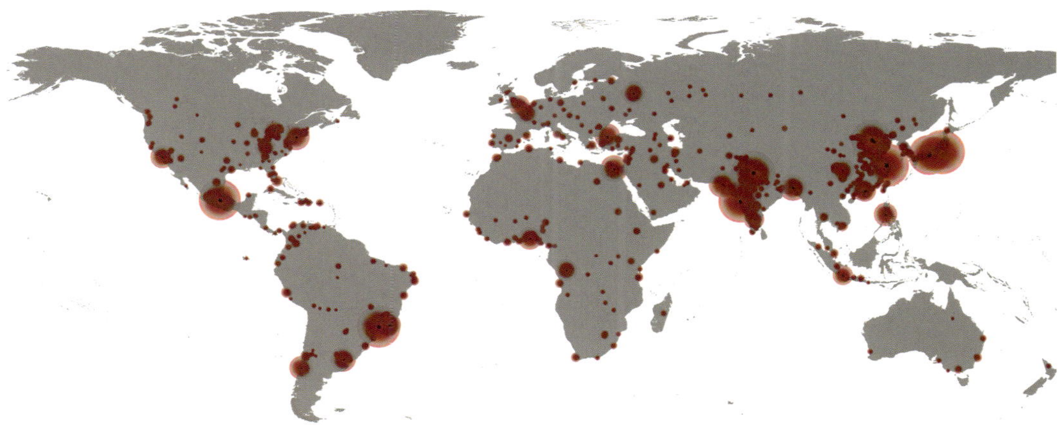

SETTLEMENTS WITH POPULATION OVER ONE MILLION, 2015

BACKGROUND: URBANIZATION

To understand the relevance of these figures, and the scale of the issues faced by urban planners and policy makers, it is important to address some of the reasons urban environments evolved into cities and megacities. While the initial formation of human settlements is difficult to precisely identify through historical records, a recent study analyzing historical settlement and population data ***(Reba et al. 2016)*** reports that the earliest record of true urbanization can be traced back to 3700 BC in Mesopotamia (modern-day Iraq), with later developments at or around the same latitude in the Indus Valley and ancient China.

The function of these early cities was diverse, ranging from religious focal points and fortresses of security, to centers of trade, to ancient political capitals. It is currently believed that the earliest settlements were built in the post-Neolithic period, prompted by the spread of organized agriculture and the decline of nomadic hunter-gatherer societies. People lived near others who farmed, forming settlements with strong agricultural productivity and crop storage that could support community development and encourage population growth. Some of these settlements grew into villages, towns, and cities, eventually developing their own economies and the capacity to trade with other regions, supporting even further expansion ***(Boundless, 2014)***. As cities matured, consistent trade links developed, and new settlements began to appear along major routes such as the Silk Road and the Via Maris. After the Industrial Revolution, cities began to develop as a result of natural resources, rather than agriculture. In the 19th Century, cities were built to support coal mining and mineral extraction industries and in the 20th Century, to support the automotive, steel, oil and gas industries.

Thousands of years after cities began to develop, their density continues to vary. While most were originally collections of one- or two-story buildings, many cities developed vertically, as horizontal expansion was restricted geographically, or by tribal rivalries. The City of Shibam in Yemen, once the capital of the Hadramaut Kingdom, for example, is often cited as the first planned vertical urban development. Its three- to eight-story houses, dating back to the 16th century, now have UNESCO World Heritage Site status

In the developing world, migration from rural areas has consistently been the main contributor to urban population growth. Mechanization of agriculture requires fewer farm laborers, forcing them to seek employment in urban areas, a pattern known as "rural flight." Additionally, many people move to cities for economic and social benefits, including increased access to education and healthcare, and a greater range of economic opportunities. Although cities continue to develop for increasingly diverse reasons, such as proximity to transportation, fiber optics networks, and recreational access, these factors are typically most common in countries with a high degree of technological sophistication. Their growth has led to the development of suburbs, which originated primarily as residential communities within traveling distance of a city. Suburbs eventually established their own identity with distinct industries, amenities, and social centers.

(Left) Originally designed in the 16th century, Shibam, Yemen

During the 1940s, after World War II and the development of the atomic bomb, there was considerable thought given to the idea of dispersing the population centers in America. With the advent of the Interstate Highway—or the "Freeway" system—and the mass production of vehicles, came the planned development of decentralized neighborhoods. Ludwig Hilberseimer was one of the first to espouse a new vision of single-family houses in a garden-like setting that also promoted industry, a strong town center, open and agriculture space, and lakes for recreation and leisure.

Similarly, Frank Lloyd Wright's Broad Acre City was presented as a new utopia. The City in the Garden movement thrived in the United States from the 1950s through the 2000s, each year increasing traffic for commuters. During the 1980s, the movement generated reverse commutes as company headquarters and industry moved to the suburbs. Suburban communities continue to expand, and thrive, as residential hubs for those who commute to urban centers and as job centers.

Some governments have attempted to mitigate continuous suburban expansion by legally protecting and preserving open land around cities and suburban towns from excessive encroachment (Figure 5). In the US, losing agricultural land to development is "the most permanently destructive of all non-farm land-use practices ***(Illinois Department for Natural Resources)***." In the Midwest agricultural belt of the United States, the Northeastern Illinois Planning Commission estimated that between 1970 and 1990, the population of the six counties around Chicago had grown by 4%, while the amount of developed land expanded 51% and resulted in a net loss of 146,000 hectares of agricultural land.

Nationally, almost 17-million hectares of rural land, including more than 9.7-million hectares of agricultural land, was converted into developed areas between 1982 and 2010 ***(Farmland Information Center, 2010)***. Much of this development was low-rise housing and retail along major road or rail corridors, with development expanding outward from the corridors as the suburbs expand.

Over time, in addition to the loss of agricultural land and watersheds, natural hydrological systems are often exacerbated by over-burdened and aging infrastructure, impacting regions well beyond the boundaries of urbanized areas. Rainwater that would naturally have recharged rivers and lakes is often collected from impermeable surfaces, such as paved areas, into combined sewers. Between 1987 and 2007, the once-agricultural area around Wuhan, a Chinese city that has experienced significant flooding over the past decade, has seen a four-fold increase in area that was previously 45–80% impervious: from 113 km^2 to 591 km^2. The area of land that was over 80% impervious increased by 221%, from 175 km^2 to 561 km^2 ***(Xie et al., 2013)***.

Ludwig Hilberseimer City in the Garden, 1944

Broad Acre City, Frank Lloyd Wright, 1950

The effect on greenhouse gas emissions is also significant and is primarily attributed to transportation and industrial uses associated with buildings like heating, air-conditioning, and lighting. Residential developments within suburban areas notoriously lack connectivity and consequently, the density of most these communities is too low to sustain public transit. In addition, many cities and suburbs have zoning laws prohibiting mixed-use development, so residents are forced to rely on transit for their daily activities.

This issue is compounded by the replacement of rural land by suburban development, which reduces the sequestration of carbon dioxide ***(Jones et al., 2013)***. Most carbon footprint studies consider emissions and not the effects of reducing carbon sequestration capacity. Some urban planners have sought to address these issues through the New Urbanism movement, which has successfully influenced a number of developments, steering them toward more walkable neighborhoods with a greater range of housing types and densities, and with more walk-to accessible retail and commercial facilities.

US Green Building Council's (USGBC) LEED Neighborhood Development, United Kingdom's BREEAM Communities, and Australia's Green Star Communities are examples of green building rating systems that seek to formalize sustainable urban development practices through their nationally and internationally recognized rating systems.

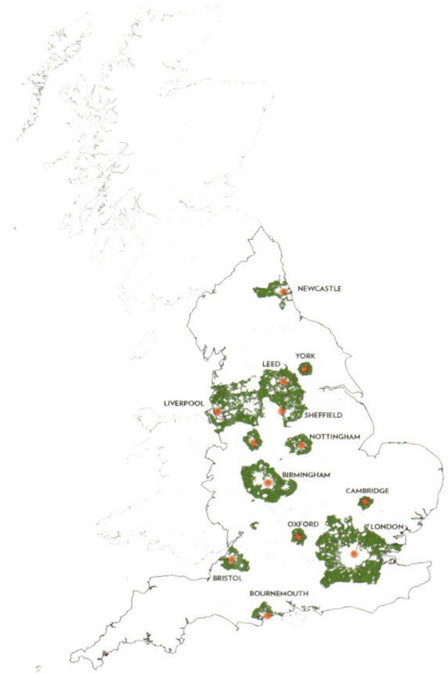

Figure 5 United Kingdom greenbelt land around major conurbations

Suburban expansion alongside infrastructure in the United States

STUDY OVERVIEW

The Residential Density study was undertaken to qualify an understanding of the relationship between residential density and several of parameters, including energy use, land use, connectivity, transportation emissions, and embodied carbon in order to relate to life cycle carbon emissions.

George Bernard Shaw once said, "No question is so difficult to answer as that to which the answer is obvious." However, there is a surprising lack of empirical information that either confirms or refutes the perceived beneficial relationship between urban density and environmental parameters. To assemble an accurate picture of these relationships, it was necessary to establish consistent measurement boundaries and measurement methodologies. In this study, prototypical buildings were designed and set within communities of different densities, as opposed to taking measurements from existing buildings and communities.

The study achieves several goals by comparing densities and their relative environmental impacts. The first was to establish a baseline against which sustainable design assessments could be compared and evaluated. The second was to establish a consistent measurement and reporting methodology that could be tested further in the future. The third was to understand the connection between urban patterns and resource consumption.

The study does not intend to conclude with a preferred residential typology, but instead aims to put the attributes of different typologies into perspective, allowing the reader to assess which attributes are most important. The information and conclusions presented can be used for land use versus density comparisons, helping people draw their own conclusions regarding the merits of one typology versus another.

The study does not intend to conclude with a preferred residential typology, but instead aims to put the attributes of different typologies into perspective, allowing the reader to assess which attributes are most important.

CHAPTER DEFINITIONS

Prototype identifies and documents nine specific building prototypes as the core of the analysis. The chapter describes the history of each prototype, the design of the prototype in relation to the study, and the key statistics about each prototype.

Land Use assembles each building prototype into a community using a Geographic Information System (GIS). The chapter answers a series of questions about each community's land use, including the capabilities of the land lost or remaining, and how the land use supports food production, energy production, and recreational use.

Energy details the energy consumption profiles of each prototype and surveys their annual overall energy use, building energy use, use by unit, use intensity, and use by the occupant. The chapter accounts for building orientation by creating an average energy profile for each prototype. The energy consumption is then evaluated by each building element's contribution to the overall energy load, concluding with a results comparison that shows relative energy use for each of the prototype communities.

Transport examines different types of transit and discusses the relationship between density, connectivity, walkability, public transport accessibility, and vehicle emissions.

Carbon studies the lifecycle carbon emissions for each typology and its supporting infrastructure. Five key attributes were examined and combined to form an overall carbon profile including operational emissions, building embodied carbon, site-wide utilities infrastructure embodied carbon, above-grade infrastructure, and service vehicle emissions, i.e. garbage collection and parcel delivery. In this chapter, each building prototype is considered in detail, with major building materials summarized for their overall carbon profile. A comparison of the nine prototypes is then presented with conclusions as to which community has the lowest life cycle carbon emissions.

STUDY APPROACH

After discussing the development and growth of cities and the environmental impacts, the study questions: what type of density-driven urban planning strategy is best for the environment?

The environmental advantages and disadvantages of these approaches have previously been considered in a number of studies of individual buildings, where the analysis has been based on comparing existing residential buildings—but not communities. The challenge in extrapolating data from such studies to answer questions regarding density is that the buildings compared often are built at different times and follow different codes and standards.

In some cases, the buildings serve an iconic function, include non-residential elements, and differ significantly in their response to environmental conditions such as climate and topography. The multiple factors that differentiate buildings and communities makes a direct comparison between them in relation to density somewhat subjective and potentially misleading.

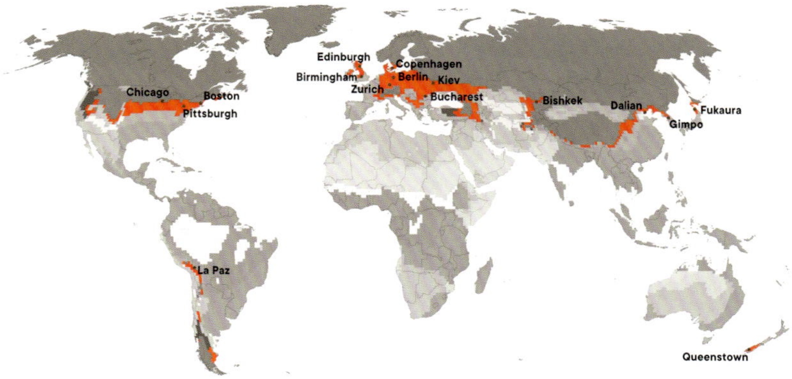

Figure 6 ASHRAE Climatic Zone 5A

Figure 7 Improvements in building Energy Use Intensity (EUI), since 1975

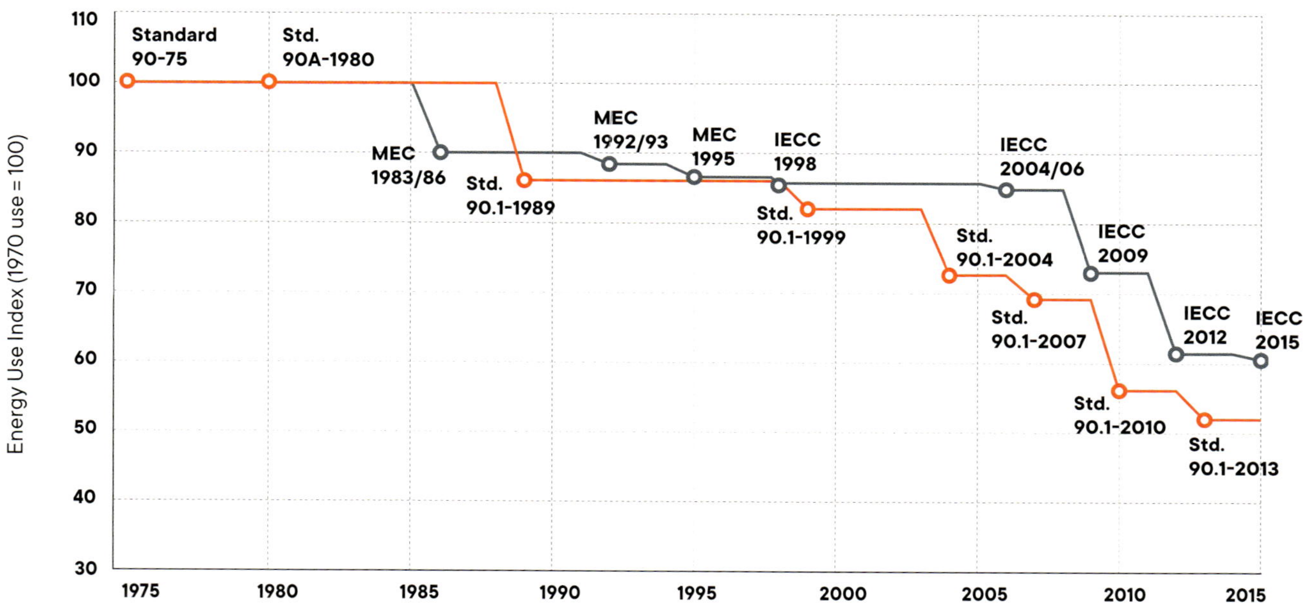

COMMUNITY AND UNIT SIZE

Buildings were first designed following a set of common rules. Because there is no "typical" housing size for an apartment, condominium, or a single-family home, the study designates an archetypal residential community of 2,000 units with an average unit size of 150 m^2, as a reasonable and representative cross section of different housing typologies.

LOCATION

A geographic location also needed to be established. We chose to make this designation as a climatic region, rather than a specific region, as any greater level of specificity would introduce a variable that might not be applied fairly across all community types. Choosing a climate region was also necessary because it would be unrealistic to design a building prototype in the absence of any constraints. Climatic considerations are the cornerstone of energy codes and something that all buildings must be designed to meet.

Many permitting authorities across the world refer to the American Society of Heating, Refrigerating and Air-Conditioning Engineers Standard 90.1 (ASHRAE 90.1) as a basis for their energy code. Within this standard, the world is divided into a number of zones, with each being assigned a different set of compliance requirements. For this study, the climatic zone chosen to design the communities in was ASHRAE Climate Zone 5A (Cool-Humid) (Figure 6).

DESIGN STANDARD

With a context identified, the study needed to establish a design standard for each building. To make comparisons between all building types possible, ASHRAE 90.1 (2010) was selected as the energy standard for the mid-rise and high-rise typologies and for all the building envelopes, with ASHRAE 90.2 (2007) as the mechanical systems standard for low-rise typologies. The ASHRAE energy standard was introduced in 1975 and has been subject to improvements every three years since 2004.

Having established these three axioms for the study, prototypical communities were designed as an unbiased representation of a monotypic built environment, each with a constant housing unit density. The following work describes the study of nine such communities, ranging from a single, megatall residential tower, through a variety of high- and mid-rise prototypes, to low-rise and single-family urban and suburban homes.

To answer each question objectively, robust study methods were developed with clear boundaries and assumptions that can be applied equally to both high- and low-density communities.

- *Which building typology has the lowest carbon emissions?*
- *Which residential community has the lowest impact?*
- *Which residential community has the lowest energy demand?*
- *Which residential community has the best access to public transportation?*
- *Which residential community has the lowest lifecycle carbon dioxide emissions?*
- *How does building efficiency effect carbon emissions?*

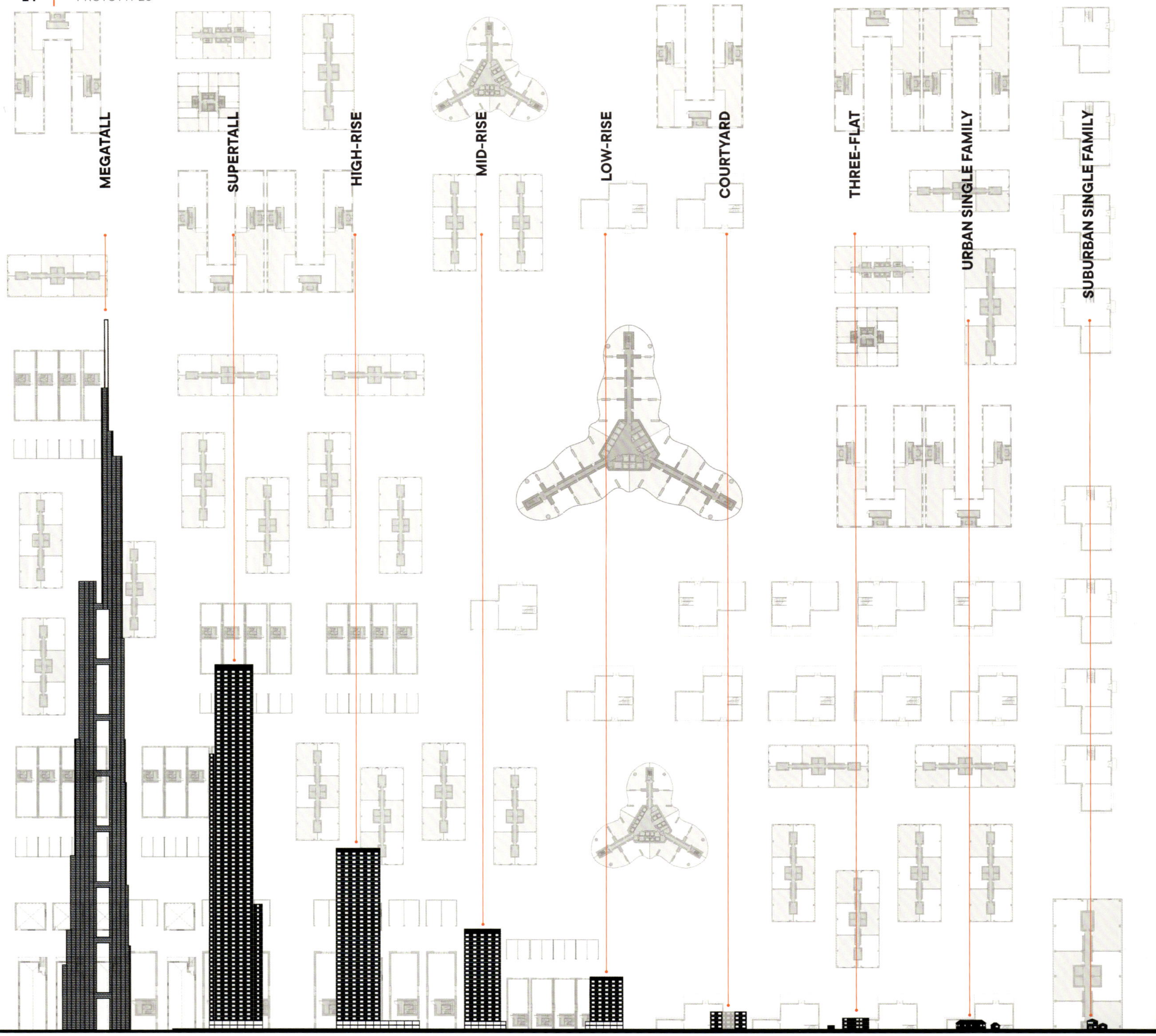
MEGATALL
SUPERTALL
HIGH-RISE
MID-RISE
LOW-RISE
COURTYARD
THREE-FLAT
URBAN SINGLE FAMILY
SUBURBAN SINGLE FAMILY

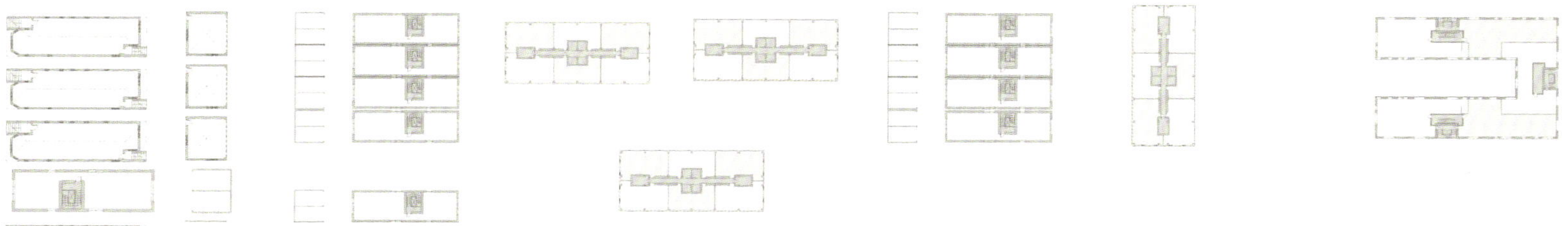

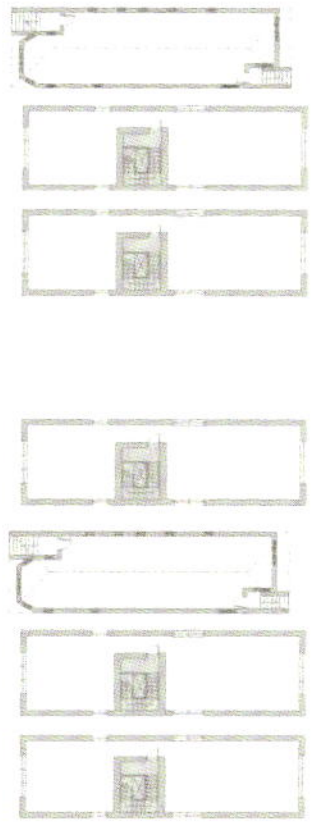

PROTOTYPES

The following is an examination and documentation of nine specific building prototypes that form the core of the analysis, describing the prototypes' history, design in relation to the study, and key statistics about each type. To answer questions regarding comparisons between different building types or communities, each typology was first examined to ensure relevancy. Data for each prototype is summarized in Table 1.

Total Area is determined by the gross enclosed floor area of the building, measured to the external face of the exterior wall.

Core Area is the floor area comprised of the access to unit circulation corridors, stairs, elevator and other shafts, and the structure enclosing them.

Efficiency is equal to the total area of the floor minus the core area, minus structural members, which are defined as walls and columns.

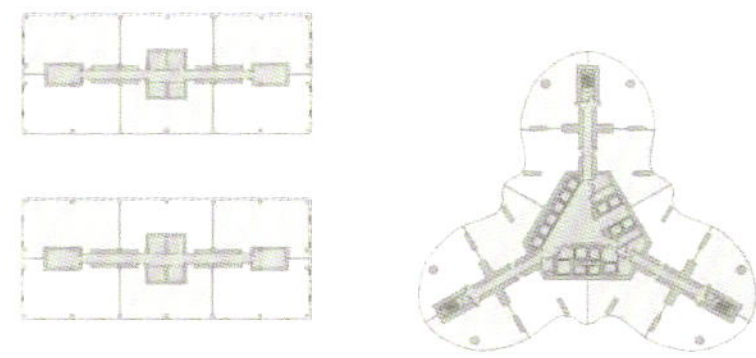

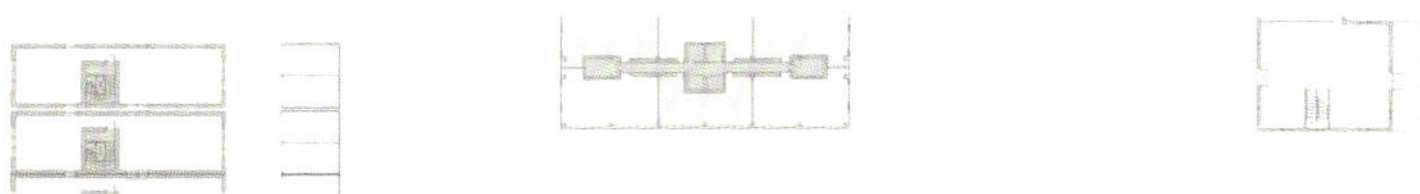

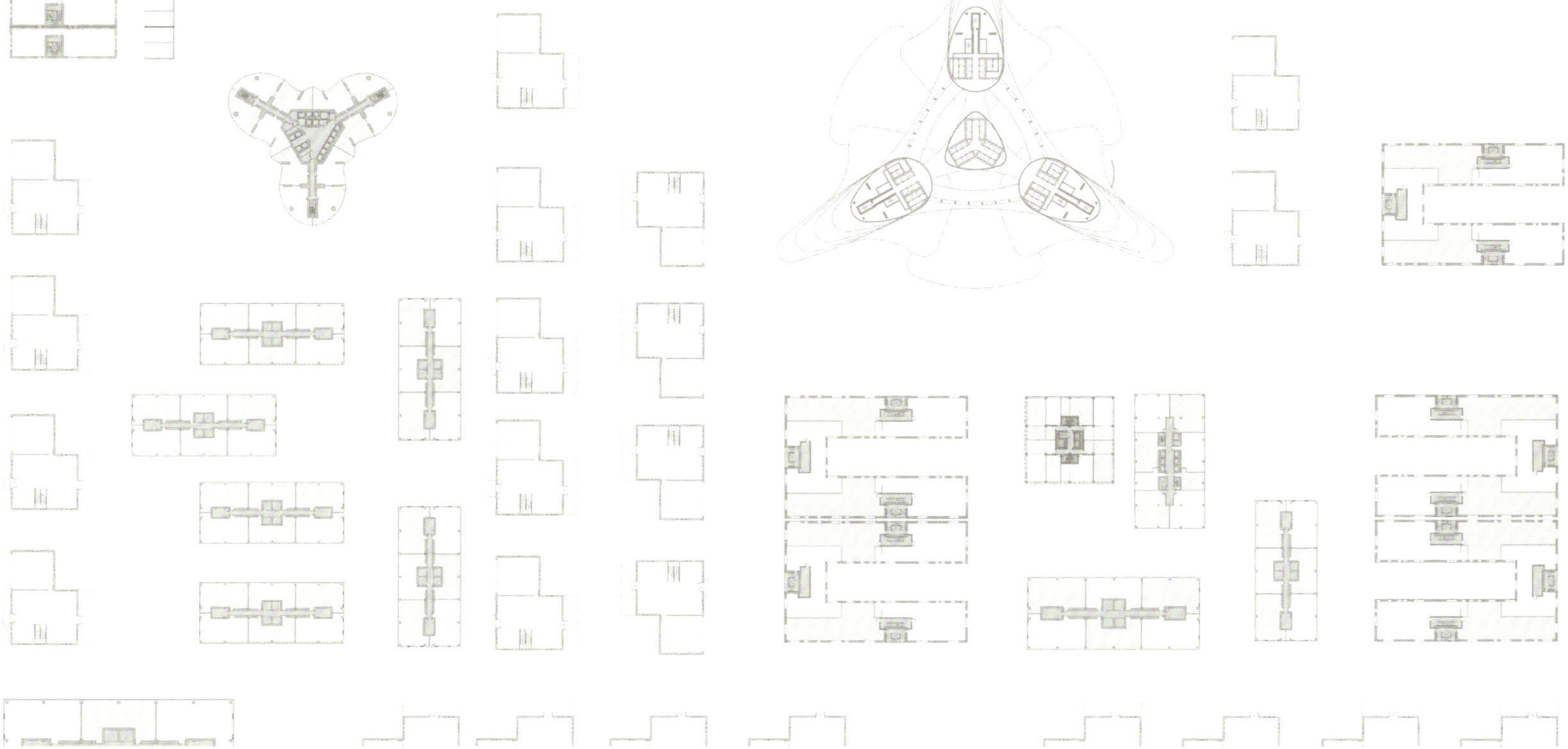

MEGATALL + SUPERTALL

Throughout history, civilizations have been trying to reach the heavens with man-made structures. The tallest buildings on earth, classified as megatall buildings, have emerged in the early 21st Century as technology has made it feasible and practical to construct buildings of this height. According to the Council on Tall Buildings and Urban Habitat (CTBUH), Megatall is described as a building over 600 meters tall. Supertall is described as a building between 300 meters and 600 meters in height ***(CTBUH, 2017)***. Both typologies are generally commissioned by large corporations and are often additionally supported by the local or national governments, with the objective of becoming the tallest in a region. Regardless of the client, a large financial investment and a highly motivated developer is required to build at these heights.

Megatall and supertall buildings are typically mixed-use with large residential components. Globally, there are three completed megatall buildings and nearly a dozen more under construction. In 2010, the first megatall building, the Burj Khalifa in Dubai, United Arab Emirates, opened at more than 160 stories and 828 meters in height; the second was the 601-meter-tall Makkah Royal Clock Tower in Mecca, Saudi Arabia, built in 2012; and third is Shanghai Tower, at 632 meters tall in China, which opened in 2015.

The next world's tallest building will be Jeddah Tower, designed by AS+GG for Jeddah Economic Company. The tower, currently under construction, is set to be over one-kilometer-tall when completed in Jeddah, Saudi Arabia.

The functionality of megatall and supertall buildings are limited by their lease span, which is the length between the core of the building and its exterior glass wall. As buildings become taller, their slenderness—or height over width ratio—becomes smaller so their structural feasibility is compromised. Therefore, the idea of the "mega building" typology within the overall genre of supertall buildings has emerged. A mega building is a grouping of supertall buildings that are structurally tied together to improve stability without compromising the lease spans.

The first supertall buildings were office towers, beginning with the Chrysler Building in 1930 and the Empire State Building in 1931, both in New York City (319 meters and 381 meters, respectively). Completed in 1969, the first mixed-use supertall building was the John Hancock Center, now known as 875 North Michigan Avenue, in Chicago, Illinois. At 457 meters tall, the tower has residential, office, retail, and observation functions. It is more common today for supertall buildings to be residential or mixed-use, over exclusively used for office functions. The typical mixed-use megatall or supertall building has office floors on the lower levels and residential and/or hotel at the higher levels. Many have special observation, amenity, or restaurant spaces at the top.

Engineering buildings over 300 meters tall is a complicated process, requiring complex vertical transportation, engineering, and structural systems, while also considering soil and seismic conditions. Despite these challenges, megatall and supertall buildings have technical and economic advantages in areas with high-population density, including their ability to accommodate more inhabitants and workers per unit of land area.

MEGATALL + SUPERTALL PROTOTYPE SYSTEMS

The prototype for the megatall and supertall typologies is based on a collective experience in designing at this scale. The structural and mechanical systems were modeled on those designed for the Burj Khalifa, the current world's tallest building. The structural systems consist of a hexagonal core with high-strength reinforced concrete, buttressed by three wings in an efficient Y-shaped plan that steps and spirals upward (Figure 8). The plan has visual and programmatic advantages that help deflect wind forces and reduce the amount of structure needed to counteract lateral loads, with structure accounting for just over 10% of the building plan.

The megatall and supertall buildings in this study are represented as a 213-story Megatall prototype and a 121-story Supertall prototype. Both prototypes were designed with a reinforced concrete mat that is supported by 1.5-meter diameter piles. Both prototypes were designed with two levels of below-grade parking, loading and mechanical spaces. The facades are enclosed with low emissivity coated (low-E) double-glazed units, set in a unitized aluminum curtain-wall system.

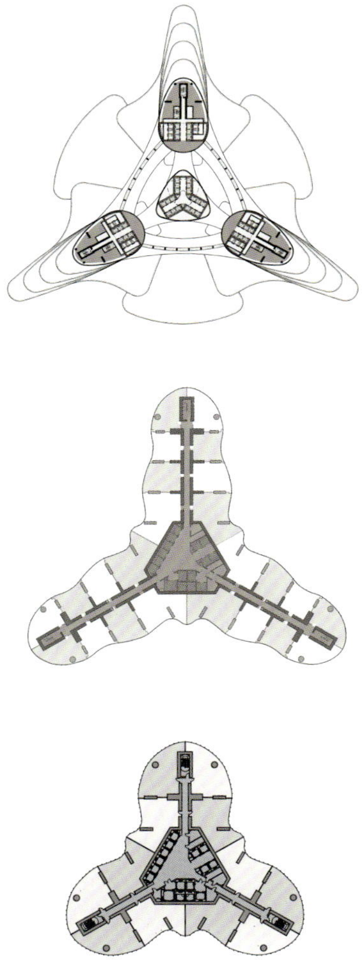

Figure 8
Typical floor plates
Megatall (top)
Supertall (middle, lower)

The building envelope performance for modeling and simulation purposes meets the prescriptive requirements of ASHRAE 90.1 (2010) standard and has a 40% glazing ratio. In reality, the vision glass ratio is greater than 40% and higher performing glazing can be used to compensate. Mechanical systems are located 20–30 stories apart and serve 10–15 stories above and below in independent zones, with vertical fan coil units providing heating and cooling to the residential floors.

Designing buildings taller than 300 meters requires a holistic team approach. The amount of structure required can be three to four times greater than that of a conventional building, and while the earliest supertall buildings were constructed of steel, many of the newer ones consist of concrete or composite structure. Column and shear wall sizes are also much larger than smaller buildings and the primary structure consumes as much as 12% of the average floor plate. Therefore, complex design solutions that balance economics, engineering, and construction management are required to push the limits of engineering, with innovations such as pumping concrete vertically during construction or robust structural systems that resist wind loads and maximize elevator travel.

JEDDAH TOWER
Jeddah, Saudi Arabia
Adrian Smith + Gordon Gill Architecture
Under construction, 2020
1000+m | 3280+ft

MILE-HIGH TOWER
Riyadh, Saudi Arabia
Adrian Smith + Gordon Gill Architecture
Proposed 2017
1609m | 5280ft

BURJ KHALIFA
Dubai, United Arab Emirates
Adrian Smith, Design Partner, Skidmore, Owings & Merrill
Completed 2010
828m | 2717ft

MEGATALL

NUMBER OF UNITS / BUILDING	2,000
NUMBER OF STORIES (ABOVE GRADE)	213
BUILDING HEIGHT	766 m
FLOOR TO FLOOR HEIGHT	3.5 m
AVERAGE UNIT SIZE	150 m^2
PARCEL AREA	14,641 m^2
TOTAL AREA (ABOVE GRADE)	451,480 m^2
GROSS RESIDENTIAL FLOOR AREA	406,342 m^2
MECHANICAL FLOOR AREA	34,762 m^2
UNDERGROUND PARKING AREA	44,400 m^2
PODIUM PARKING AREA	N/A
PARKING SPACES	1,268
EFFICIENCY	74%
STRUCTURE	10.3%
WINDOW / WALL RATIO	40%

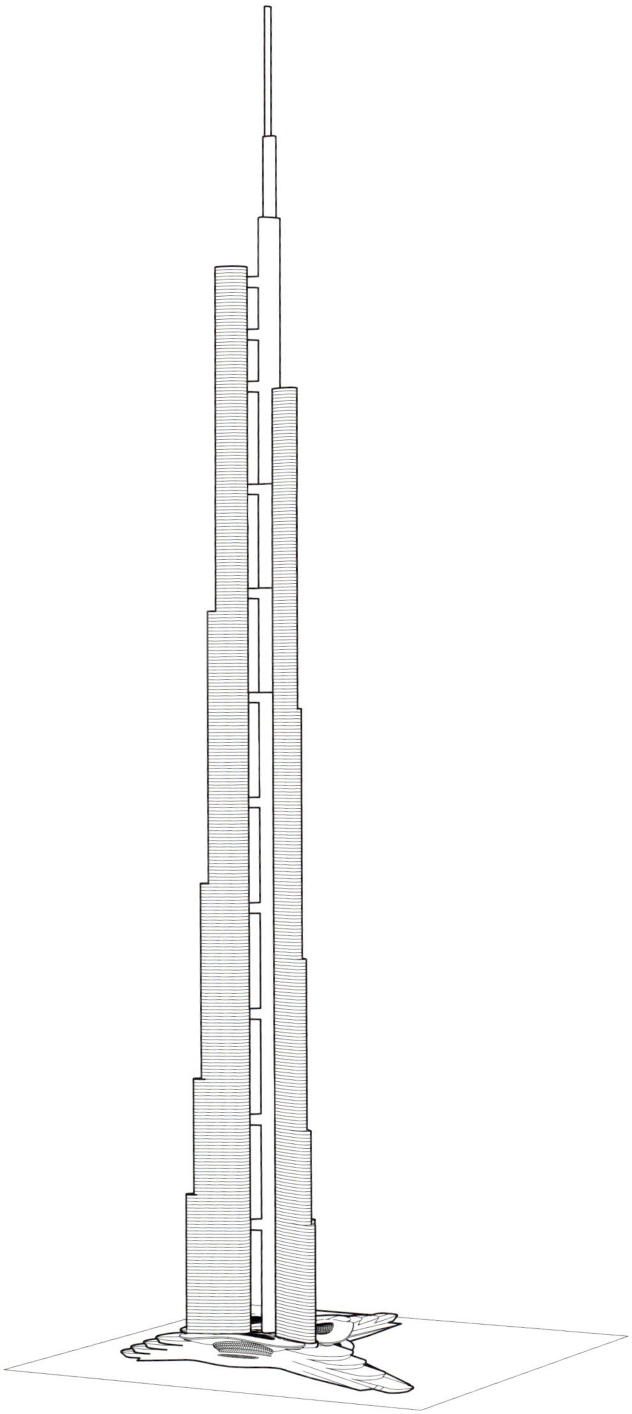

Megatall and supertall sites include large parcels of land around the base of the towers as a viewing platform for adjacent properties, drastically increasing their land values. They are also typically built on special or combined plots that have larger areas for landscape and supporting podium structures. For the purpose of this study, ancillary structures normally within the site boundary, such as small office buildings, have not been included but a generous parcel size of nearly 15,000 m^2 has been used due to elaborate drop off sequences, access points, podium functions, and security needs.

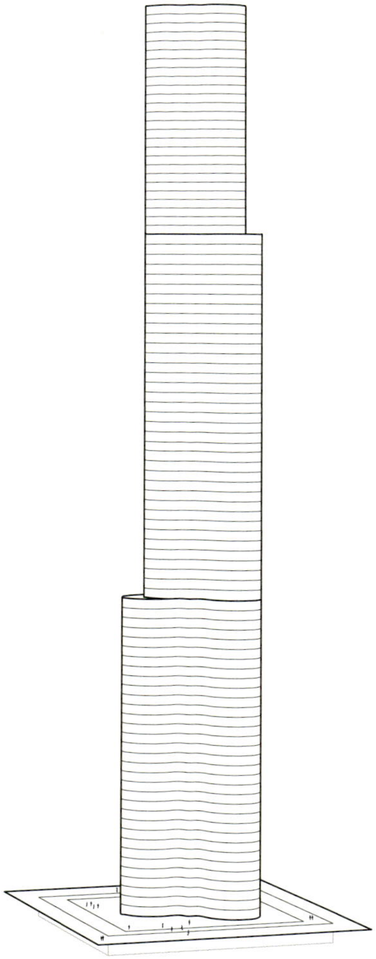

SUPERTALL	
NUMBER OF UNITS / BUILDING	1,000
NUMBER OF STORIES (ABOVE GRADE)	121
BUILDING HEIGHT	435 m
FLOOR TO FLOOR HEIGHT	3.5 m
AVERAGE UNIT SIZE	150 m^2
PARCEL AREA	8,944 m^2
TOTAL AREA (ABOVE GRADE)	231,869 m^2
GROSS RESIDENTIAL FLOOR AREA	205,710 m^2
MECHANICAL FLOOR AREA	19,618 m^2
UNDERGROUND PARKING AREA	23,600 m^2
PODIUM PARKING AREA	N/A
PARKING SPACES	575
EFFICIENCY	76%
STRUCTURE	9.8%
WINDOW / WALL RATIO	40%

As towers become taller, their mechanical systems become increasingly complex. For example, the ability to move water to upper floors requires the use of pump sets to raise water pressure from municipal levels, typically 400kpa, while plumbing drains require valves to reduce the speed and pressure of waste water traveling down the building. The systems assigned for the prototypical megatall building were those that are commonly used in this typology. Fan coil units were employed for both heating and cooling. Ventilation rates were compliant with ASHRAE 62.1 (2010).

TRUMP INTERNATIONAL HOTEL & TOWER
Chicago, Illinois
Adrian Smith, Design Partner
Skidmore, Owings & Merrill, LLP
Completed 2010
415m | 1,171sf

TOWER PALACE III
Seoul, Republic of Korea
Adrian Smith, Design Partner
Skidmore, Owings & Merrill, LLP
Completed 2004
264m | 865sf

HIGH-RISE + MID-RISE

Although becoming increasingly common in the modern era, the idea of high-rise living has actually existed since ancient times. The first forms appeared in ancient Rome's stacked insula apartments. Ruins of these structures are evident at Ostia, where insulae were ten stories and higher. Lower floors were occupied by stores or wealthier residents, while higher floors contained less expensive rental units.

High-rise residential buildings were also found in many important medieval cities, often built by the wealthy for defense and prestige. In 12th Century Bologna, there were upward of 100 high rises, including the 97.2 meter Two Towers. The medieval Egyptian city of Fustat had high-rise residential buildings that were up to 14 stories tall. In the 16th and 17th Centuries, high-rise buildings could be found in a variety of cities including Cairo, Shibam (Yemen), and Edinburgh, each reaching as high as 14 stories.

Modern skyscrapers first began to appear in the US in the late 19th Century in both New York City and Chicago. This new typology became associated with the aspirations of ordinary people who moved into cities from rural areas in search of jobs and a higher quality of life. Tall buildings became symbols of capitalism and economic power.

In the 19th Century the creation of the passenger elevator, and the development of steel-framed structures, contributed to the widespread construction of high-rises. The upper floors, which were now conveniently accessible, became luxurious and desirable for their views.

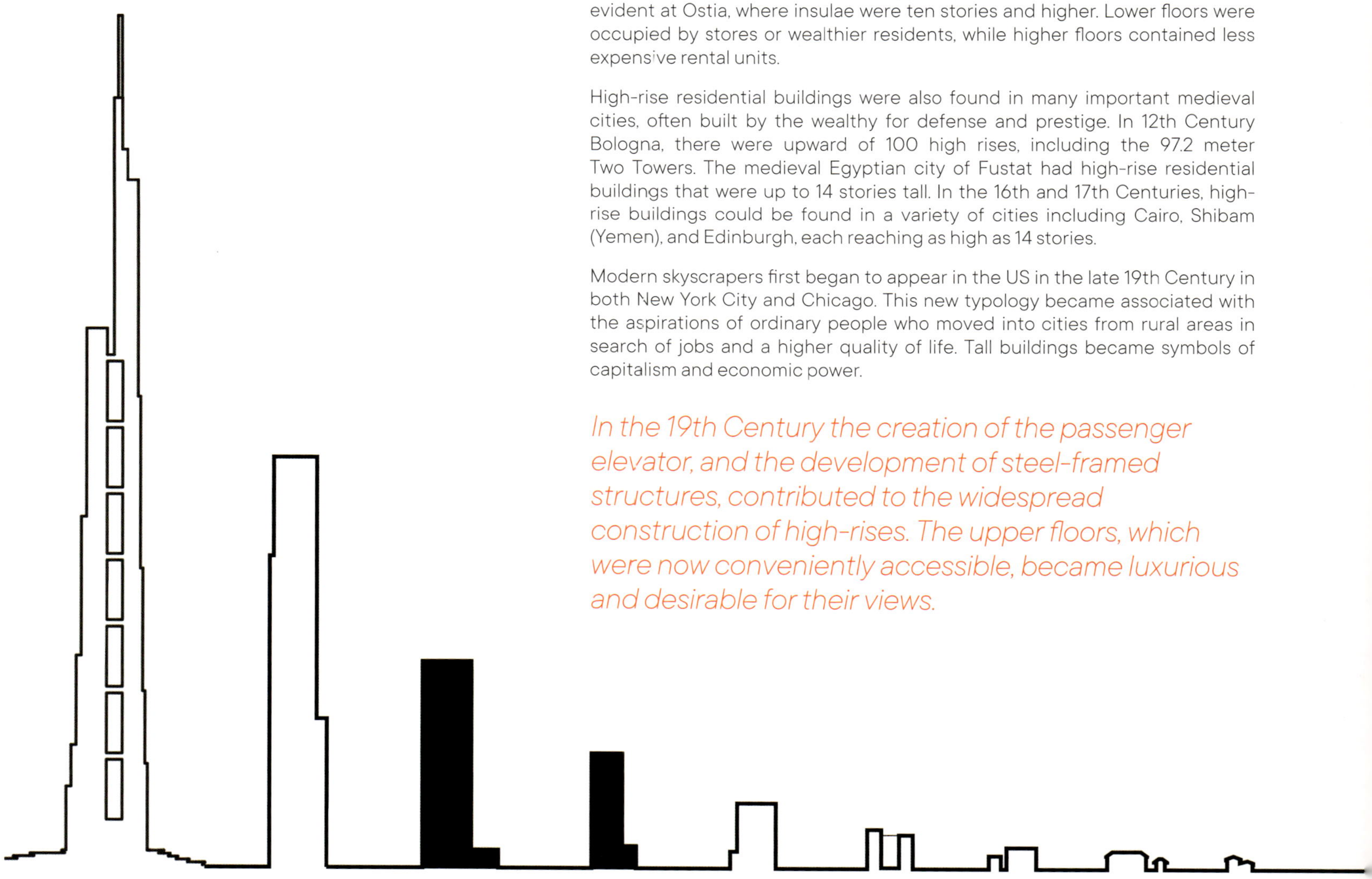

Chicago became the birthplace of the high-rise typology when the first modern high-rise, the 10-story Home Insurance Building designed by William LeBaron Jenney, opened in 1185. Once completed it was the catalyst to build higher with the 14-story Tacoma Building in 1889, and the 22-story Masonic Temple in 1892. In the 1950s, the International Style emerged and many high-rise buildings were built using structural steel frame construction and lightweight glass curtain walls. As concrete technology advanced, more residential buildings were built using reinforced concrete.

Many of these early 10-to-20 story buildings are still in use today and the typology has continued to evolve by becoming more efficient—and taller—as the years progressed. Pre-air-conditioned buildings have proven to be excellent for residential use. Initially designed using operable windows, they have effective cross ventilation, allowing residents to bring fresh outside air naturally into their living spaces.

Today's urban high-rise structures use more conventional structural systems than their megatall and supertall counterparts. In North American and European cities, many of the residential towers of this height use two-way flat plate construction. While some of the taller high-rises have complex shapes and require some lateral systems to resist wind loads, this typology is becoming increasingly simple and therefore more economical as developers in each city learn which heights are ideal to maintain structural efficiency and the best rentable-to-core ratio of the plans. High-rise construction is also becoming more slender and commonly is used for residential development on constrained sites where land value may be at a premium.

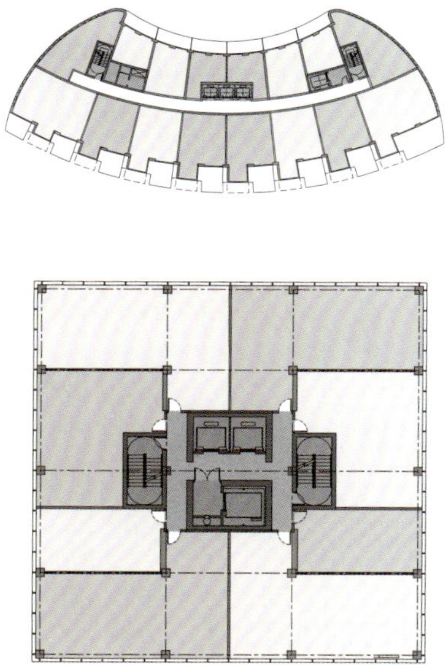

Figure 9

Typical floor plates
High-Rise (top)
Mid-Rise (lower)

Widely considered an efficient urban typology that can take a variety of forms, high-rise buildings built in the 1950s and 1960s still dominate the building stock found in major Western cities, along with a wide variety of mid-rise steel-frame buildings built in the 1920s and 1930s. These buildings tend to be decorative, clad with ornate terracotta, stone, or brick, or with traditional designs that include elaborate cornices and window detailing. Much of this building stock remains intact because there are zoning laws in historic older cities that prohibit taller buildings.

Today, this prototype is used for new developments on the outskirts of urban centers. As cities expand, it is logical that residential developments on their periphery may include high-rise buildings because of their economic efficiency and rising premiums on the cost of land. High-rise residential developments can share amenity and parking podiums, allowing for phased, master planned developments. In the suburban context, this typology is increasingly used to add density to a downtown village, making the typology more viable and vibrant.

OLYMPIA CENTER
Chicago, Illinois
Adrian Smith, Design Partner
Skidmore, Owings & Merrill
Completed 1986
221 m | 725 sf

BURJ VISTA
Dubai, United Arab Emirates
Adrian Smith + Gordon Gill Architecture
Completed 2018
272 m | 892 sf

HIGH-RISE + MID-RISE PROTOTYPE SYSTEMS

For the purposes of this study, the High-Rise prototype is a 65-story tower and the Mid-Rise prototype is a 38-story tower. These prototypes adopt an economical flat-plate system on an efficient six- or nine-meter grid with a transfer-free, three-story parking podium and multiple residential unit configurations. A rectilinear plan was designed for the High-Rise prototype and a square plan was designed for the Mid-Rise prototype.

Each prototype consists of a central core and minimum corridor (Figure 9). Columns are placed inside the exterior wall with concrete core walls encasing the elevator, stair and mechanical shafts as well as corridor walls, with the structure accounting for approximately 4% of the building plan. The building has a facade this is compliant with an ASHRAE 40% window-to-wall.

HIGH-RISE

NUMBER OF UNITS / BUILDING	500
NUMBER OF STORIES (ABOVE GRADE)	65
BUILDING HEIGHT	229 m
FLOOR TO FLOOR HEIGHT	3.5 m
AVERAGE UNIT SIZE	150 m^2
PARCEL AREA	4,212 m^2
TOTAL AREA (ABOVE GRADE)	110,184 m^2
GROSS RESIDENTIAL FLOOR AREA	91,255 m^2
MECHANICAL FLOOR AREA	6,293 m^2
UNDERGROUND PARKING AREA	N/A
PODIUM PARKING AREA	8,424 m^2
PARKING SPACES	263
EFFICIENCY	82%
STRUCTURE	4%
WINDOW / WALL RATIO	40%

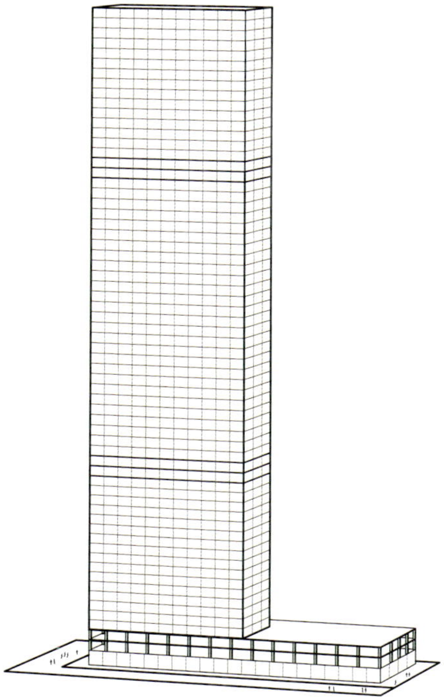

Due to their height and strength requirements needed to resist wind loads, as well as for basic economic reasons and to limit floor-to-floor height, the structural system material used in both prototypes is standard reinforced concrete. Most high-rise residential blocks that are not located in high-seismic zones are constructed either from concrete or composite construction, so for the purposes of this study, a concrete flat plate construction is assumed.

Unlike taller buildings, High-Rise and Mid-Rise structures have more flexibility in their facades and can consist of floor-to-ceiling glazed curtain walls, glass, and metal facades, or punched openings in precast or stone. Window wall systems that sit directly on the concrete slabs are common in this typology. It is assumed that a window-to-wall ratio of 40%, reflects current energy codes and is an economical wall design that is typically used in buildings of this scale today. Most facades in this typology are designed with operable windows or operable mullions.

Servicing the 65-story High-Rise prototype requires three discrete mechanical zones in each tower. Mechanical systems are designed on levels 2, 30, and 57, allowing them to be spaced 20–30 stories apart and serve 10–15 stories above and below, with vertical fan coil units to provide heating and cooling. The Mid-Rise 38-story prototype requires two discrete mechanical zones and occurs from the top and the base of the building, servicing 18 stories above and below.

HILAL TOWER
Riyadh, Saudi Arabia
Adrian Smith + Gordon Gill Architecture
Under Construction
78m | 256m

Fan coil unit systems are the most common mechanical system used in high-rise residential buildings today. The three major components of a typical ventilation system are the bathroom exhaust, the kitchen exhaust and the makeup air systems. In most cases, the air is circulated within the residences by a series of duct risers terminating with a fan or makeup air handler. Pumping energy is needed to move chilled water and domestic water up and down the building, but this energy load is less than would be required for a supertall building.

High-rise buildings also serve as visual markers within urban skylines. Compared with mega and supertall structures, high-rise sites tend to be more compact and set within existing urban contexts. The sites are often tight and are packed with drop-offs, parking ramps, and servicing areas. In this prototype, a plot similar to a typical city block is applied. For the mid-rise prototype, a smaller site the size of approximately half of a city block is used.

OCT SHENZHEN
Shenzhen, China
Adrian Smith + Gordon Gill Architecture
Proposed 2012
80m | 262sf

MID-RISE

NUMBER OF UNITS / BUILDING	200
NUMBER OF STORIES (ABOVE GRADE)	38
BUILDING HEIGHT	134.5 m
FLOOR TO FLOOR HEIGHT	3.5 m
AVERAGE UNIT SIZE	150 m^2
PARCEL AREA	2,005 m^2
TOTAL AREA (ABOVE GRADE)	42,896 m^2
GROSS RESIDENTIAL FLOOR AREA	34,774 m^2
MECHANICAL FLOOR AREA	2,108 m^2
UNDERGROUND PARKING AREA	N/A
PODIUM PARKING AREA	4,010 m^2
PARKING SPACES	124
EFFICIENCY	81%
STRUCTURE	4%
WINDOW / WALL RATIO	40%

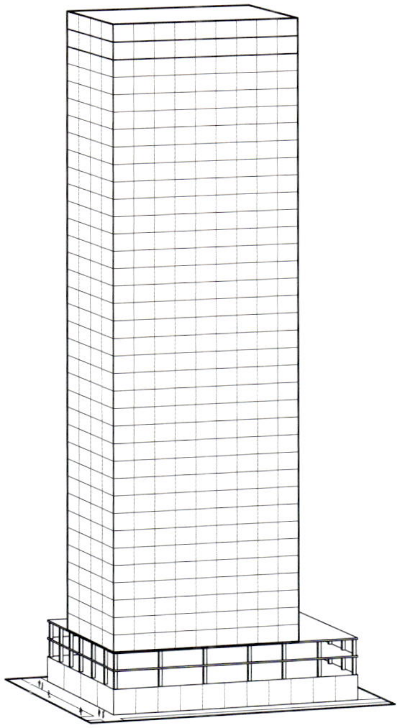

LOW-RISE

The low-rise typology includes some of the first 10- to 20-story "skyscrapers" ever constructed. Many early skyscrapers in city centers still exist today and have been renovated and restored to new uses. In our modern era, these buildings are now classified as low-rise buildings as cities have risen around them. Some consist of steel framed structures, but others are built of heavy timber, brick, or stone bearing walls.

Low-rise buildings are those that are 8- to 20-stories tall and are common in both dense areas as well as outside the city center. They are increasingly found in suburban areas, but it is also common for a low-rise building or group of low-rise buildings to anchor an urban neighborhood.

Low-rise buildings also have the widest variety of potential configurations. They can have small floor plates and be located on small sites in the middle of city blocks or they can be stand-alone corporate headquarters or hotels that are hundreds of feet long (Figure 10). However, due to the small floor plate size, low-rise buildings are slightly less efficient than the High-Rise or Mid-Rise prototype.

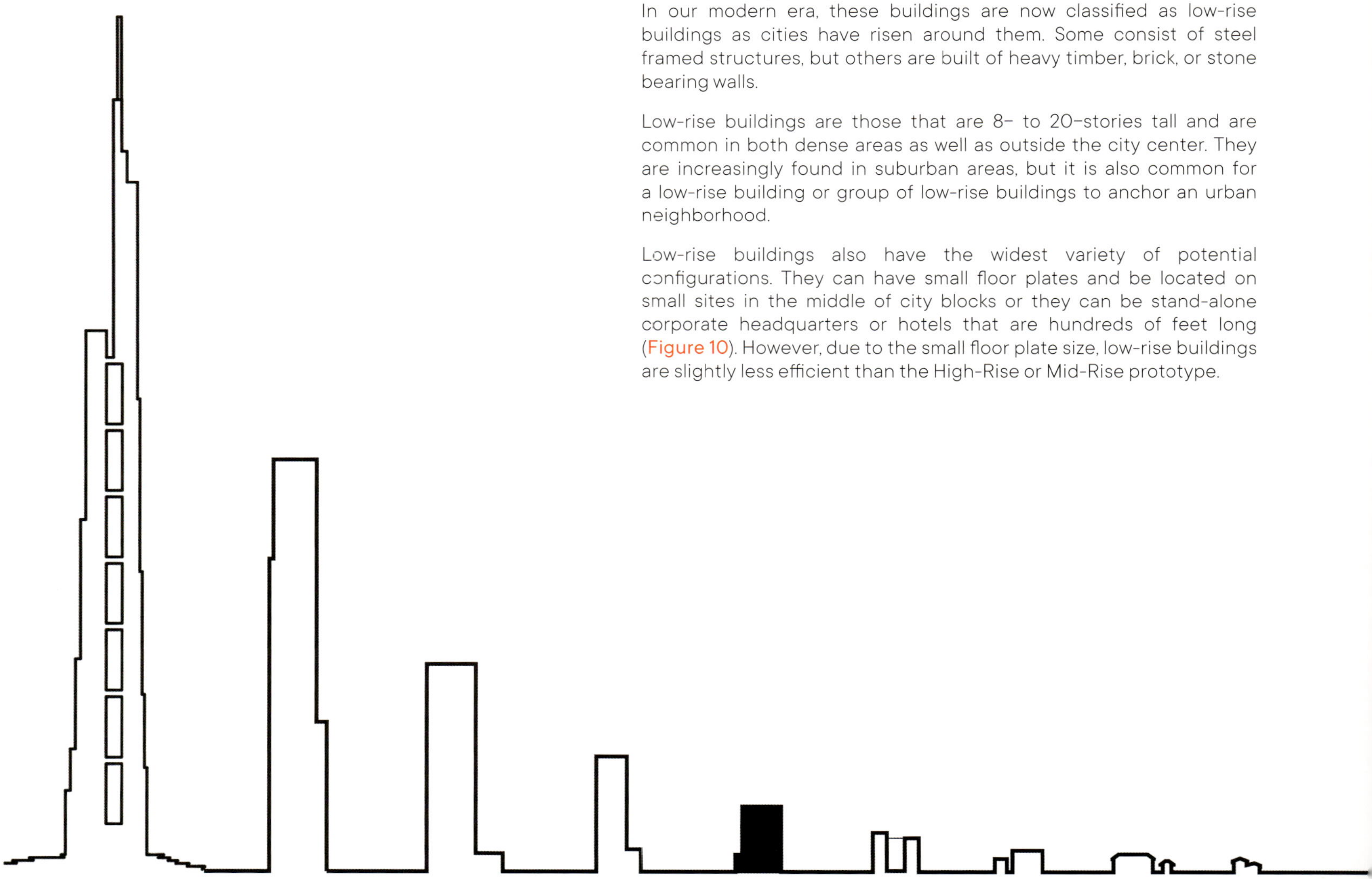

The materials used for the structural system are reinforced concrete, steel, or heavy timber. Due to the low amount of lateral loads and limited height, it is possible to use a variety of materials of construction. The window-to-wall ratio is typically 40% or lower, depending on views and orientation. It is also common for a parking podium to be incorporated into the building.

A variety of facade materials can be used effectively in low-rise buildings. Due to a lower emphasis on distant views, it is less important to have large expanses of glass so many low-rises have facade materials of brick, terracotta, or stone. Mid-century, low-rise buildings and many office buildings of this scale are clad with metal panels. Today, many of the newer low-rise residential and hotel developments are clad with synthetic materials such as pre-cast concrete panels, stucco, or brick. Contemporary materials such as metal and traditional materials such as wood are also used. Additionally, most buildings in this typology have operable windows.

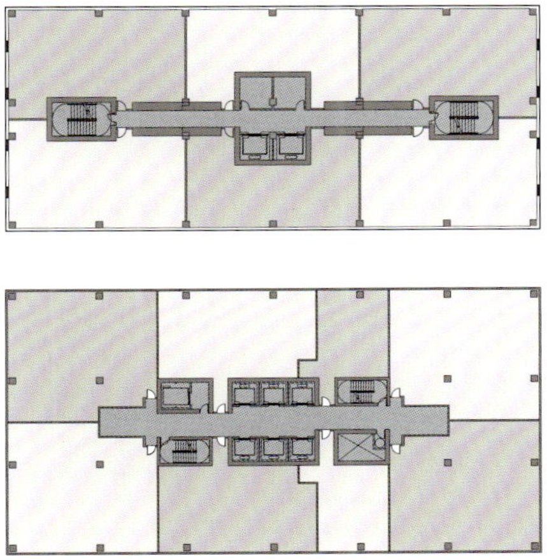

Figure 10

Typical floor plates
High-Rise (Top)
Low-Rise

CHENGDU GREAT CITY
Chengdu, China
Adrian Smith + Gordon Gill Architecture
Proposed 2012

The potential site area for a low-rise building has a wide variety, as these buildings can be located in urban areas, suburban areas, or as stand-alone buildings. In well-established cities it is not uncommon for a low-rise building to be built on a small site in an older neighborhood. However, many of today's low-rise buildings, especially in the United States, include a podium at the base with retail and parking. For the purposes of this study, a site approximately the size of a small city block is used.

The principles of heating and cooling urban low-rise buildings have changed over the last century. Early skyscrapers and low-rise residential dwellings utilized natural ventilation because air-conditioning was not yet widespread. Cross ventilation and access to adequate natural light was an important element in the design. Early heating systems were typically a central boiler. With the proliferation of mechanical air conditioning, these prototypes have switched to gas-fired, forced air heating systems and central air conditioning. These systems are segregated at the unit to provide individual controls and separate metering where necessary.

LOW-RISE PROTOTYPE SYSTEMS

For this study, the Low-Rise prototype is a 20-story residential building with a small core that has four elevators and two sets of stairs. Core walls are minimized, and shear walls are able to double as tenant partitions (Figure 10). Like the High-Rise and Mid-Rise prototypes, the Low-Rise prototype uses a two-way flat plate system on a six- or nine-meter grid, with a transfer-free, two-story parking podium and the ability to create numerous residential unit configurations.

Also like the High-Rise prototype, this typology is designed with a rectangular plan and a central core with a double-loaded corridor. Columns are placed inside the exterior wall with core walls encasing the elevator, stair, and mechanical shafts. The structure accounts for approximately 6% of the building plan. Servicing the 20-story prototype requires only one mechanical zone that is located at the top of each building, which services downward with fan coil units to provide heating and cooling.

LEXINGTON AVE RESIDENCES
New York, New York
Adrian Smith + Gordon Gill Architecture
Proposed 2015

LOW-RISE

NUMBER OF UNITS / BUILDING	100
NUMBER OF STORIES (ABOVE GRADE)	20
BUILDING HEIGHT	71.5 m
FLOOR TO FLOOR HEIGHT	3.5 m
AVERAGE UNIT SIZE	150 m^2
PARCEL AREA	2,005 m^2
TOTAL AREA (ABOVE GRADE)	24,300 m^2
GROSS RESIDENTIAL FLOOR AREA	17,856 m^2
MECHANICAL FLOOR AREA	2,232 m^2
UNDERGROUND PARKING AREA	N/A
PODIUM PARKING AREA	2,106 m^2
PARKING SPACES	66
EFFICIENCY	81%
STRUCTURE	6%
WINDOW / WALL RATIO	40%

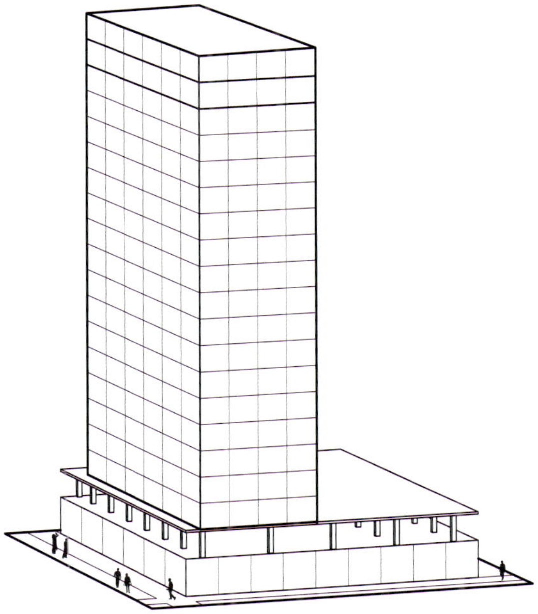

COURTYARD

Courtyard typologies can be found throughout the world and date back to ancient history. In the ancient Roman empire courtyard buildings appeared as a series of rooms that surrounded a central court. In China, Korea, and Japan—where linear buildings are often designed around central outdoor spaces—this typology has been used for centuries as traditional palaces and houses. Courtyard buildings allowed the expansion of dense city dwellings, without the loss of access to natural light and air.

Chicago has an abundance of courtyard buildings in the city center and in its surrounding suburbs. Aided by the explosion in Chicago's population and the increase of congestion, noise, and pollution in the late 19th and early 20th Centuries, the courtyard building helped lead the outward expansion of Chicago's population from the city core. Residents moved into areas such as Lakeview, Lincoln Park, Edgewater, and Rogers Park, where courtyard and three-flat buildings offered greener, less congested living environments than those downtown.

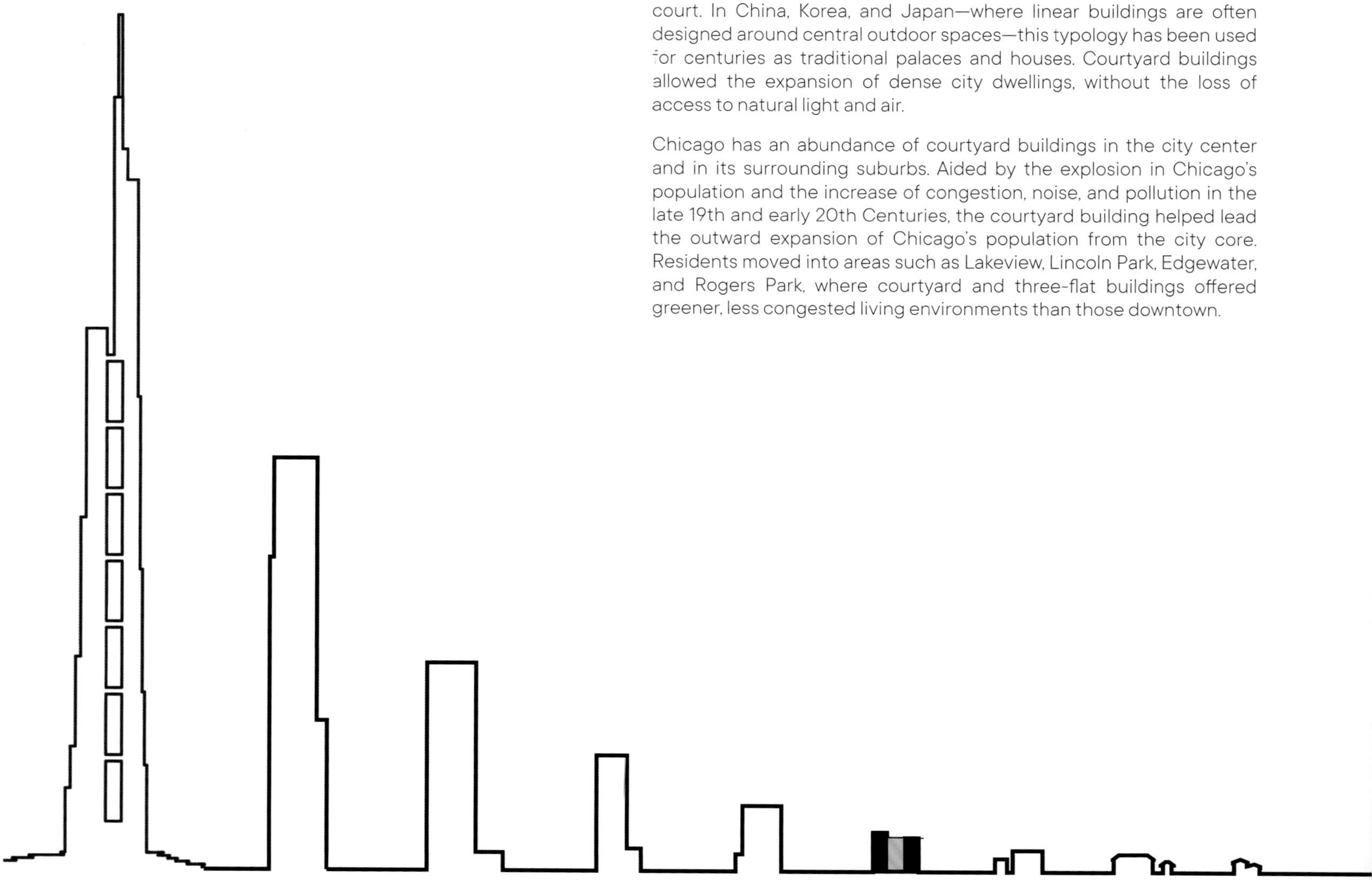

Courtyard buildings can take on a variety of heights and configurations, but they are typically three-to-four story buildings with apartments surrounding a central outdoor space. They are commonly configured as L-shaped on street corners or U-shaped on internal lots. The U-shaped configuration is particularly beneficial because it enables a developer to build two full wings that extend to the edge of a lot with a courtyard space in the middle, which ensures light and air will continue to reach the apartments despite any adjacent future development.

The typology is functional as both single- and multi-family residences, as well as government forums and retail markets and are used in many of today's traditional houses and newer apartment designs.

A key benefit of courtyard buildings is the central court: a semi-private green space within an otherwise dense urban environment that helps reduce noise and offers landscaped views to occupants. The buildings are commonly grouped with four to eight apartments per level, with two of the units per level sharing a stairwell. The building seems smaller and more intimate than a traditional apartment complex because of the multiple private entrances and the shared courtyard.

Although the Courtyard prototype is not the most efficient use of land, it maximizes natural light and ventilation, while providing a usable outdoor courtyard space as an amenity. The arrangement also eliminates the need for an internal corridor, allowing natural through ventilation and lighting and therefore minimizing the need for mechanical ventilation and air conditioning. Because their height is limited to four stories, courtyard buildings do not require fire proofing or elevators, reducing construction costs and promoting an economically ethical design.

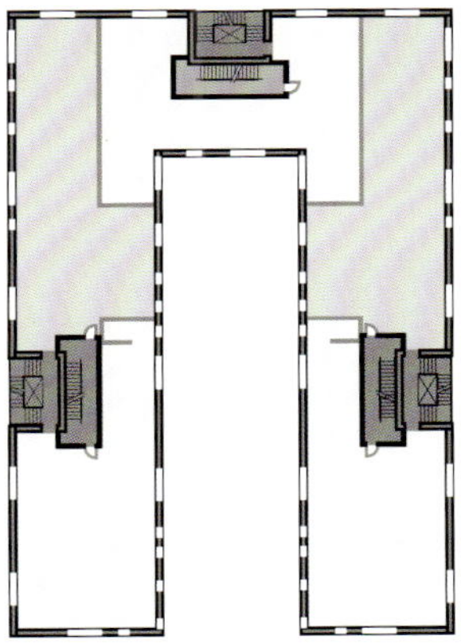

Figure 11

Typical floor plate
Courtyard

COURTYARD PROTOTYPE SYSTEMS

For this study, the Courtyard prototype is configured in a U-shaped plan and consists of five decentralized stair cores that climb four floors (Figure 11). Eight units share each stair core and external stairs are used as a secondary means of egress. Concrete core walls encase the stairs, with the U-plan also resistant against lateral forces.

Courtyard and three-flat buildings—see next prototype—are typically the same construction type, with masonry load-bearing walls on the perimeter and timber floor and roof construction. The courtyard and street elevations of the building are frequently stone or face brick, while less expensive finishes are on the alley and rear elevations. This type of fire resistive construction is permitted by zoning laws because the prototypes are four stories or less. In some cases, such buildings have concrete/steel frames with block infill and brick cladding.

VANCOUVER RESIDENCES
Vancouver, British Columbia
Adrian Smith + Gordon Gill Architecture
Proposed 2009

Windows are punched openings with the largest facing the courtyard. Front elevations and smaller openings are found along the back alleys and rear elevations. For the purposes of this study, a window-to-wall ratio of 14.5% was used. In total, the structure only accounts for approximately 2% of the building plan. Framed punched aluminum windows with low-E double glazing are set within the brick veneer facade, providing the prototype with an 18% window-to-wall ratio. Each unit has an independent mechanical system using gas-forced air heating and packaged condenser units on the roof for cooling.

The Courtyard prototype in the study is located on an approximately 2,000m^2 city lot and multiple units are 150m^2 in size. This prototype typically has gas-fired, forced-air heating systems and central air conditioning that are segregated by unit to provide individual thermostat controls, as well as separate metering. Courtyard buildings are built using a variety of construction methods and for this study the courtyard prototype is designed using a concrete frame with block infill, with a two-way flat plate system on a nine-meter grid to maximize flexibility for interior fit-out.

400 GROVE STREET
San Francisco, California
Fougeron Architecture
Completed 2016

COURTYARD

NUMBER OF UNITS / BUILDING	20
NUMBER OF STORIES (ABOVE GRADE)	4
BUILDING HEIGHT	14 m
FLOOR TO FLOOR HEIGHT	3.5 m
AVERAGE UNIT SIZE	150 m^2
PARCEL AREA	2,075 m^2
TOTAL AREA (ABOVE GRADE)	3,756 m^2
GROSS RESIDENTIAL FLOOR AREA	3,756 m^2
MECHANICAL FLOOR AREA	N/A
UNDERGROUND PARKING AREA	N/A
PODIUM PARKING AREA	2,465 m^2
PARKING SPACES	16
EFFICIENCY	89%
STRUCTURE	2%
WINDOW / WALL RATIO	14.6%

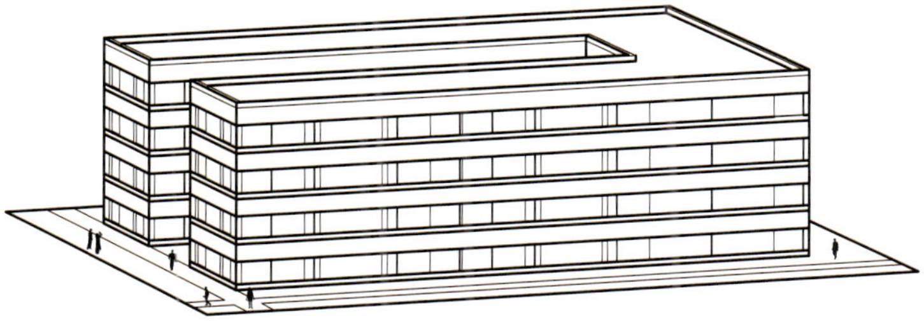

THREE-FLAT

Today, nearly every city—and many dense suburban environments—has multi-unit apartment buildings situated next to each other on narrow urban lots, forming a neighborhood. These long, narrow multi-unit buildings are found around the world but are most successful in cities with efficient street layouts that have street access at the front of the building and alley or service entrances at the back. Blocks can be several hundred feet long, allowing for greater density; a neighborhood of multi-unit buildings can be more dense than a courtyard neighborhood.

Multi-unit buildings have anywhere from two to ten apartments, or flats, and can reach up to four floors above grade. When multi-unit buildings face a major commercial street, it is common to have retail on the first floor with residential units above. When one faces a residential street, it typically has a basement or garden apartment that is depressed four to five feet below grade so that the owner can maximize the number of units. It is also possible for the floors to be divided into front, middle, and rear tenants if a separate egress is provided, further maximizing the unit space for the owner.

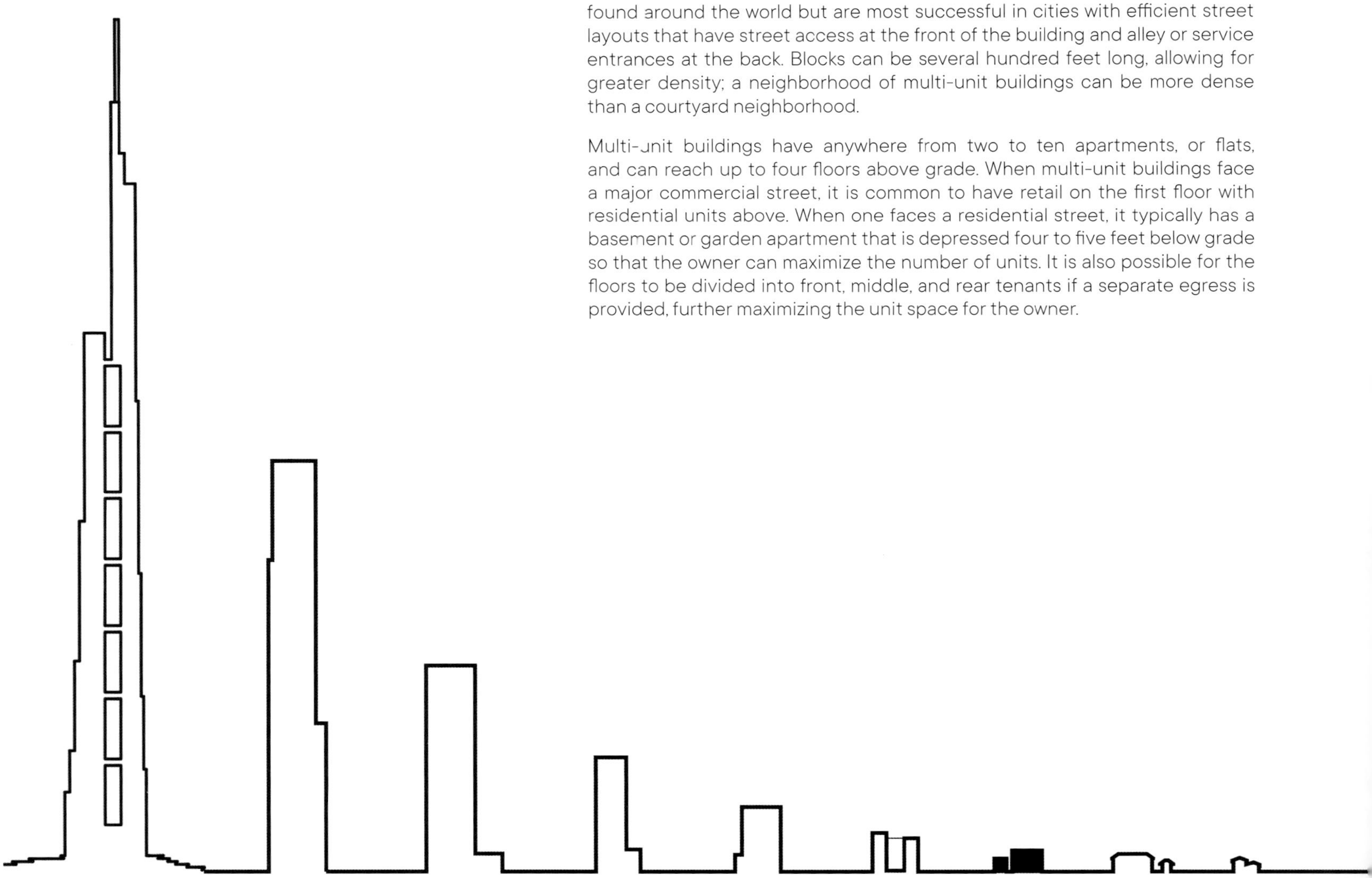

Unlike the Courtyard prototype, the Three-Flat's position is on a typical 9.25m x 42.5m (31' x 140') lot and does not have access to a landscaped courtyard, instead sharing a modest rear garden and front yard. The open space is typically about 20% of the lot area. If the lot size allows, a garage is located at the rear of the lot and accessed from the alley.

It is common for three-flat buildings to have multi-story front porches or balconies, as well as rear balconies, which may be integrated with the second exit stair (Figure 12). The mechanical systems use gas-forced air and packaged condenser units on the roof for cooling. The system is zoned floor-by-floor with a separate condenser for each unit, and individual controls for heating.

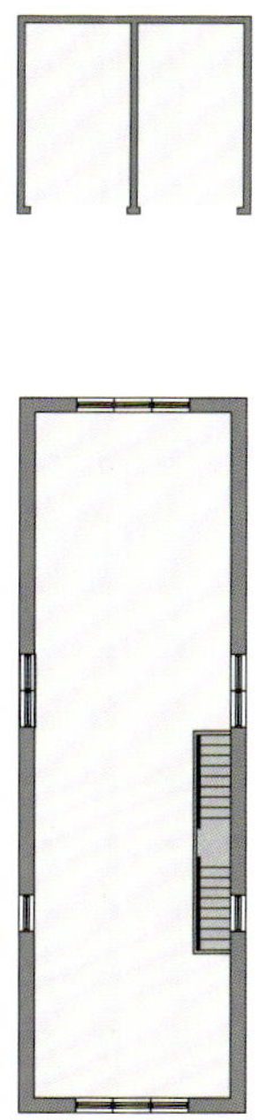

Figure 12

Typical floor plate
Three-Flat

THREE-FLAT PROTOTYPE SYSTEMS

For the purposes of our study, the multi-unit building is represented as a Three-Flat prototype with three stories and structural block walls along the length of the lot. Timber trusses for joists span the width of the structure, accounting for 3% of the building plan. Because the structure spans in the short direction, column-free spaces are achieved for flexibility in the internal layout. Typically, the living space is in the front, with the internal stair and two rooms fitting narrowly across the back of the plan.

The Three-Flat has similar advantages to the Courtyard prototype. It occupies a narrow lot with a shot-gun layout and shares internal entry stairs at the front and an external stair at the back. It can utilize a simple wood frame, composite construction, steel, or even metal or bar-joist framed systems.

For this study, the Three-Flat's facade system is a brick veneer over a block wall backup with punched aluminum-framed windows that have low-E double-glazing set within the brick veneer facade. Large windows face the street and garden, while smaller windows occupy the side walls, resulting in a window-to-wall ratio of 9%.

TYPICAL THREE-FLAT
Chicago, Illinois

THREE-FLAT	
NUMBER OF UNITS / BUILDING	3
NUMBER OF STORIES (ABOVE GRADE)	3
BUILDING HEIGHT	10.5 m
FLOOR TO FLOOR HEIGHT	3.5 m
AVERAGE UNIT SIZE	150 m^2
PARCEL AREA	414 m^2
TOTAL AREA (ABOVE GRADE)	554 m^2
GROSS RESIDENTIAL FLOOR AREA	554 m^2
MECHANICAL FLOOR AREA	N/A
UNDERGROUND PARKING AREA	N/A
PODIUM PARKING AREA	51 m^2
PARKING SPACES	2
EFFICIENCY	91%
STRUCTURE	2%
WINDOW / WALL RATIO	9.6%

TYPICAL THREE-FLAT
Chicago, Illinois

URBAN SINGLE-FAMILY

Just outside of a city's urban core, entire neighborhoods—with identical lot sizes—exist in the Urban Single-Family typology. Sometimes in a dense urban environment, tall, narrow single-family houses are mixed on a block with multi-flat buildings.

A wide variety of these homes can be found in Zone 5 cities including flat-fronted row houses, greystones, and several varieties of historical houses such as Craftsman bungalow, Cape Cod, and Federalist. Zoning laws typically control the scale of these neighborhoods, therefore when older neighborhoods have empty lots, infill construction of similar scale is utilized between the existing properties, often consisting of new urban single-family homes.

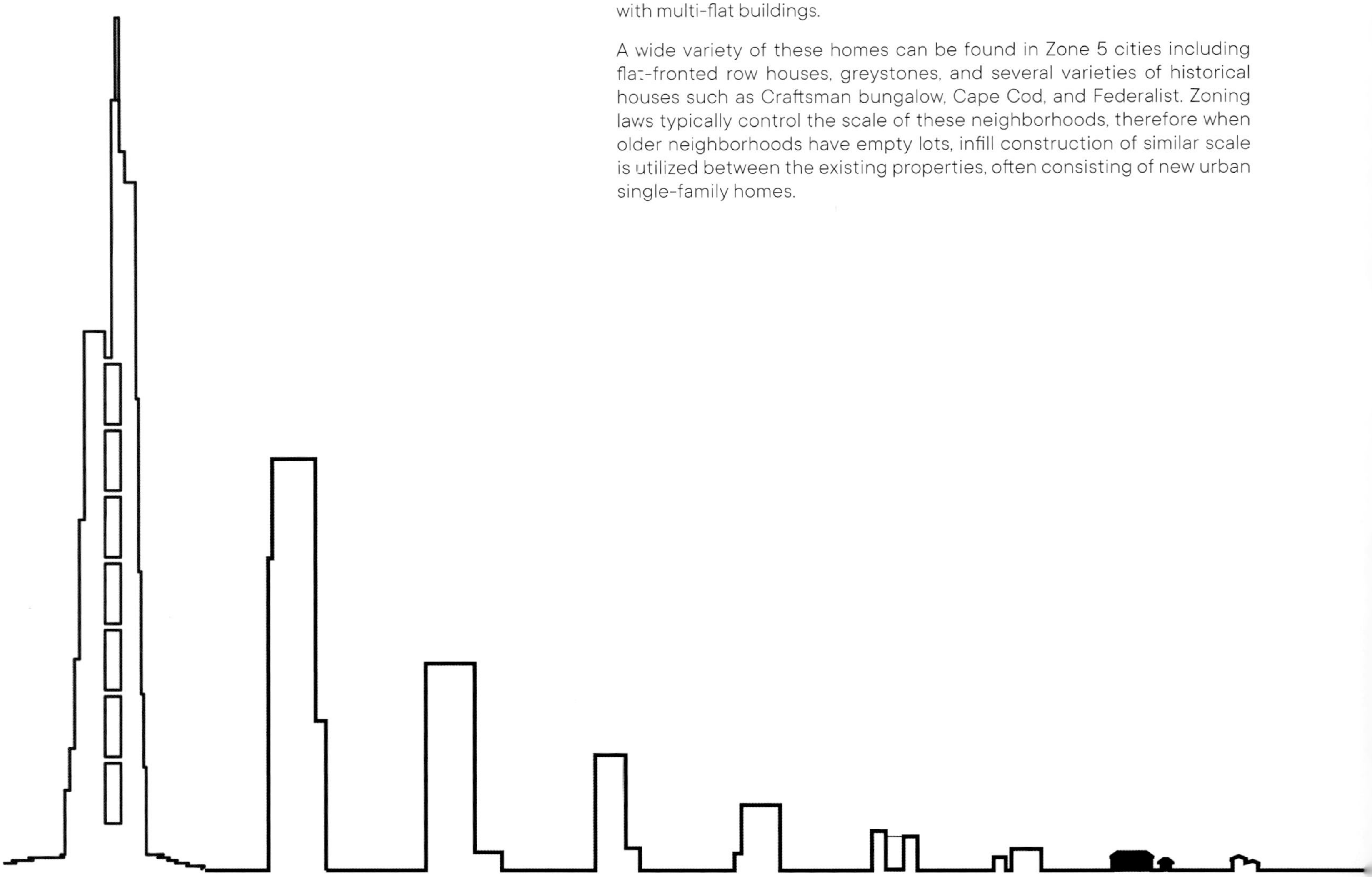

URBAN SINGLE-FAMILY PROTOTYPE SYSTEMS

For this study, the Urban Single-Family prototype is represented by a two-story, narrow building that is approximately 8m x 23m (26' x 75'), with a 150m^2 total area. The prototype has a living room, dining room, and kitchen, with three bedrooms located on the second story (Figure 13). The site is compact, with a small front and backyard and five to ten-foot side yards.

The Urban Single-Family prototype is modeled with timber frame stick-built walls and a timber floor structure, with structure accounting for approximately 1% of the building plan. The exterior facade is clad with masonry, which is typical for the standard urban single-family house, although other materials such as stone, metal siding, and insulated EIFS panels are also used. Construction types range from timber balloon-frame, to masonry bearing walls, to composite wall types that are more modern. In should be noted here, modern fire codes no longer allow wood-framed houses to be built using wooden cladding due to the proximity of one lot to another.

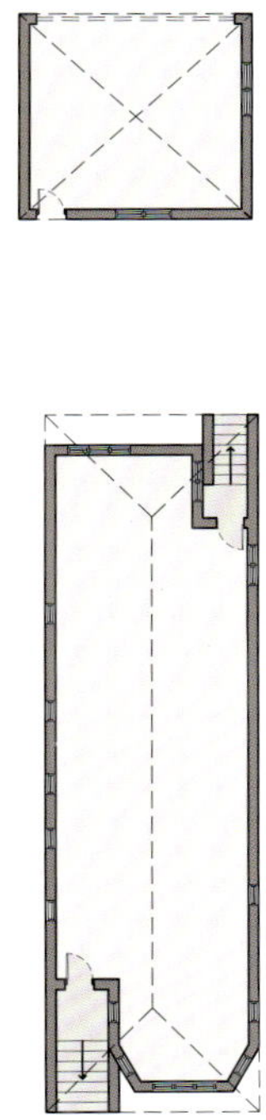

Figure 13

Typical Floor Plate
Urban Single-Family

TYPICAL URBAN SINGLE FAMILY
Chicago, Illinois

The Urban Single-Family prototype assumes that the windows, which are punched aluminum and framed with low-E double glazing, are set within the brick veneer facade. Large windows face the street and backyard with smaller windows along the demising walls. The window-to-wall ratio is at 7%.

Similar to the Three-Flat prototype, the site of the Urban Single-Family prototype is a 440m^2 city lot and consists of a house and a rear-facing garage that is accessible from the rear alley. Also similar to the Three-Flat prototype is the mechanical system, which has radiant or forced-air heat and air conditioning. The mechanical systems include a gas forced-air furnace in the basement for heating and a condenser unit at the rear of the house.

TYPICAL URBAN SINGLE-FAMILY BLOCK
Chicago, Illinois

URBAN SINGLE-FAMILY	
NUMBER OF UNITS / BUILDING	1
NUMBER OF STORIES (ABOVE GRADE)	2
BUILDING HEIGHT	5.6 m
FLOOR TO FLOOR HEIGHT	3.1 m
AVERAGE UNIT SIZE	150 m^2
PARCEL AREA	440 m^2
TOTAL AREA (ABOVE GRADE)	216 m^2
GROSS RESIDENTIAL FLOOR AREA	175 m^2
MECHANICAL FLOOR AREA	N/A
UNDERGROUND PARKING AREA	N/A
PODIUM PARKING AREA	41 m^2
PARKING SPACES	2
EFFICIENCY	98%
STRUCTURE	1%
WINDOW / WALL RATIO	7%

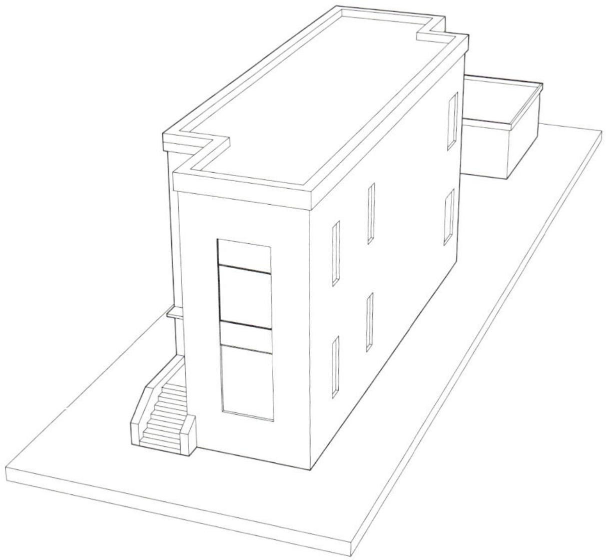

SUBURBAN SINGLE-FAMILY

Zoning laws have greatly influenced the spread of housing outside city limits by creating wide zones where only residential development was permitted. Suburban areas have larger lot sizes, and consequently larger houses, than the city center.

The Suburban Single-Family house typically has a generous lawn space in the front and back, a private driveway and an attached garage. Over the years the suburban house in America has changed in size: older houses from the 1800s which houses several generations may be over 3,000 sf, whereas small houses from the 1950s and 1960s may be only 2,000 sf (200m^2).

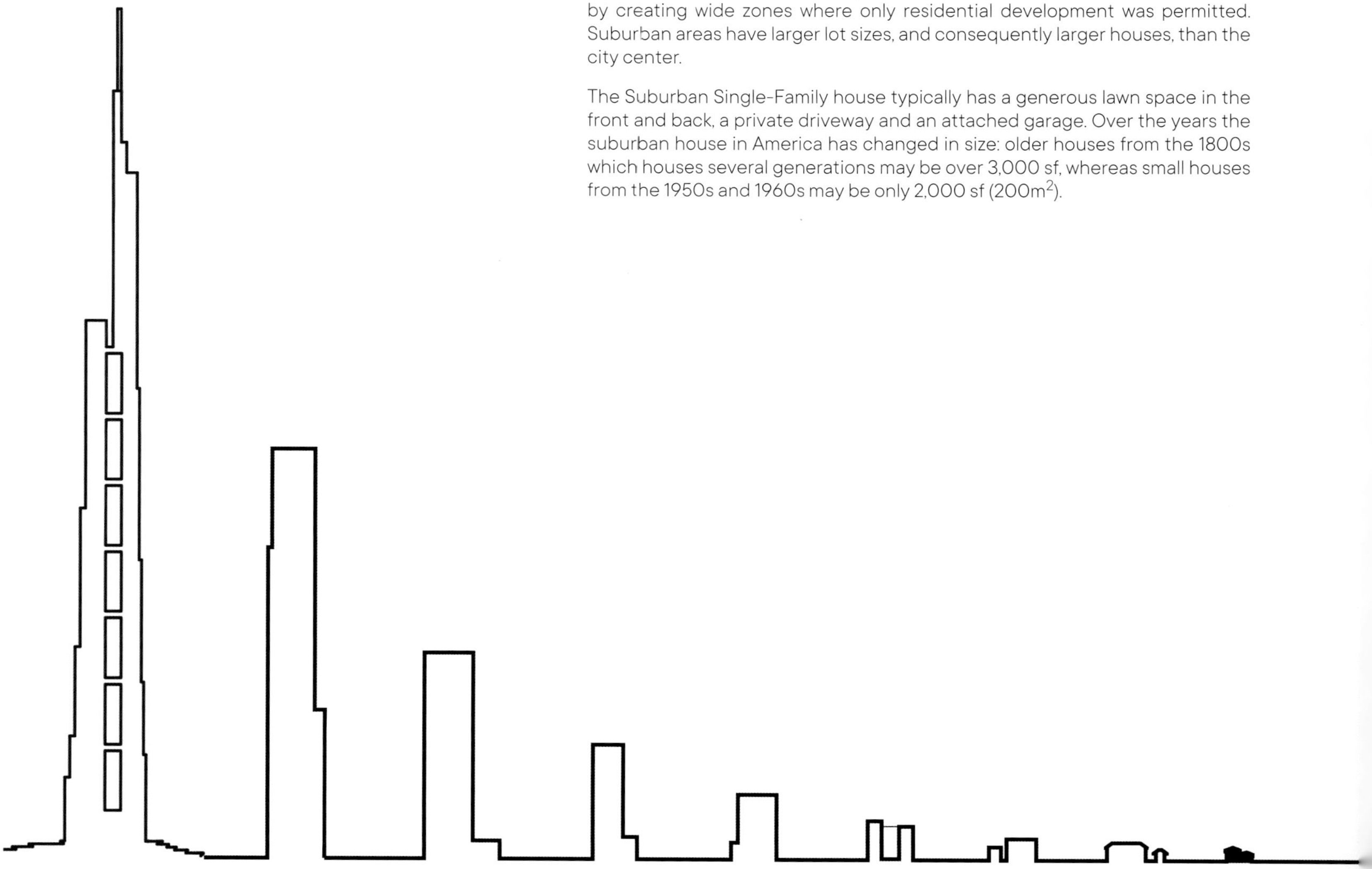

SUBURBAN SINGLE-FAMILY PROTOTYPE SYSTEMS

For this study, the Suburban Single-Family prototype reflects most typical North American suburban houses as a two-story building with a gross area of 233m^2, three bedrooms, and an attached garage (Figure 14). It is modeled with timber-frame stick-built walls and a timber floor structure, reducing the structure to a mere 0.7% of the building plan.

The Suburban Single-Family prototype has punched wood-framed windows, with low-E double glazed windows that are set within a brick veneer facade. Large windows face the street and backyard with smaller windows along the side walls, minimizing views of neighboring parcels and providing a 12% window-to-wall ratio.

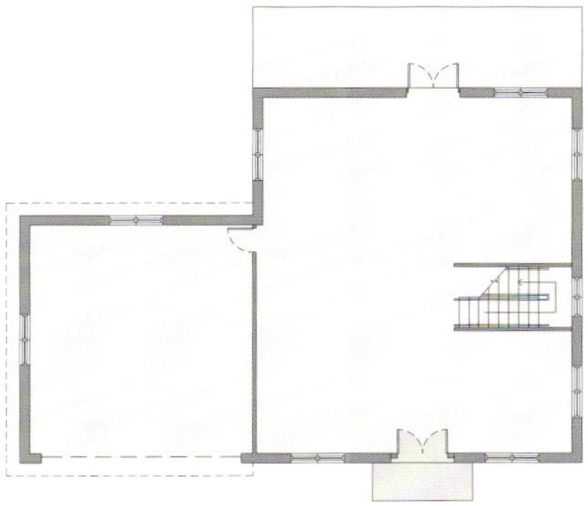

Figure 14

Typical Floor Plate
Suburban Single-Family

For ease of construction and economy of cost, the suburban single-family house is most commonly wood-framed construction, but the construction type allows for a variety of external cladding veneers. They are often clad with wood or metal siding, brick, stone, or a combination of these materials. The mechanical system includes a gas forced air furnace in the basement for heating, and a condenser unit on grade for cooling.

The Suburban Single-Family prototype was modeled on a lot that is slightly over 1,000m^2, with a generous front yard, backyard, and a private driveway to an attached two-car garage. The large yards provide enough space for outdoor activities, decks, gardening, and children's play areas. Trees typically shade the front and the backyards.

TYPICAL ZONE 5
Suburban Single Family

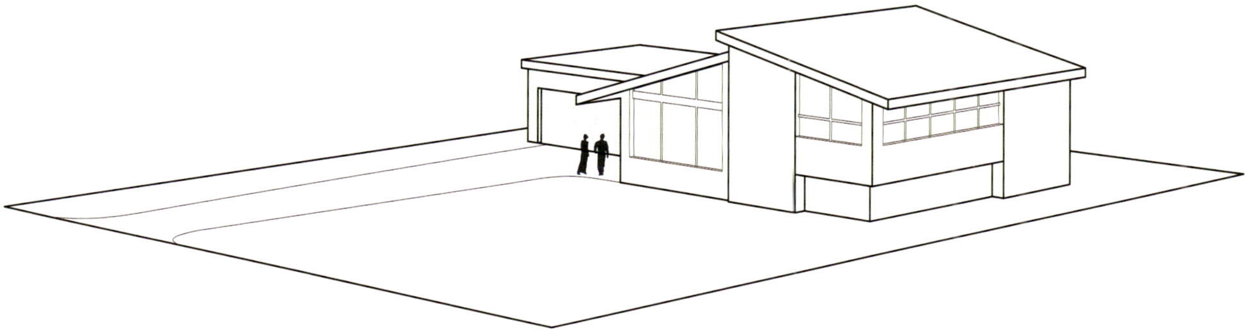

SUBURBAN SINGLE-FAMILY

NUMBER OF UNITS / BUILDING	1
NUMBER OF STORIES (ABOVE GRADE)	2
BUILDING HEIGHT	8.6 m
FLOOR TO FLOOR HEIGHT	3.2 m
AVERAGE UNIT SIZE	150 m^2
PARCEL AREA	1,076 m^2
TOTAL AREA (ABOVE GRADE)	233 m^2
GROSS RESIDENTIAL FLOOR AREA	233 m^2
MECHANICAL FLOOR AREA	N/A
UNDERGROUND PARKING AREA	N/A
PODIUM PARKING AREA	53 m^2
PARKING SPACES	2
EFFICIENCY	98%
STRUCTURE	.7%
WINDOW / WALL RATIO	10.9%

TYPICAL ZONE 5
Chicago, Illinois
Suburban Single Family

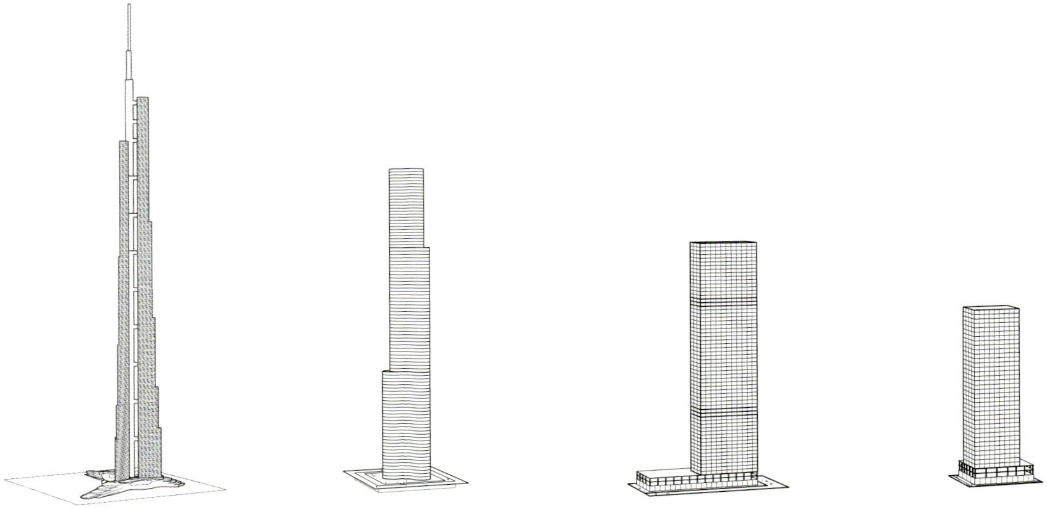

MASSING STUDY

TYPICAL FLOOR PLATE

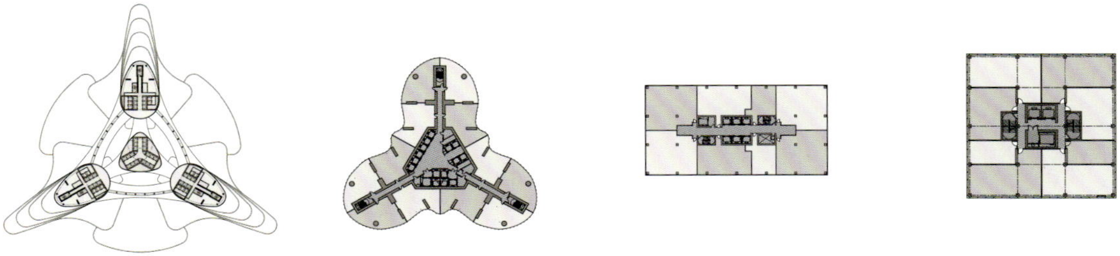

	MEGATALL	SUPERTALL	HIGH-RISE	MID-RISE
NUMBER OF UNITS / BUILDING	2,000	1,000	500	200
NUMBER OF STORIES ABOVE GRADE	213	121	65	38
BUILDING HEIGHT (M^2	766	435	229	134.5
FLOOR TO FLOOR HEIGHT (M)	3.5	3.5	3.5	3.5
TOTAL ABOVE GRADE AREA (M^2)	451,480	231,869	110,184	42,896
GROSS RESIDENTIAL FLOOR AREA (M^2)	406,342	205,710	91,255	34,774
MECHANICAL FLOOR AREA (M^2)	34,762	19.618	6,293	2,108
UNDERGROUND PARKING AREA (M^2)	44,400	23,600	N/A	N/A
PODIUM PARKING AREA	N/A	N/A	8,424	4,010
NUMBER OF PARKING SPACES	1,268	575	263	124
EFFICIENCY	74%	76%	82%	81%
STRUCTURE	10.3%	9.8%	4%	4%
WINDOW / WALL RATIO	40%	40%	40%	40%

Table 1 Prototype Data

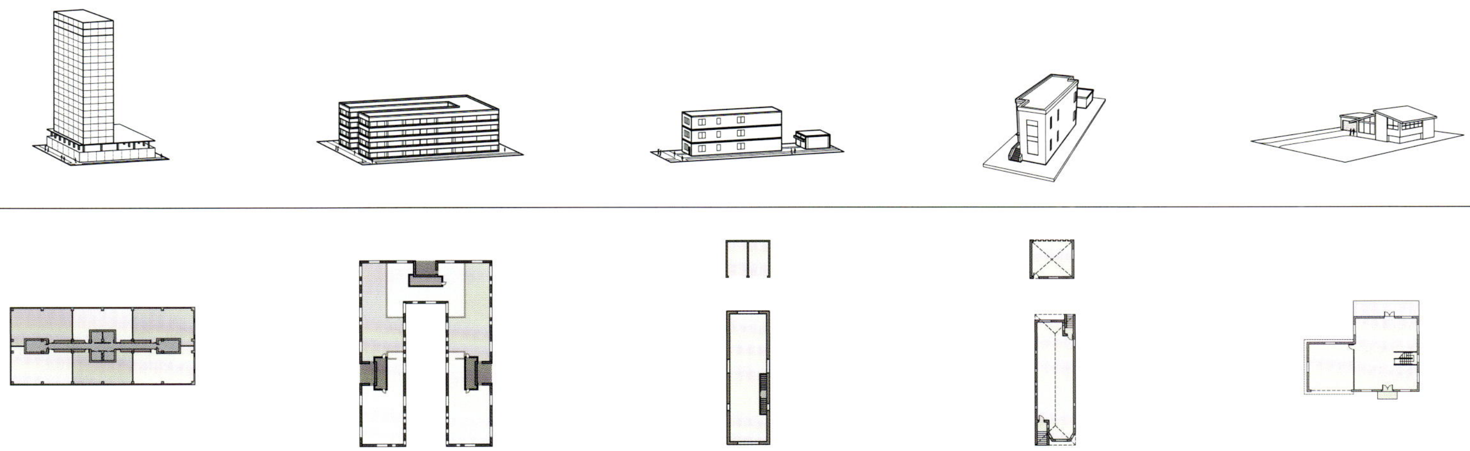

LOW-RISE	COURTYARD	THREE-FLAT	URBAN SINGLE-FAMILY	SUBURBAN SINGLE-FAMILY
100	20	3	1	1
20	4	3	2	2
71.5	14	10.5	5.6	8.6
3.5	3.5	3.5	3.1	3.2
24,300	3,756	554	216	233
17,856	3,756	554	175	233
2,232	N/A	N/A	N/A	N/A
N/A	N/A	N/A	N/A	N/A
2,106	2,465	51	41	53
66	16	2	2	2
81%	89%	91%	98%	94%
6%	2%	3%	1%	0.7%
40%	14.6%	9.6%	7%	10.9%

LAND USE

Although it has changed considerably through the ages, the development, spread, and expansion of cities is not a recent phenomenon. Ancient cities grew to defend groups of people or protect valuable land; others were strategically built along trade routes or shipping ports. If a city's population continually expands it needs to adapt by creating areas of increased density and improved transportation.

The development of open land has historically impacted the human condition. Land use is an acute issue in western nations, such as the United Kingdom and Japan, and can be even more critical in newly industrialized and developing nations where there is an opportunity to learn from earlier trends. But the United States continues to serve as an interesting example of urban development at a relatively young age.

LAND-USE PATTERNS

In the United States, urban growth has moved outward from dense industrial centers, expanded around personal transportation. The widespread adoption of the automobile in the early 20th Century prompted the contemporary phenomenon of the commuter suburb. Unlike the densely inhabited regions around European cities, American suburbs had more open space and were further encouraged by heavy investments in infrastructure. People began moving to the suburbs in search of the "American Dream."

This trend has accelerated over the last century; today more than 55% of the US population lives in the suburbs compared with 31% living in urban areas and the trend toward suburban living is increasing (***Pew Social trends, based on US census data, 2018***). This pattern has several societal implications, touching on major issues including natural and agricultural land loss as well as transportation. When urban regions expand as suburbs, large areas of rural and agricultural land are lost. In the united states between 1992 and 2012, 12.5 million Ha (31 million acres) of agricultural land was lost to urban development or low-density residential use (***Farmland Information Center, 2018***).

The corollary to this is that even with improvements in agricultural productivity through intensification and horticultural technology, continued agricultural land loss in the United States will lead to further conversion of forest and natural land elsewhere in the world to provide food for the domestic population. There is also an ever-increasing area of agricultural land this is given over to production of crops such as corn and soybean for biofuel. 5.6 million hectares of agricultural land was used solely for corn ethanol production in 2011 (***Mumm et al., 2014***), so land loss to urbanization is not just an environmental issue. It will soon become a food security issue as well.

Another result of changes in land use and the resultant pollution from cities is that water sources have become contaminated or have been altered throughout history. In terms of land and water, it is clear that the finite amount of natural resources available are being stressed but it is also becoming increasingly apparent that planners, politicians, and populations are faced with the problem of land use as outward expansion continues without checks.

Development is typified by its expansion outward from a city center, as people search for access to more land along transportation corridors. Most suburban developments are characterized by their low-population density and dependence on automobiles for both commuting long distances as well as short in-town trips. Land uses such as housing, commercial, recreational, and public spaces, are typically zoned separately. Planning in all density patterns should maximize accessibility of basic services within walking or biking distance in order to minimize automobile use.

The land-use patterns associated with low-density development can lead to a car-dependent culture that results in one of the most environmental and financially costly impacts of expansion. A 2002 study of vehicle ownership in Los Angeles, San Francisco, and Chicago showed that as population density decreases, vehicle miles traveled per individual exponentially increases ***(Holtzman et al., 2002)***. Low-density residential developments are typically unable to support commuter-friendly public transit and, through necessity, must invest more (per capita) in roadways to support the needs of the community. If people lived closer their place of employment—as is increasingly being facilitated by improved communication technologies—it is possible for a dispersed workplace, effectively eliminating the need for daily employee in-person interaction. This technological development has the potential to have a profound impact on society, and in terms of transportation, bears some relationship to the time before the car.

HUMAN HEALTH

Increased use of fossil fueled cars affects human health through two mechanisms. First, by causing a deterioration in air quality through exhaust emissions and second, by leading to a decrease in physical activity. Over the past century, an overwhelming amount of research has shown a causal relationship between air pollution—notably oxides of nitrogen (NOx), sulfur oxides (SOx), organic chemicals, metals, and particulates—and negative health effects, linking particulate matter with respiratory problems, asthma attacks, and increased mortality. Continued tightening of vehicle emissions standards have sought to address this impact and it is predicted that following the implementation of the latest emissions standards across the G20 countries, PM2.5 emissions will be reduced by two thirds and 60,000 early deaths in urban areas can be avoided by 2030 ***(ICCT, 2017)***.

Small measures can add up; during the 1996 Atlanta Summer Olympics, residents and visitors were encouraged not to drive, which decreased morning peak traffic by 22.5%. The result was a significant decrease in the number of asthma associated emergency room visits—as much as a 44.1% reduction ***(Friedman et al., 2001)***. Similarly, prior to and during the 2008 Beijing Summer Olympics, roadway restrictions were implemented in order to cut air pollution and alleviate traffic congestion. The result was a reduction in the daily volume of traffic by more than one million cars and a reduction in emissions of between 45.7% and 56.8% ***(Zhou et al., 2009).***

COMMUNITY PROTOTYPES

Each building prototype is now placed in comparable communities of 2,000 residential units that were designed to comply with relevant building codes for a cool-humid location. The community prototypes are based on GIS data obtained from the City of Chicago and surrounding suburbs. This data, along with local building code and practical knowledge, informed the design assumptions regarding the lot size, parking capacity and structure, roads, alleys, footpaths, and water infrastructure. Nine communities were designed to ensure a fair and consistent analysis across all prototypes. Building structures and the infrastructure required to support them are also included.

The study seeks to answer questions related to the land area that each community occupies by examining parameters associated with the communities' land use, including the capability of remaining land to support food, energy production, and recreational use. Lot size was determined by typical Chicago standards based on building type, height, and occupancy. Prototypes that are 20 stories or higher follow standards within the downtown area. Courtyard, Three-Flat, and Urban House prototypes look to urban residential zones outside of the downtown area and the Suburban House prototype follows the typical size of outer suburban lots.

Parking requirements were also determined on predetermined zoning. Prototypes follow the standards of the downtown zone, which has 0.55 parking spots per unit. Multi-family buildings located outside a downtown area have one parking spot per unit, and all single-family houses have a 2-car garage. Sidewalks and alleys were designed based on GIS data that was found to be typical depending on the assumed neighborhood. Footpaths were included for the Three-Flat and Urban Single-Family since they have detached garages for parking, while all other prototypes have direct access to parking.

The amount of infrastructure to support a community is relevant to the embodied carbon calculations in future analyses. For this study, the supporting infrastructure is included for the area within the dimensions of the community, up to the boundary of each building, and includes sidewalks and roadways, as well as potable water, sanitary sewer, and stormwater piping.

After the building prototypes were designed, their footprints and the resulting lots were imported into ESRI ArcMax to create prototypical communities. The land use of each community was analyzed using the software's measurement tools to allow the generation of information about total land use as well as a breakdown by use type. The analysis focuses on the difference in land use between the nine prototypes, with each prototype compared to the criterion of the suburban single-family home, providing an equal baseline for all communities in terms of the land occupied by 2,000 residences.

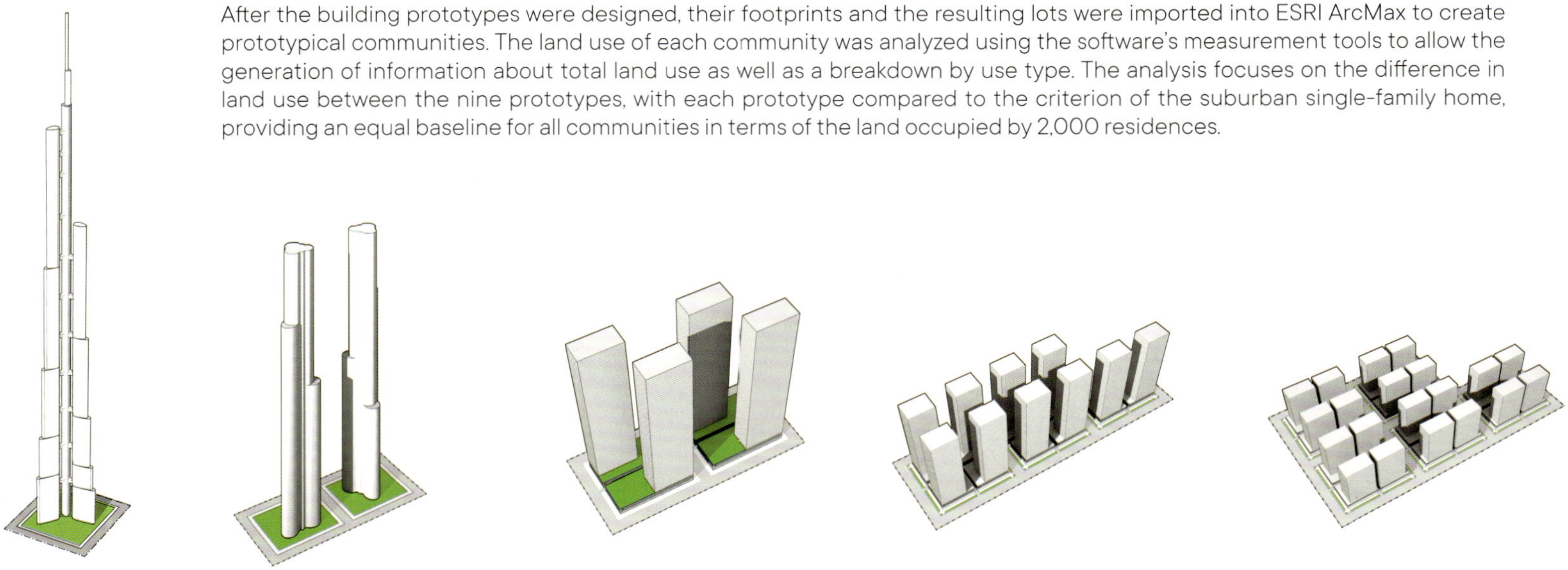

GLOSSARY

FAR. The Floor Area Ratio is calculated by dividing the gross floor area by the total land area.

Total Land Area. The Total Land Area is defined as the area the entire community occupies, including total parcel area plus all public and paved areas (1+2+3+4+5).

Total Parcel Area. The Total Parcel Area is defined as all the building lots, excluding public spaces such as sidewalks, alleys, and roads (1+2).

Total Building Footprint. The Total Building Footprint is the total land area that is covered by buildings, as defined by the perimeter of the exterior walls of the building (1).

Total Infrastructure Length. The Total Infrastructure Length is the total length of the pipe infrastructure within the community, up until the entrance of the building.

Total Unpaved Area. The Total Unpaved Area is the area of the community that is not paved or part of the building; i.e. permeable or green spaces (5).

Total Paved Area. The Total Paved Area includes all roads, alleys, sidewalks, and footpaths.

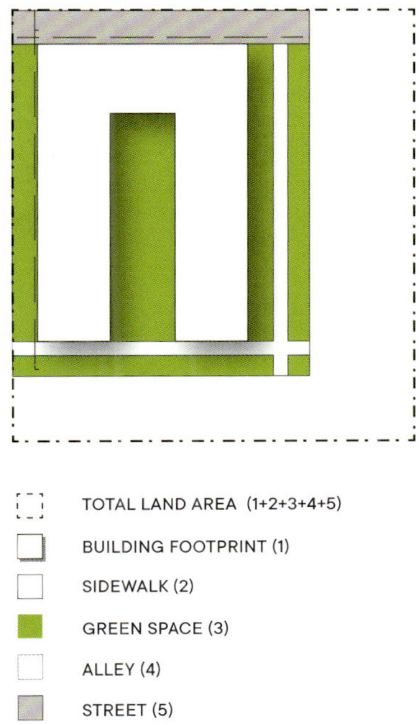

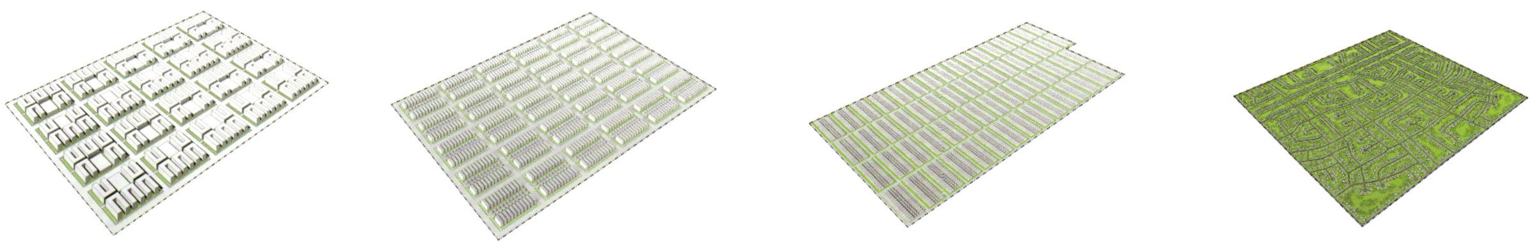

MEGATALL

0.9% ***LAND USE OF THE SUBURBAN PROTOTYPE***

Land Area of Suburban Single- Family Prototype

Land Area of Megatall Prototype

The Megatall prototype is a 213-story tower with 2,000 units occupying a total land area of approximately 2.7 Ha. The site is designed to accommodate the structure and all necessary infrastructure to support the needs of the building's services. It has a relatively large area (43%) of open space surrounding the tower's base (1.1 hectares), as is typical of developments anchored by megatall towers. This land which is above the below grade parking garage can be used for recreational use such as a children's play area or landscaped as an amenity for the residents.

The surrounding asphalt roads are designed with an external four-lane road measuring 15m wide with a generous 7m wide concrete pedestrian sidewalk that can accommodate a dedicated bike lane. Pathways were not designed within the site because occupants have direct access to below-grade parking and it was assumed that open space landscape would include them. Below-grade and buried infrastructure includes potable water, stormwater and sewer piping within the site and was designed to the boundary of the building in consultation with plumbing engineers.

The Megatall occupies the least amount of land, at just 0.9% of the Suburban Single Family's total land use. The building footprint occupies 12% of the land area, with paved and unpaved sections covering 45% and 43%, respectively. Although it is intuitive that the Megatall prototype would have the smallest total building footprint, it is worth noting how great the difference is when compared with the Suburban prototype.

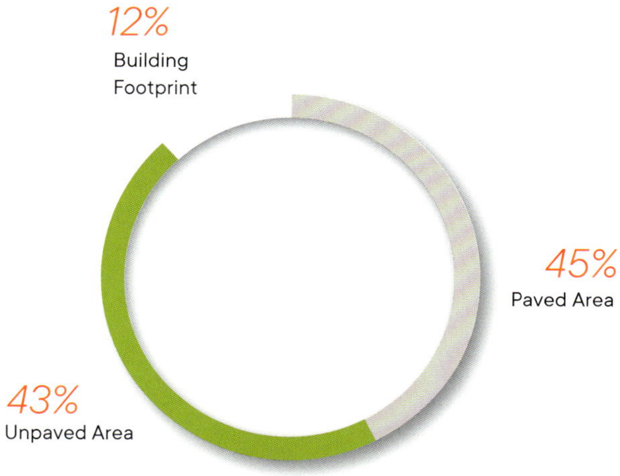

MEGATALL

TOTAL LAND AREA	26,896 m^2
NUMBER OF BUILDINGS	1
NUMBER OF STORIES (ABOVE GRADE)	213
AVERAGE LOT SIZE	14,641 m^2
TOTAL BUILDING FOOTPRINT	3,177 m^2
TOTAL INFRASTRUCTURE LENGTH	1,646 m
TOTAL SIDEWALK AREA	3,584 m^2
TOTAL DRIVEWAY AREA	N/A
TOTAL ALLEY AREA	N/A
TOTAL STREET AREA	8,672 m^2
BUILDING COVERAGE	3,177 m^2 (12%)
TOTAL UNPAVED AREA	11,464 m^2 (43%)
TOTAL PAVED AREA	12,256 m^2 (45%)
LAND DIFFERENCE FROM SUBURBAN	2,940,241 m^2

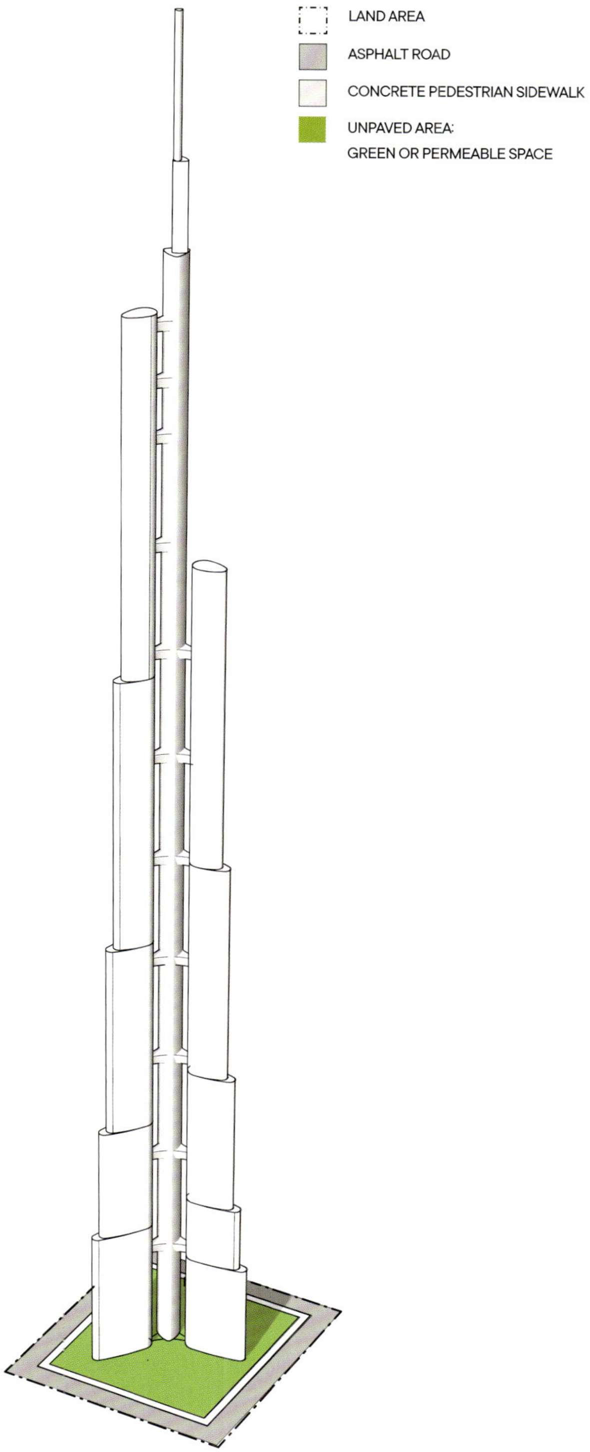

SUPERTALL

1.2% ***LAND USE OF THE SUBURBAN PROTOTYPE***

Land Area of Suburban Single-Family Prototype

Land Area of Supertall Prototype

The Supertall prototype consists of two 121-story buildings with a total of 2,000 units. The community occupies a total land area of approximately 3.7 hectares. As with the Megatall prototype, the site is designed to accommodate the structure and the necessary infrastructure to support the building's services. It also has a relatively large area of open space (37%) surrounding the tower's base (1.3 hectares), and although is a smaller percentage than the Megatall prototype, the overall area is greater. Also, like the Megatall, the land above the below-grade parking garages can be used for recreational uses including a children's play areas or landscaped amenity spaces.

The surrounding asphalt roads are designed with an external four-lane road measuring 15m wide with a 7m wide concrete pedestrian sidewalk that can accommodate a dedicated bike lane. The two parcels are separated by a similarly dimensioned road and sidewalk. Internal footpaths were not designed across the site because occupants have direct access to below-grade parking and it is assumed that open space landscape includes them. Below-grade and buried infrastructure includes potable water, stormwater, and sewer piping within the site and was designed to extend to the boundary of the building in consultation with plumbing engineers.

The two parcels can conceivably be combined, with a shared parking garage and some shared infrastructure. The twin tower format is common in several major cities, however both buildings would typically be built by the same developer, at the same time, and for the purposes of this study we wanted each building to maintain a degree of autonomy not possible with twin towers.

The height of the Supertall is 43% less than the Megatall, necessitating two towers with a combined building footprint occupying 12% of the land area. The paved and unpaved areas cover 51% and 37%, respectively. The total land use of the Supertall prototype is 1.2% of the Suburban Single-Family prototype.

SUPERTALL	
TOTAL LAND AREA	36,530 m^2
NUMBER OF BUILDINGS	2
NUMBER OF STORIES (ABOVE GRADE)	121
AVERAGE LOT SIZE	8,944 m^2
TOTAL BUILDING FOOTPRINT	4,529 m^2
TOTAL INFRASTRUCTURE LENGTH	2,676 m
TOTAL SIDEWALK AREA	5,712 m^2
TOTAL DRIVEWAY AREA	N/A
TOTAL ALLEY AREA	N/A
TOTAL STREET AREA	12,930 m^2
BUILDING COVERAGE	4,529 m^2 (12%)
TOTAL UNPAVED AREA	13,359 m^2 (37%)
TOTAL PAVED AREA	18,642 m^2 (51%)
LAND DIFFERENCE FROM SUBURBAN	2,930,607 m^2

HIGH-RISE

1.2% ***LAND USE OF THE SUBURBAN PROTOTYPE***

Land Area of Suburban Single-Family Prototype

Land Area of High-Rise Prototype

The High-Rise prototype consists of four 65-story towers each with 500 units that occupy a total land area of approximately 3.7 hectares. The four high-rise buildings use the same land area as the two supertall towers. As with the preceding prototypes, the site is designed to accommodate the structure and all necessary infrastructure to support the needs of the four buildings' services.

However, there is no open space surrounding the tower's base. Instead, there is a podium roof, which can still be used for recreational use such as a children's play area or landscaped as an accessible green roof or swimming pool. The four podium roofs have a combined area of 1.0 hectares, or 28% of the site area.

The surrounding asphalt roads are designed with an external four-lane road measuring 15m wide, with a generous 7m wide concrete pedestrian sidewalk, that like the previous prototypes, can accommodate a dedicated bike lane. The four parcels are separated on the short axis by a similarly dimensioned road and sidewalk and on the long axis by a 5m wide service alley. Below-grade and buried infrastructure includes potable water, stormwater, and sewer piping within the site and is designed to the boundary of the building in consultation with plumbing engineers.

The four towers have a combined building and podium footprint occupying 46% of the land area, with the paved area covering 54%. The total land use of the High-Rise prototype is 1.2% of the Suburban Single-Family prototype.

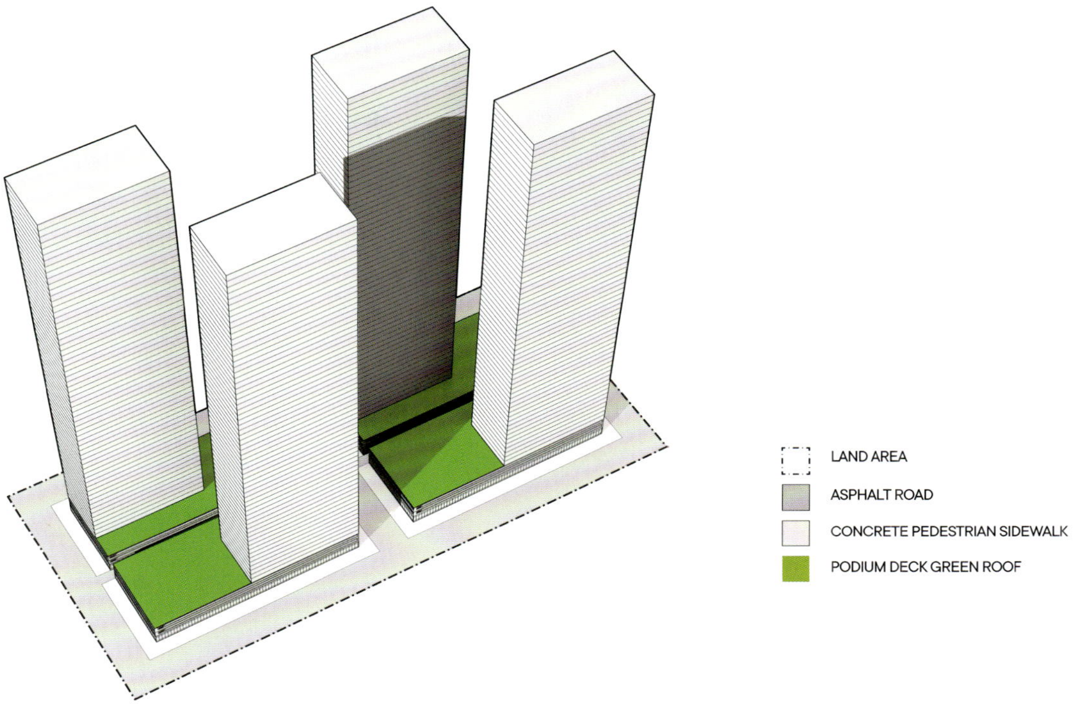

HIGH-RISE	
TOTAL LAND AREA	36,530 m^2
NUMBER OF BUILDINGS	4
NUMBER OF STORIES (ABOVE GRADE)	65
AVERAGE LOT SIZE	4,212 m^2
TOTAL BUILDING FOOTPRINT	16,848 m^2
TOTAL INFRASTRUCTURE LENGTH	2,204 m
TOTAL SIDEWALK AREA	5,573 m^2
TOTAL DRIVEWAY AREA	N/A
TOTAL ALLEY AREA	1,180 m^2
TOTAL STREET AREA	12,930 m^2
BUILDING COVERAGE	16,848 m^2 (46%)
TOTAL UNPAVED AREA	N/A
TOTAL PAVED AREA	19,683 m^2 (56%)
LAND DIFFERENCE FROM SUBURBAN	2,930,607 m^2

MID-RISE

1.5% LAND USE OF THE SUBURBAN PROTOTYPE

Land Area of Suburban Single-Family Prototype

Land Area of Mid-Rise Prototype

The Mic-Rise prototype is a collection of ten 38-story towers, each with 200 units that occupies a total land area of approximately 4.6 hectares. Each site is compactly aggregated with a parking podium that extends out to the street, as is typical of mid-rise buildings in a downtown area. The podium roof is similar to the High-Rise and can be used for recreation such as a children's play area or landscaped as an accessible green roof or swimming pool. The ten podium roofs have a combined area of 1.0 hectares, or 21% of the site area.

The surrounding asphalt roads are designed with a four-lane road measuring 15m wide, a 4m wide concrete pedestrian sidewalk, and a 3m wide landscaped parkway. The individual sites are separated by 5m wide service alleys. Below-grade and buried infrastructure includes potable water, stormwater, and sewer piping within the site and was designed to the boundary of the building in consultation with plumbing engineers.

The Mid-Rise community has a combined building footprint occupying 44% of the land area, with paved and unpaved sections covering 50% and 6%, respectively. The total land use of the Mid-Rise prototype is still low at 1.5% of the Suburban Single-Family prototype.

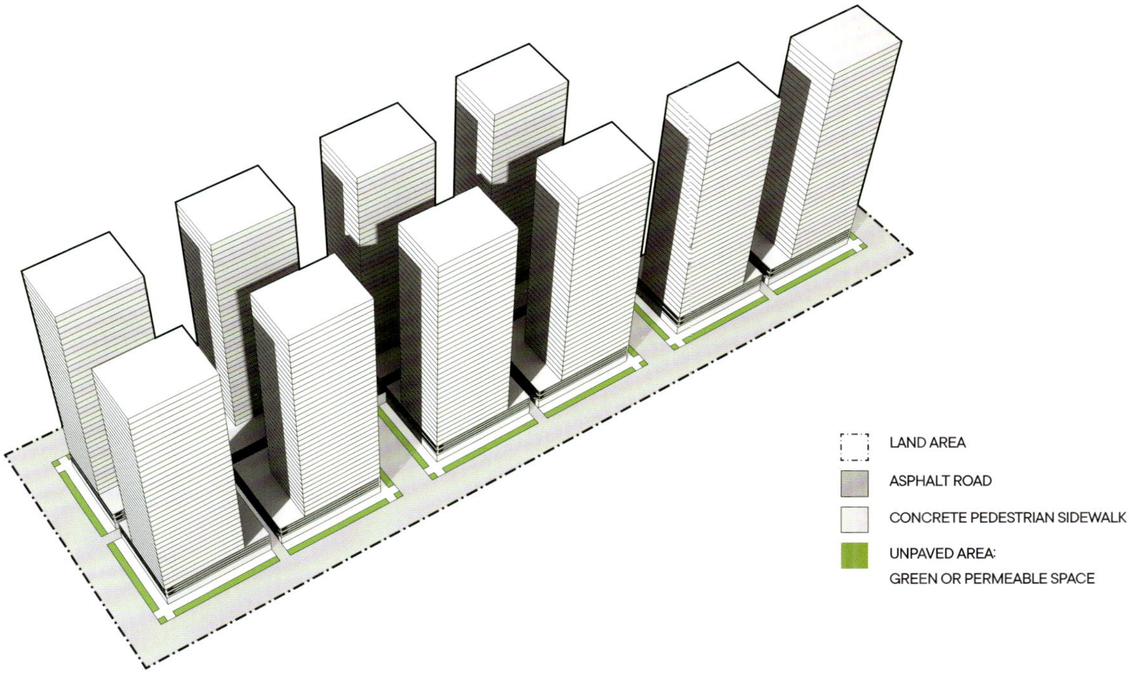

MID-RISE

TOTAL LAND AREA	45,508 m^2
NUMBER OF BUILDINGS	10
NUMBER OF STORIES (ABOVE GRADE)	38
AVERAGE LOT SIZE	2,005 m^2
TOTAL BUILDING FOOTPRINT	20,048 m^2
TOTAL INFRASTRUCTURE LENGTH	2,823 m
TOTAL SIDEWALK AREA	4,004 m^2
TOTAL DRIVEWAY AREA	N/A
TOTAL ALLEY AREA	2,958 m^2
TOTAL STREET AREA	15,713 m^2
BUILDING COVERAGE	20,048 m^2 (44%)
TOTAL UNPAVED AREA	2,779 m^2 (6%)
TOTAL PAVED AREA	22,674 m^2 (50%)
LAND DIFFERENCE FROM SUBURBAN	2,921,629 m^2

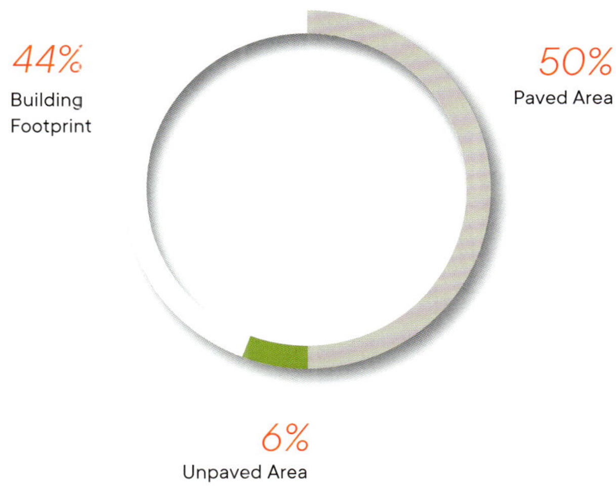

LOW-RISE

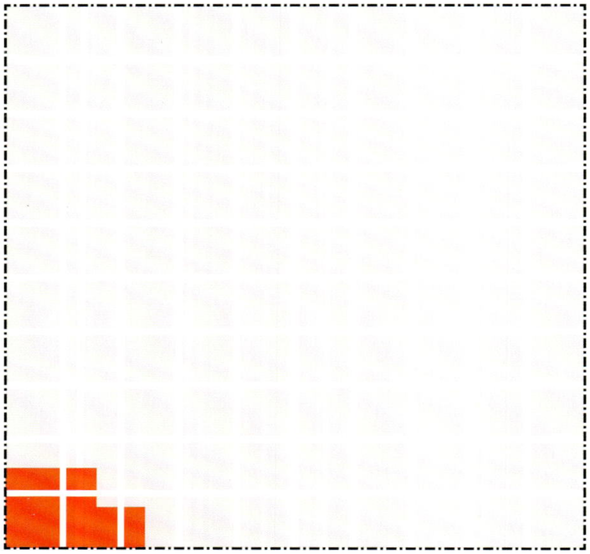

2.9% ***LAND USE OF THE SUBURBAN PROTOTYPE***

Land Area of Suburban Single-Family Prototype

Land Area of Low-Rise Prototype

The Low-Rise prototype consists of twenty 20-story towers with 100 units each, occupying a total land area of approximately 8.6 hectares. Each site includes a parking podium that extends out to the street, typical in low-rise buildings in a downtown area. The podium roof can be designed for recreational uses as with the previous prototypes. The 20 podium roofs have a combined area of 1.8 hectares, or 21% of the site area.

The asphalt streets are designed with four-lane roads measuring 15m wide, with adjacent 4m wide concrete pedestrian sidewalks and a 3m wide landscaped parkway. The individual sites are separated by 5m wide service alleys. Below-grade and buried onsite infrastructure includes potable water, stormwater, and sewer piping and is designed to the boundary of the building in consultation with plumbing engineers.

A main pipe was placed under the streets onsite, with connections to the individual buildings for potable and sewage systems. A stormwater system has been designed with a main pipe running north-south and east-west catch basins every 40m.

The Low-Rise community has a combined building footprint that occupies 47% of the land area, with paved and unpaved sections covering 47% and 6%, respectively. The total land use of the Low-Rise is the greatest of the tower prototypes, but still low at 2.9% of the Suburban Single-Family prototype.

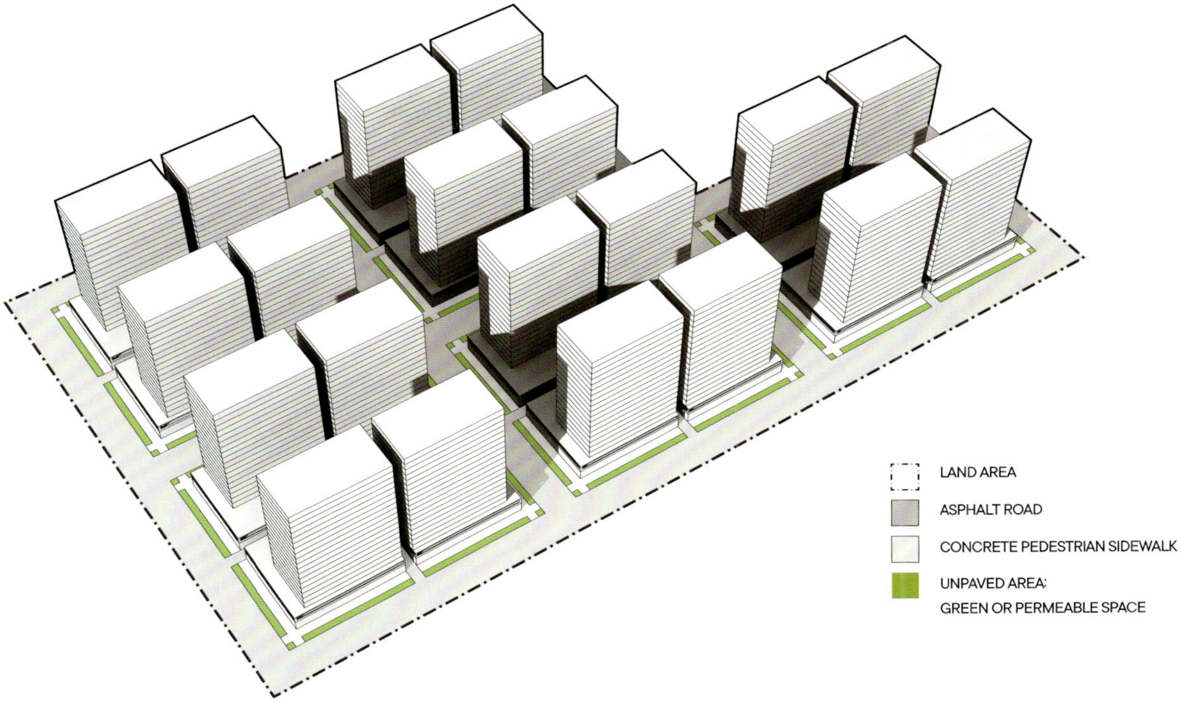

LOW-RISE	
TOTAL LAND AREA	86,135 m^2
NUMBER OF BUILDINGS	20
NUMBER OF STORIES (ABOVE GRADE)	20
AVERAGE LOT SIZE	2,005 m^2
TOTAL BUILDING FOOTPRINT	40,095 m^2
TOTAL INFRASTRUCTURE LENGTH	6,170 m
TOTAL SIDEWALK AREA	8,000 m^2
TOTAL DRIVEWAY AREA	N/A
TOTAL ALLEY AREA	5,325 m^2
TOTAL STREET AREA	27,135 m^2
BUILDING COVERAGE	40,460 m^2 (47%)
TOTAL UNPAVED AREA	5,580 m^2 (6%)
TOTAL PAVED AREA	40,460 m^2 (47%)
LAND DIFFERENCE FROM SUBURBAN	2,881,002 m^2

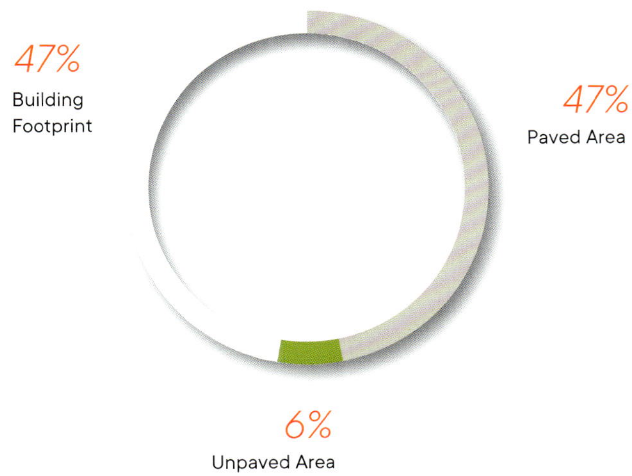

COURTYARD

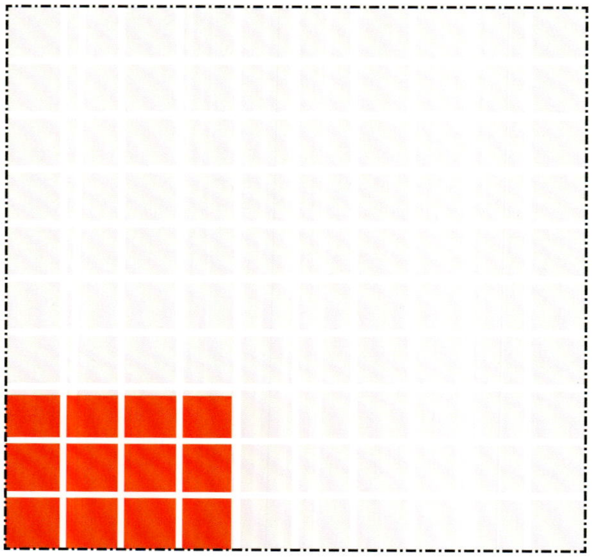

10.9% ***LAND USE OF THE SUBURBAN PROTOTYPE***

Land Area of Suburban Single-Family Prototype

Land Area of Courtyard Prototype

The Courtyard prototype consists of 100 buildings, each with four stories and 20 units. This can be considered the first true low-density prototype in the study, occupying a total land area of 32.3 hectares. Each site is approximately 1,500m^2 and sites are grouped together on an 11,800m^2 block of five buildings and a car parking structure. Each block has 0.44 hectares of green space within the property line and each courtyard building has almost 300m^2 of private open space. Parking garages, which replace the podiums of the previous prototypes, have one spot provided per unit, for a total of 100 spaces.

The surrounding asphalt streets are designed with roads measuring 15m wide to allow for street parking, with adjacent 2m wide concrete pedestrian sidewalks, a 3m wide parkway and 5m wide alleys running through the center of each block with access to the parking garages. Onsite below-grade and buried infrastructure includes potable water, stormwater and sewer piping and is designed to the boundary of the building, in consultation with plumbing engineers.

The Courtyard community has a combined building footprint occupying 37% of the land area, with paved and unpaved sections covering 36% and 28%, respectively. Despite the increased green space and decreased density of the Courtyard prototype, the total land use is relatively low at 10.9% of the Suburban Single-Family prototype.

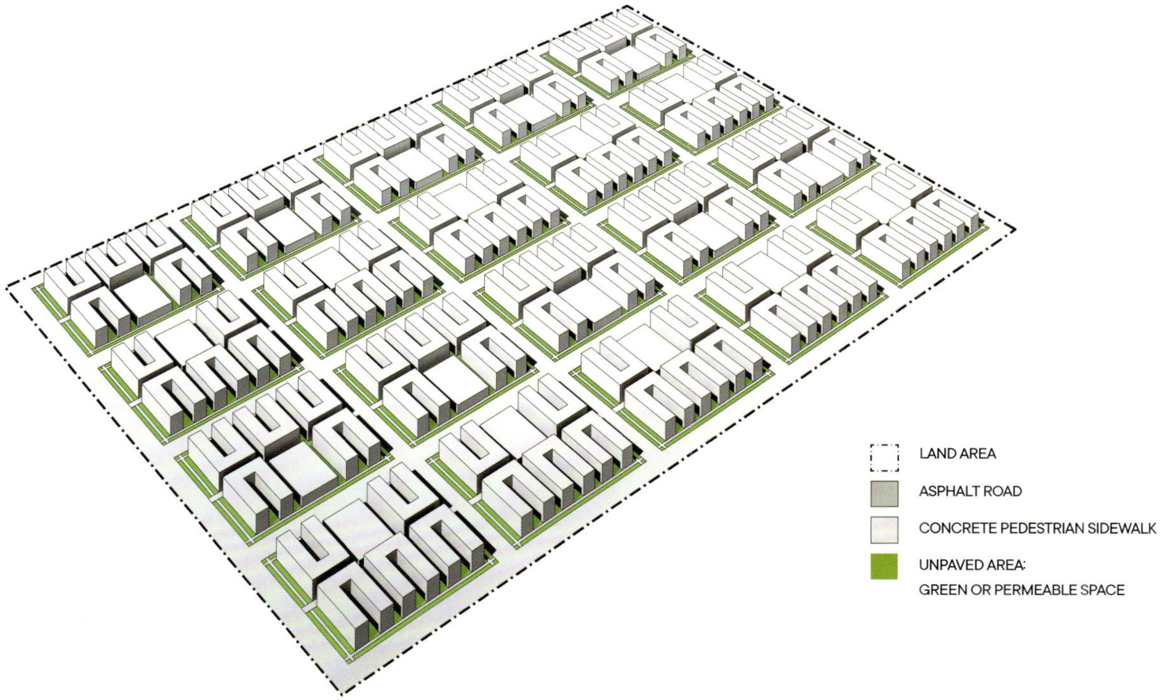

COURTYARD	
TOTAL LAND AREA	323,000 m^2
NUMBER OF BUILDINGS	100
NUMBER OF STORIES (ABOVE GRADE)	4
AVERAGE LOT SIZE	2,075 m^2
TOTAL BUILDING FOOTPRINT	118,560 m^2
TOTAL INFRASTRUCTURE LENGTH	25,074 m
TOTAL SIDEWALK AREA	16,720 m^2
TOTAL DRIVEWAY AREA	N/A
TOTAL ALLEY AREA	11,800 m^2
TOTAL STREET AREA	86,989 m^2
BUILDING COVERAGE	118,560 m^2 (37%)
TOTAL UNPAVED AREA	88,920 m^2 (27%)
TOTAL PAVED AREA	115,509 m^2 (30%)
LAND DIFFERENCE FROM SUBURBAN	2,644,137 m^2

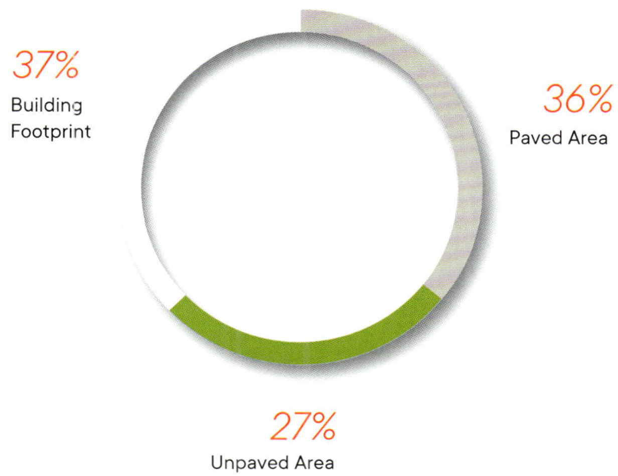

THREE-FLAT

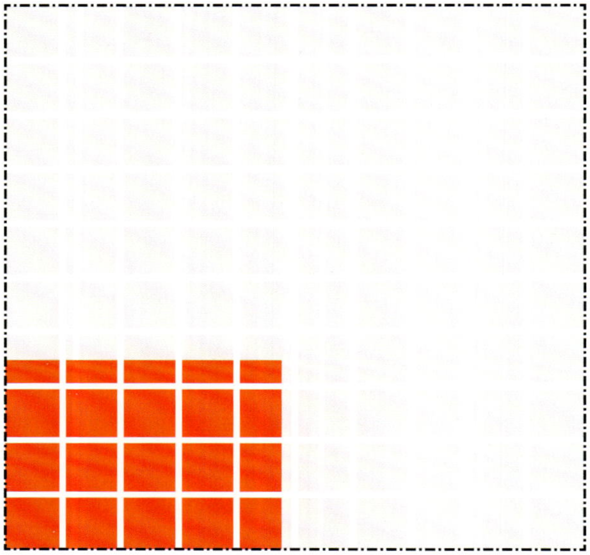

16% LAND USE OF THE SUBURBAN PROTOTYPE

Land Area of Suburban Single-Family Prototype

Land Area of Three-Flat Prototype

The Three-Flat prototype consists of 667 buildings, each with three floors, with one unit per floor. The total land area is approximately 48.5 hectares. Typical for an urban residential zone, each Three-Flat is situated on a block that measures 118m x 47.5m, with 16 lots per block. The average lot size is 414m^2 with a typical lot measuring 9.65m x 42.5m and 67m^2 of open space within the property line.

The surrounding asphalt streets have roads that measure 15m wide to allow for street parking, with adjacent 2m wide concrete sidewalks, a 3m wide parkway and 5m wide alleyways running through the center of each block. Shared, detached garages located at the back of each lot are accessible from the alleys and connect to the house by a path through the shared rear garden. Onsite below-grade and buried infrastructure includes potable water, stormwater and sewer piping and is designed to the boundary of the building in consultation with plumbing engineers.

The Three-Flat community has a combined building footprint occupying 30% of the land area, with paved and unpaved sections covering 40% and 30%, respectively. The total land use is 16% of the Suburban Single-Family prototype.

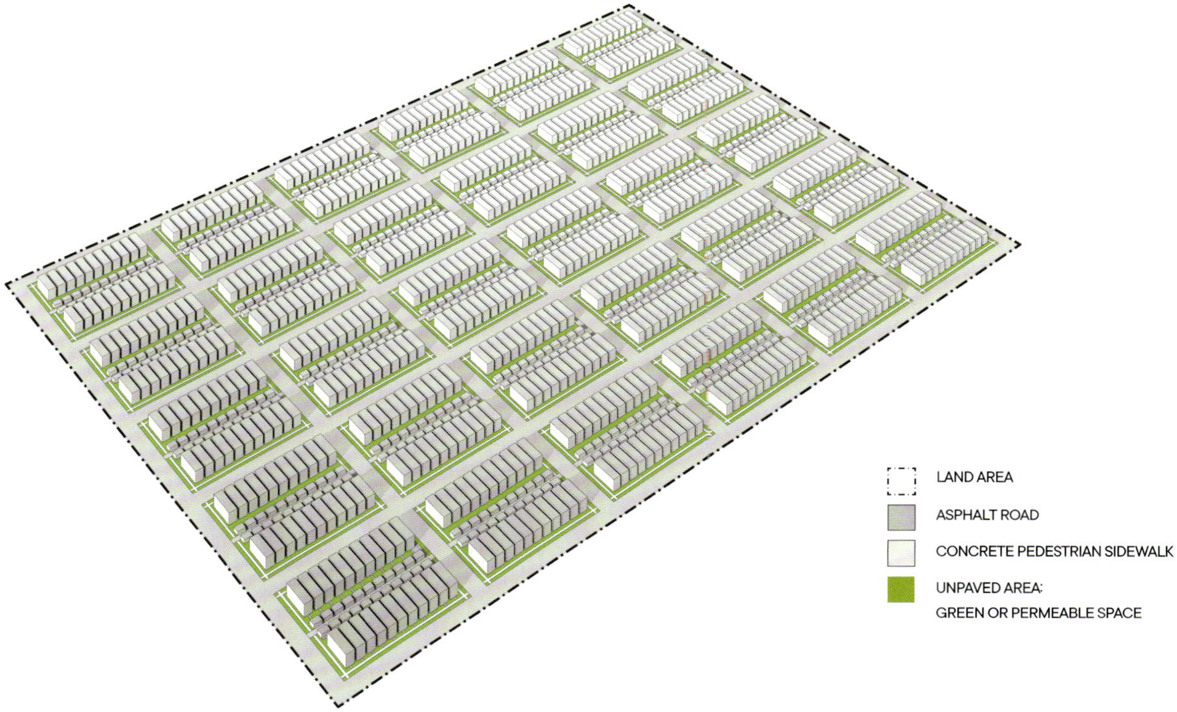

THREE-FLAT	
TOTAL LAND AREA	485,408 m^2
NUMBER OF BUILDINGS	667
NUMBER OF STORIES (ABOVE GRADE)	3
AVERAGE LOT SIZE	414 m^2
TOTAL BUILDING FOOTPRINT	147,974 m^2
TOTAL INFRASTRUCTURE LENGTH	57,005 m
TOTAL SIDEWALK AREA	25,498 m^2
TOTAL DRIVEWAY AREA	19,660 m^2
TOTAL ALLEY AREA	18,290 m^2
TOTAL STREET AREA	127,243 m^2
BUILDING COVERAGE	147,974 m^2 (30%)
TOTAL UNPAVED AREA	147,014 m^2 (30%)
TOTAL PAVED AREA	190,690 m^2 (40%)
LAND DIFFERENCE FROM SUBURBAN	2,481,729 m^2

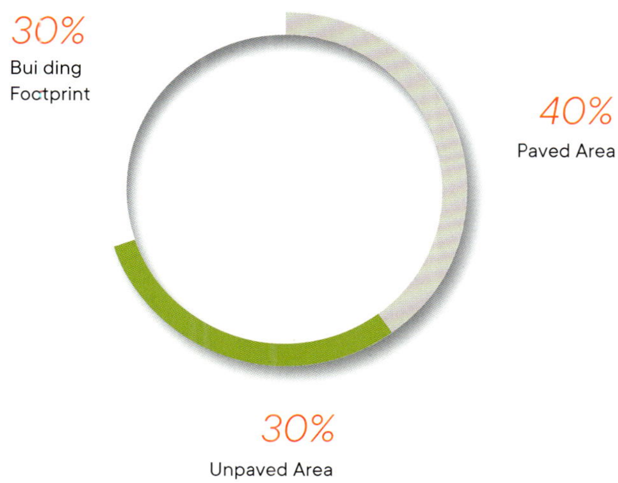

URBAN SINGLE-FAMILY

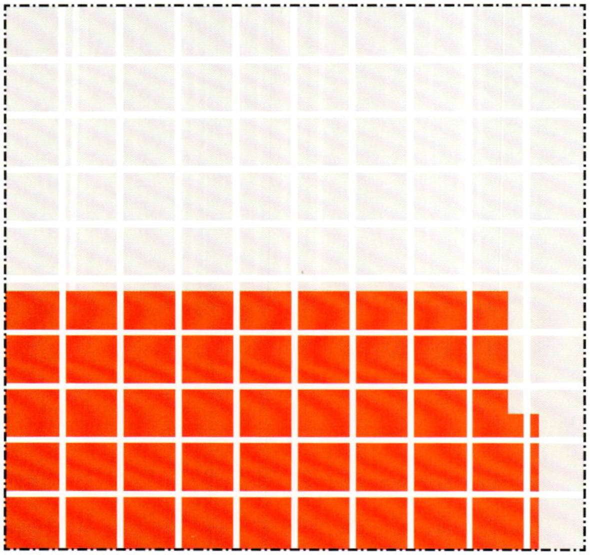

43% ***LAND USE OF THE URBAN PROTOTYPE***

Land Area of Suburban Single-Family Prototype

Land Area of Urban Single-Family Prototype

The Urban Single-Family prototype consists of 2,000 one-story, single-family houses, occupying a total land area of approximately 128 hectares. Each house is located on an urban residential lot of 11.4m x 38.5m, with 16 lots on a 194m x 44m block.

The surrounding asphalt streets are designed with roadways measuring 7.5m wide to allow for limited street parking, with adjacent 2m wide concrete sidewalks, a 3m wide parkway, and 4.5m wide alleys running through the center of each block. Detached two-car garages located at the back of each lot are accessible from the alley and connect to the house by a path through the shared rear garden. Onsite below-grade and buried infrastructure includes potable water, stormwater and sewer piping and was designed to the boundary of the building in consultation with plumbing engineers.

The Urban Single-Family community has a combined building footprint occupying 33% of the land area, with paved and unpaved sections covering 25% and 42%, respectively. The relatively lower density of the Urban Single-Family gives it the highest total land use when compared to the Suburban Single-Family prototype, however at 43%, it is still less than half of the area.

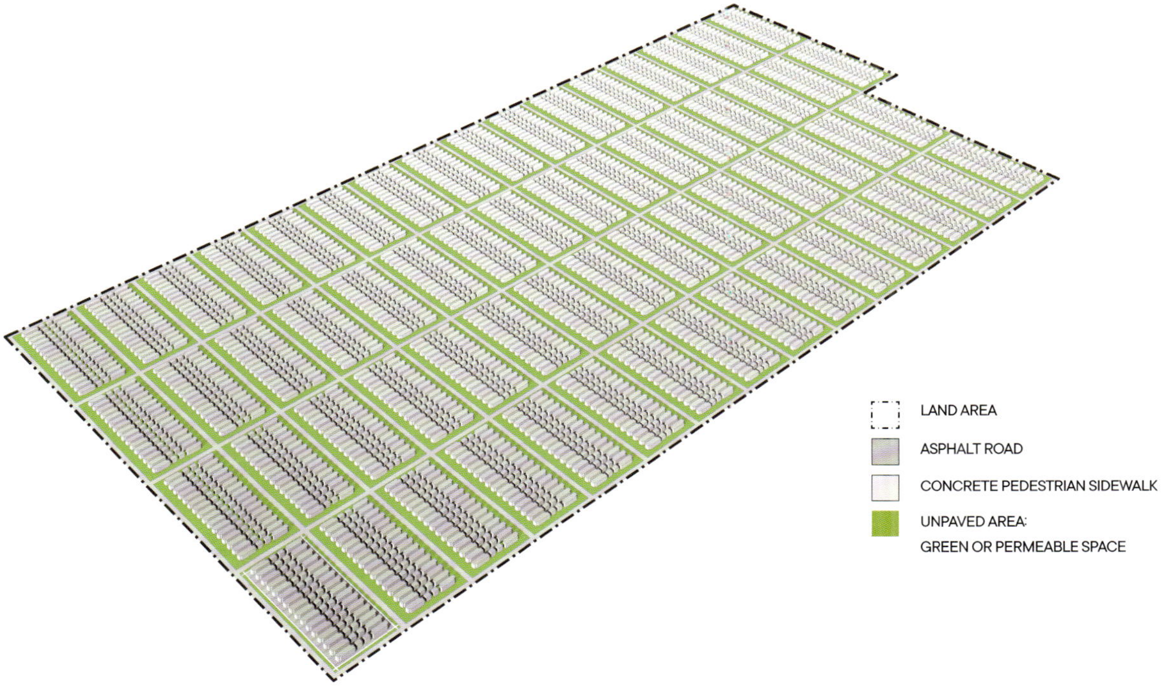

URBAN SINGLE FAMILY	
TOTAL LAND AREA	1,277,174 m^2
NUMBER OF BUILDINGS	2,000
NUMBER OF STORIES (ABOVE GRADE)	1
AVERAGE LOT SIZE	440 m^2
TOTAL BUILDING FOOTPRINT	417,247 m^2
TOTAL INFRASTRUCTURE LENGTH	139,302 m
TOTAL SIDEWALK AREA	69,500 m^2
TOTAL DRIVEWAY AREA	42,300 m^2
TOTAL ALLEY AREA	54,999 m^2
TOTAL STREET AREA	155,175 m^2
BUILDING COVERAGE	417,247 m^2 (33%)
TOTAL UNPAVED AREA	537,953 m^2 (42%)
TOTAL PAVED AREA	321,974 m^2 (25%)
LAND DIFFERENCE FROM SUBURBAN	1,689,963 m^2

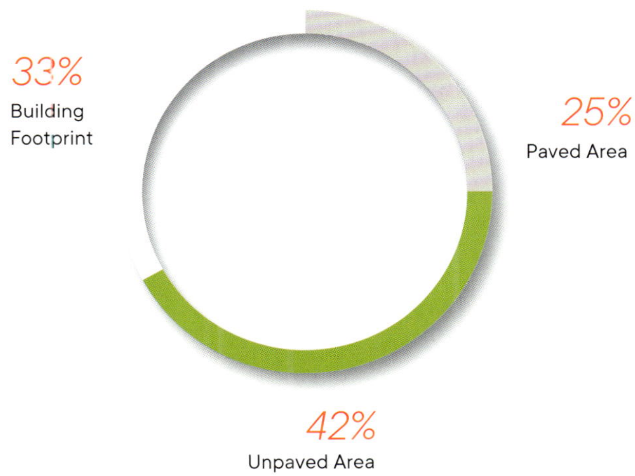

SUBURBAN SINGLE-FAMILY

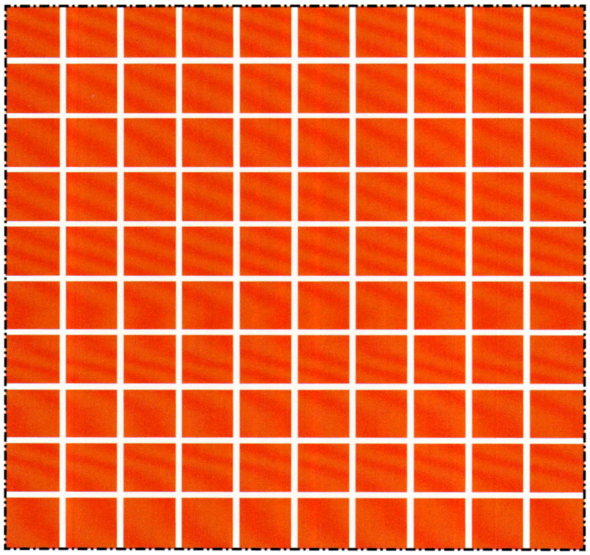

100% ***LAND USE OF THE SUBURBAN PROTOTYPE***

Land Area of Suburban Single-Family Prototype

The Suburban Single-Family prototype consists of 2,000 two-story, single-family houses over a total 296.7 hectares, in a low-density, suburban setting with each house located on a typical lot of 1076m^2 (1/4 acre). Parcel green space is typically in the range of 850m^2.

The surrounding asphalt streets are designed at 8m to 19m wide. The streets are designed in the winding or cul-de-sac fashion that is typical of a suburban development, with adjacent 2m wide concrete pedestrian sidewalks and a 3m wide parkway. Large, attached two-car garages connect to the street by a private driveway that runs through the front yard. Onsite below-grade and buried infrastructure includes potable water, stormwater and sewer piping and was designed to the boundary of the building in consultation with plumbing engineers.

The Suburban Single-Family community has a combined footprint that occupies 13% of the land area. This prototype has the greatest amount of green space per unit, with paved and unpaved sections covering 21% and 66%, respectively.

SUBURBAN SINGLE FAMILY	
TOTAL LAND AREA	2,967,137 m^2
NUMBER OF BUILDINGS	2,000
NUMBER OF STORIES (ABOVE GRADE)	2
AVERAGE LOT SIZE	1,076 m^2
TOTAL BUILDING FOOTPRINT	394,716 m^2
TOTAL INFRASTRUCTURE LENGTH	202,338 m
TOTAL SIDEWALK AREA	106,493 m^2
TOTAL DRIVEWAY AREA	163,452 m^2
TOTAL ALLEY AREA	N/A
TOTAL STREET AREA	353,041 m^2
BUILDING COVERAGE	394,716 m^2 (30%)
TOTAL UNPAVED AREA	1,956,769 m^2 (30%)
TOTAL PAVED AREA	622,986 m^2 (40%)
LAND DIFFERENCE FROM SUBURBAN	0

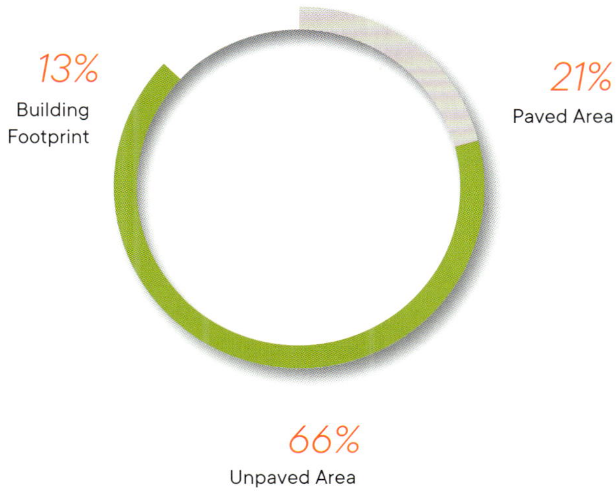

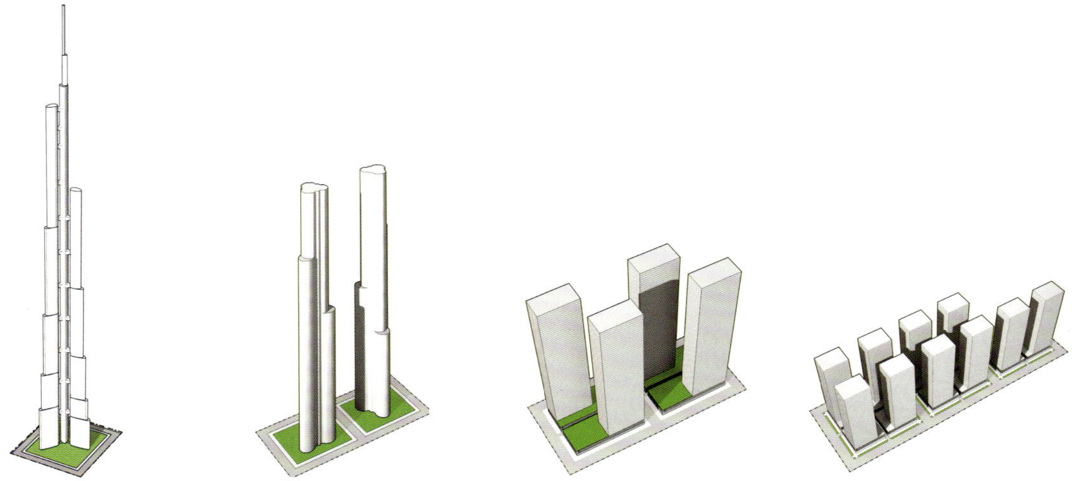

MASSING STUDY

TYPICAL FLOOR PLATE

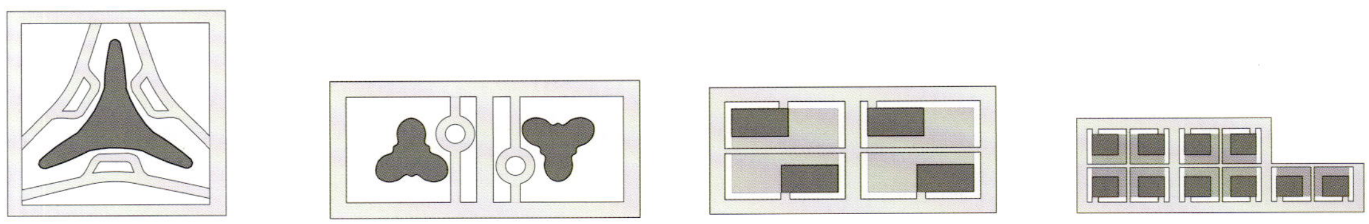

SUMMARY	MEGATALL	SUPERTALL	HIGH-RISE	MID-RISE
TOTAL LAND AREA (M^2)	26,896	36,530	36,530	45,508
NUMBER OF BUILDINGS	1	2	4	10
AVERAGE LOT SIZE (M^2)	14,641	8,944	4,212	2,005
TOTAL BUILDING FOOTPRINT (M^2)	3,177	4,529	16,848	20,048
TOTAL INFRASTRUCTURE LENGTH (M)	1,646	2,676	2,204	3,823
TOTAL SIDEWALK AREA (M^2)	3,584	5,712	5,573	4,004
TOTAL DRIVEWAY AREA (M^2)	N/A	N/A	N/A	N/A
TOTAL ALLEY AREA (M^2)	N/A	N/A	1,180	2,958
TOTAL STREET AREA (M^2)	8,672	12,930	12,930	15,713
BUILDING COVERAGE (M^2)	3,177 (12%)	4,529 (12%)	16,848 (46%)	20,048 (44%)
TOTAL UNPAVED AREA (M^2)	11,464 (43%)	13,359 (37%)	0 (0%)	2,779 (6%)
TOTAL PAVED AREA (M^2)	12,256 (45%)	18,642 (51%)	19,683 (54%)	22,674 (50%)
LAND DIFFERENCE FROM SUBURBAN (M^2)	2,940,241	2,930,607	2,930,607	2,921,629

Table 2 Building prototype data

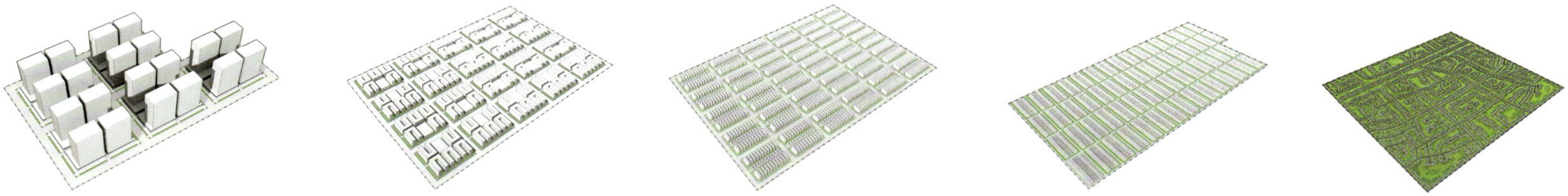

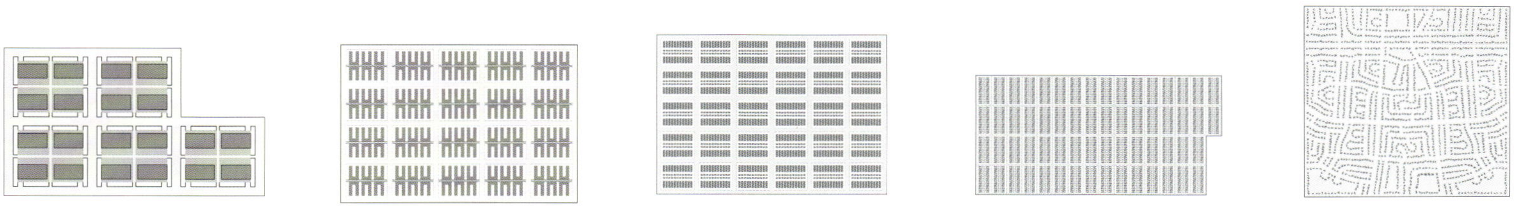

LOW-RISE	COURTYARD	THREE-FLAT	URBAN SINGLE-FAMILY	SUBURBAN SINGLE-FAMILY
86,135	323,000	485,408	1,277,174	2,967,137
20	100	667	2,000	2,000
2,005	2,075	414	440	1,076
40,095	118,560	147,974	417,247	394,716
6,170	25,074	57,005	139,302	202,338
8,000	16,720	25,498	69,500	106,493
N/A	N/A	19,660	42,300	163,452
5,325	11,800	18,290	54,999	n/a
27,135	86,989	127,243	155,175	353,041
40,095 (47%)	115,509 (37%)	147,974 (30%)	417,247 (33%)	394,716 (13%)
5,580 (6%)	88,920 (28%)	147,014 (30%)	537,953 (42%)	1,956,769 (66%)
40,460 (47%)	115,509 (36%)	190,690 (40%)	321,974 (25%)	622,986 (21%)
2,881,002	2,644,137	2,481,729	1,689,963	0

DISCUSSION

Humans have significantly changed our planet's landscape. According to the Millennium Ecosystem Assessment, over the past half-century we have changed ecosystems more rapidly and intensely than at any other point in history. One of the major contributors has been land-use changes related to rapid urban expansion. Over the past 100 years the world population has grown by 400%, often in a pattern characterized by discontinuous, low-density growth away from a developed city center.

As cities expand outward, there is an increased need to the establish industry and business in "satellite city" centers to decentralize housing and places of employment. Satellite cities can help minimize long commutes and help suburban environments become smaller, more manageable towns that support a more diverse lifestyle.

The study data puts land-use issues into perspective. As our population faces depletion of space and resources, it is clear that new solutions need to be found for urban development. The date shows that a suburban community can take up 110 times as much land as a megatall tower that houses the same amount of units. Undeveloped land could be preserved for natural wildlife habitats and water sources, while naturally sequestering carbon emissions. Alternatively, undeveloped land from the denser prototypes could be used as farmland to support the demands of the growing population for food or as a renewable clean-energy source, such as wind and solar (**Figure 15, 16**).

Illinois, located in the Midwestern United States, was the basis for the land-use data gathered. It makes an interesting case study in the relationship of residential development density to other land uses such as agriculture, natural ecosystems, energy and recreation, and is discussed in the following pages.

LAND USE FOR AGRICULTURE

In Illinois, glaciers formed the soil and flat topography during the last ice age. When they melted, a thick layer of loess—sediment with a high concentration of minerals—was left behind, creating a nutrient-rich soil. In Illinois, the natural prairie biome has deep root systems, which sequester carbon and nutrients in the soil and help generate some of the most productive farmland in the world. The rich soil attracted settlers who established farms, passing the history and culture of farming down for generations—95% of Illinois corn farms are family-owned. But when there is a migration from rural areas, as we have seen in the last century, there is a corresponding loss of skills and land used for farming.

Today, 9% of the land in Illinois is developed, with 85% used for agriculture and 6% government-owned. Most large farms in Illinois are devoted to grain crops, while 33% raise livestock. Illinois is the second-largest crop producer in the country. Major crops are corn and soybeans, although the state produces a variety of others, wheat and potatoes for example.

According to the Illinois Farm Bureau Information Center (***IFB, 2017***), Illinois is the second highest crop producing state in the country, producing the most soybean and the second most corn. A high degree of mechanization, the use of genetically engineered seeds (89% of corn and 92% of soybean), as well as application of more than four million tons of fertilizer annually (***Illinois Dept. of Agriculture, 2017***), are needed to support an ever-increasing demand for productivity. In 2017, the state produced over 57 million tons of corn and over 16 million tons of soybeans.

Most of the corn produced in Illinois in the 2015–2016 season was grown for bio-ethanol production (79%), with the by-products used as animal feed. The second highest use (7%) was high-fructose corn syrup. Soybeans are primarily used for animal feed (73%) but are also made into soybean oil (18%) that is used in human-consumption food products. Once the oil has been extracted, crushed soybeans are used as a high-protein meal for animal feed. Soybeans are a global commodity. According to the Illinois Soybean Association (2017) the United States exports 30 million tons of soybean to China annually.

Illinois is the fourth-largest swine producer in the country and supports a substantial beef and dairy industry. In 2016, Illinois had 5,100,000 pigs, produced 837 million liters of cow's milk, and 1.5 billion eggs. High-quality feed, such as corn or soybeans from Illinois, is a vital part of healthy and economical meat, dairy, and poultry production industry.

Data from our study shows that the land remaining from building a high-density development rather than a lower density development—up to 294 hectares—could be used for such agriculture to help support population growth and an increasing demand for meat. Potential agricultural outputs from the land are shown in Table 3.

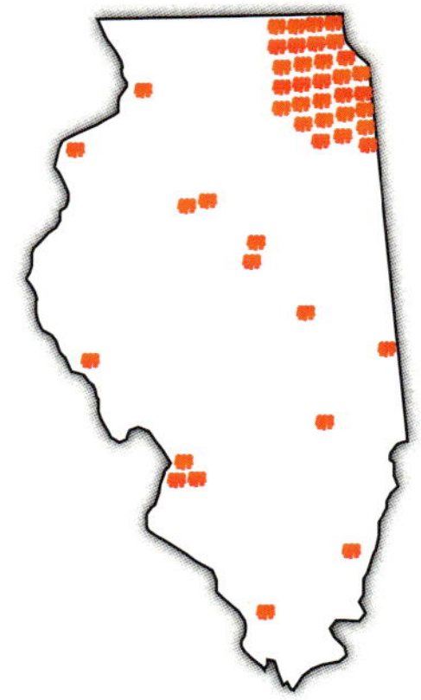

Figure 15 Current Population Distribution (Illinois)

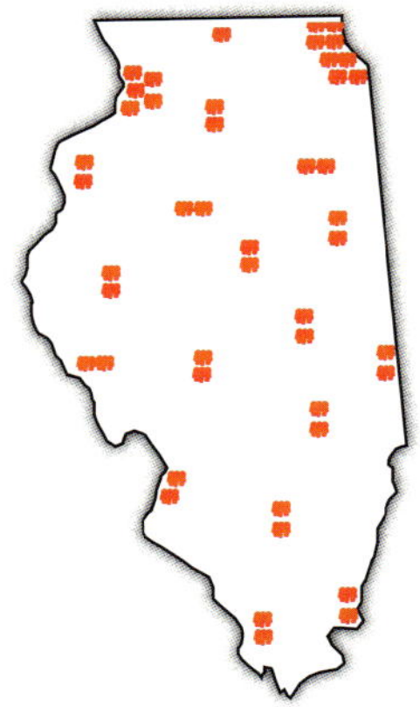

Figure 16 Decentralized Population Hypothesis (Illinois)

Obviously, these are just examples of what could be done. Rearing livestock on the remaining land or using it for intensive greenhouse based or hydroponic vertical horticulture are two other options. The point is that through increasing residential density, land is freed up to be used for potentially providing food for the community, reversing the trend where communities expand at the cost of losing agricultural land.

	MEGATALL	SUPERTALL	HIGH-RISE	MID-RISE	LOW-RISE	COURTYARD	THREE-FLAT	URBAN	SUBURBAN
LAND DIFFERENCE (HECTARES)	294	293	293	292	288	264	248	169	0
CORN (TONS)	3,636	3,623	3,623	3,611	3,561	3,265	3,067	2,090	0
SOYBEANS (TONS)	1,167	1,163	1,163	1,159	1,143	1,047	984	671	0

Table 3 Potential agricultural outputs from "saved" land

LAND USE FOR NATURAL HABITAT

The natural ecosystem in Illinois is tall-grass prairie, a type of temperate grassland that once dominated the Great Plains of North America, covering the northern two-thirds of Illinois. Following the settlement of the region by European farmers, much of this highly fertile land has been transformed into agricultural land for corn cultivation. In recent years however, there has been an effort to repurchase the lands for restoration to its pre-settlement condition. Beyond the historic, cultural, and aesthetic of prairie land, it also fills a critical role in supporting and maintaining significant biodiversity in North America.

Tall grass prairie vegetation in Illinois and Iowa includes vegetation that once supported a community of grazing animals such as buffalo, elk, and antelope, along with predators such as wolves and cougars. The only larger mammals to survive within the relatively small prairie reserves are white-tailed deer, coyotes, foxes, and badgers. Still, small prairie reserves are able to support an immense variety of bird and insect life.

Most tall grass prairie biomass is below ground with an extensive root system that can reach 3m or more, giving the land a considerable carbon-sequestration capability. While the exact amount of sequestration depends on a number of factors, such as species mix, rainfall, or management, the consensus is that the prairies are significant carbon sinks with net ecosystem productivity being reported as 794g of carbon/m^2/year ***(West and Haake, 2014)***. This is equivalent to a sequestering rate of 2.91 $kgCO_2$ per square meter per year. This equates to a potential for sequestering 8,555 tons of carbon dioxide per year in the Megatall prototype. According to the United States EPA, this is enough to offset the emissions of 1,833 passenger cars or 924 single-family homes.

LAND USE FOR ENERGY PRODUCTION

Renewable energy is now widely expected to become the cheapest means of generating power by 2020. Installation of onshore wind has fallen by around 23% since 2010 and the cost of solar photovoltaic (PV) electricity has fallen by 73% over the same period. According to statistics published by the International Renewable Energy Agency (***IRENA, 2018***), globally, onshore wind schemes cost an average of $0.06 per kWh—some schemes are as low as $0.04 per kWh—while the cost of solar PV is $0.10 per kWh. In comparison, the cost of electricity generation based on fossil fuels typically falls in a range of $0.05 to $0.17 per kWh.

Year on year advancements in PV technology allow more electricity to be generated per kWh of sunlight and the cost of wind turbines, per installed MW, has continued to fall. The power generation landscape has changed to the point where in Germany the levelized cost of electricity from utility scale PV and onshore wind is less than from coal or natural gas (***Fraunhofer ISE, 2018***). In 2017, a consortium of Chinese and Japanese manufacturers bid the lowest price ever recorded ($0.024 per kWh) to build a PV installation in the United Arab Emirates. The plant, which is currently under construction, is reported to be 2–19% cheaper than building a gas fired power station in the same region.

There is no doubt that within the next decade, renewable energy will continue to fall in price and that energy density—the amount of power that can be generated per hectare—will increase. Consequently, when considering land use, we should ask the question, what is the energy generation potential of the land that we have saved by building at a higher density?

If the land saved by the denser typologies was used for PV electricity production, assuming a 19.5% efficient panel anc 50% land coverage, the electrical productivity would be 161 kwh/m2/yr (calculated using NREL PVWatts calculator). In the case of the Megatall, with 294 hectares of "saved land", this equates to 474 GWh of electricity per year, more than enough to meet the energy needs of the community (see next chapter for detailed information in community energy demand). Table 4 illustrates how much electricity could be generated from the open space and how much is needed to meet the demand of the community and how much would be left over. As can be seen every single non-suburban community, if it were to be built on the land typically occupied by a suburb, could potentially be self-sufficient, in terms of energy, if the open space was used for power generation.

The land remaining from building a supertall development instead of a suburban development—727 acres—could be used for producing biofuels. The acres remaining can be used for recreational purposes to ensure adequate space for interaction with nature and physical activity.

As an alternative to PV electricity production, the open space could be used to grow biofuel—potentially as a byproduct of another agricultural product such as soybean. However, there remain a number of questions around the ethics of using agricultural land for fuel production. A quarter of the corn grown in Illinois is used to produce ethanol. Frequently asked questions include, should we really use this high-quality farm land to grow carbon emitting fuel? Do we want energy security or food security? Can we have both? Biofuel combustion emits CO2 just the same as petroleum-based fuels, so why use land to grow fuel and not food? Illinois has several native cellulosic crops, such as switchgrass and miscanthus, that produce good yields. Cellulosic crops, although less developed than starch-based crops, are seen as key to the success of biofuel production as they do not compete with food crops (one of the key criticisms of biofuel production), and they can also be grown on marginal land and support natural biodiversity.

	MEGATALL	SUPERTALL	HIGH-RISE	MID-RISE	LOW-RISE	COURTYARD	THREE-FLAT	URBAN	SUBURBAN
LAND DIFFERENCE (HECTARES)	294	293	293	292	288	264	248	169	0
ENERGY DEMAND OF COMMUNITY (MWH)	58,429	60,777	47,494	49,533	50,438	31,326	33,012	36,347	35,104
PV GENERATION POTENTIAL 50% LAND COVERAGE (MWH)	474,121	472,508	472,508	470,895	464,445	425,741	399,938	272,539	0
LAND NEEDED TO MEET COMMUNITY ENERGY NEEDS (HECTARES)	181	188	147	154	156	97	102	113	109
LAND AVAILABLE FOR OTHER USES	113	105	146	138	132	167	146	56	-109

Table 4 Potential PV generation capacity of "saved" land

LAND USE FOR RECREATION

The relationship between health and longevity and physical activity has been studied extensively. In a comprehensive study of the health benefits of increased activity levels, it was found that an increased level of physical activity reduced overall risk of death by 20–35% (***Warburton, 2006***). Conversely, physical inactivity and a sedentary lifestyle have been identified as risk factors for a variety of diseases, including cardiovascular disease, diabetes, cancer, obesity, hypertension, bone disease, and depression. These findings, combined with the fact that obesity is steadily rising around the globe, have forced an emphasis on the importance of physical activity.

Access to green space has been linked to improved physical and mental health in people and has shown to decrease overall stress levels. A 1991 study done by Roger Ulrich showed that patients with a view of nature recovered faster and easier than those without such a view. Green space also has been proven to restore focus abilities, increasing overall productivity. When designing urban environments, it is therefore imperative for professionals to consider the impact of the built environment on human health and well-being, and practices that decrease access to nature.

The 796 acres of land remaining from the most dense development could be used for recreational purposes to ensure adequate space for interaction with nature and physical activity, such as placing bike trails within a dense urban environment. Leftover land can then be preserved for prairie use, which can further harness the environmental benefits of the prairie ecosystem.

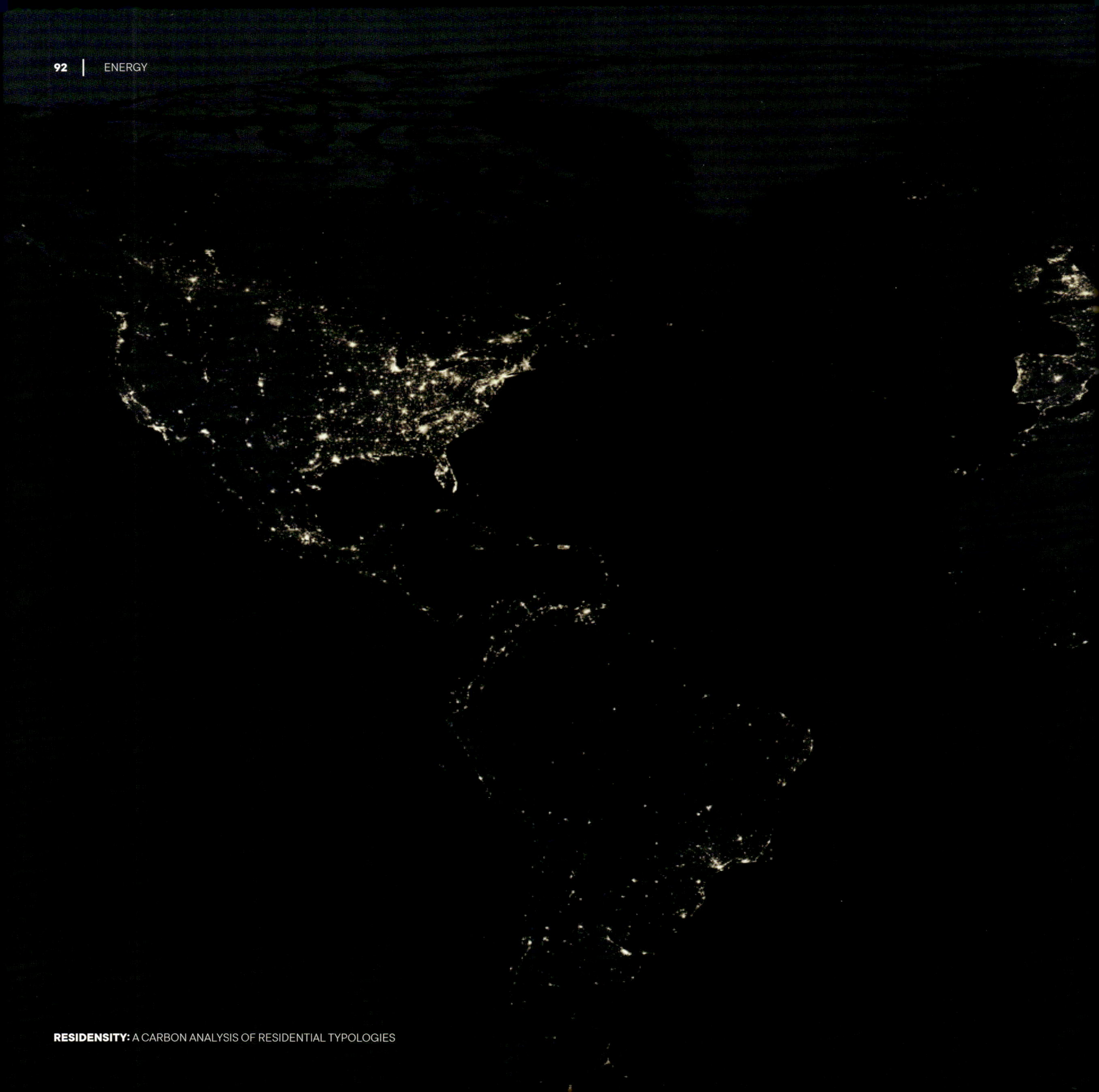

ENERGY

The energy chapter is a technical assessment of the energy-consumption profiles of each building prototype, and investigates the annual energy use, building energy use, energy-use intensity, use per unit, and use per occupant. The study analyses the relative energy use and annual energy consumption of each prototype, measuring specific design elements that can affect energy performance, such as building geometry, glazing ratio, and overshadowing. The energy consumption is then analyzed by the contribution that each building element adds to the overall energy load, concluding with a comparison that addresses if density is a potential solution for reducing energy demand.

Energy Use Intensity (EUI), measured in kWh/m^2/year, is an indicator of energy efficiency; in this study, where EUI values are used to make relative comparisons between prototypes, it is defined as the Total Energy Demand of the building, as determined through simulation modeling, divided by the Gross Residential Floor Area. By using this method, we eliminate any bias from having large, unconditioned spaces, such as mechanical floors and naturally ventilated parking podiums or large public circulation spaces that have a relatively low energy demand per m^2.

While building design aspirations have driven new innovations in structural steel, elevators, and curtain walls, historically little consideration was given to the rising energy consumption of these buildings. In the 1950s and 1960s, energy costs were low, and many buildings used heat-by-light systems. The higher glazing ratios of the first full single-glazed curtain walls provided much less solar protection and thermal insulation than buildings with other types of envelopes—and they often lacked natural ventilation. The energy embargo of the late 1970s exposed these inefficient systems. Designers and engineers began to develop new attitudes toward the energy problem, responding with building solutions that included insulated glazing units, Low-E coatings, and integrating shading elements.

Today increasing fossil fuel costs, and a greater awareness of the effects that CO_2 has on the environment, have shifted the world's attention to improving energy efficiency and developing alternative energy sources. Pressure is now being placed on the architectural and engineering world, and with good reason: global energy consumption in 2008 totaled 147,875 terawatt hours (TWh) or 504.7 quadrillion Btu (quads), as reported in the 2011 International Energy Outlook (published by the US EIA) and accounted for 30.2 billion metric tons of CO^2, with over 10% of this global energy consumption associated with residential buildings.

INTRODUCTION

According to the US Department of Energy's 2012 Buildings Energy Data Book, the US residential energy consumption in 2009 totaled 6,150 TWh, (20.99 quads), accounting for 54% of the total consumption in the buildings sector and 22% of the country's total primary energy consumption—an increase of 24% from 1990. In this context, it is important to note that building designers have the ability to control most of the decisions that dictate how a building will perform. More stringent energy codes require higher-performing envelopes and systems that help reduce a building's overall energy consumption, making most new buildings stronger performers than their predecessors. The New Buildings Institute in collaboration with Pacific Northwest National Laboratory have determined that buildings that comply with the ASHRAE 90.1–2016 Standard perform 50% better than an average commercial building, as established in the 2003 Commercial Building Energy Consumption Survey (CBECS).

INLAND STEEL BUILDING
Skidmore, Owings & Merrill
Completed 1956
Double-glazed glass systems
Tinted glass
Shading devices

Global energy reduction targets have become increasingly ambitious and often confusing, with regional codes sometimes exceeding national targets. The European Union, under its Energy Performance of Buildings Directive set a target for all new buildings to be Nearly Zero-Energy Buildings (NZEBs)—defined as a building that consumes very little energy and is powered exclusively by renewable sources—by the end of 2020. Some European countries have set their own targets that exceed the EU goal. Ireland required new residential buildings to be net zero by 2013 and the United Kingdom set the same requirement for 2016; commercial and public buildings will have the same requirements in 2019.

Subsequent EU-wide policy changes led to a re-engineering of United Kingdom policy in favor of a more strategy and initiative-based approach towards achieving a decarbonized building stock, both new and existing. All EU countries are required to provide national plans for increasing the number of NZEBs. In the United States, the ASHRAE 90.1 Energy Standard for Buildings Except Low-Rise Residential Buildings is the basis for most building codes and has been regularly updated since 1975. Figure 7 illustrates how changes to ASHRAE 90.1 over the past 40 years have brought about a 50% reduction in energy use for compliant new buildings. British Columbia in Canada has one of the most progressive building codes; the BC Energy Step Code outlines an optional path for incremental code improvements that will lead to all new buildings being net zero energy by 2032. By May 2018, this code was adopted by a number of districts in Vancouver with 23 local governments either incorporating it into their bylaws or consulting with industry on its implementation.

Many countries are mandating that newly constructed buildings satisfy their energy demands through a target percentage of alternative sources. England has proposed that all new commercial buildings in London produce or purchase 20% of their energy requirements from renewable sources. Spain requires the installation of photovoltaic panels on the rooftops of all new commercial buildings, varying between regions with more or less solar availability. The Republic of Korea's energy code requires that at least 5% of the total construction cost of any new building be allocated to renewable energy generation on site, and that the building should source at least 5% of its energy consumption from renewables.

Most cities and public institutions demonstrate their commitment to reducing energy consumption by offering benefits and incentives, including tax credits, expedited permitting, reduced energy prices, feed-in tariffs, and loans and grants for new constructions or retrofits. In France, tax credits for retrofits and on-site renewables have been offered since 2002 and continue to increase. Italy has had a tax incentives program for improvements on building structures working toward energy efficiency since 2007. In the US, a similar program was effective until 2012, with incentives now determined on a per-state basis or through the purchase of efficient products and appliances.

Despite regulations and incentives, most new buildings only meet the minimum requirements necessary to comply with local codes and do not include any additional measures to further reduce their energy demand. There is, however, a growing level of understanding within the building industry, that performative design solutions can have an impact, not just for a single building, but for an entire community and at a global scale.

Design professionals are now creating the next generation of buildings that aim to reduce energy demand and improve the built environment. These new buildings incorporate measures that consider successful historical precedents, such as natural ventilation and daylighting, while applying new technologies like energy-efficient envelope design, reduced glazing ratios, high-efficiency mechanical systems, and smart building controls that reduce energy demand when not in use. Additionally, energy-harvesting strategies such as photovoltaics, solar water heating, and wind turbines are being integrated into buildings to help meet their high-energy demands.

In addition to codes and targets, green building rating systems—like BREEAM™ and LEED™ and energy efficient design philosophies such as Passivhaus™—have become popular tools to assess and certify the sustainability of buildings by evaluating how they perform in terms of energy efficiency, as well as water usage, material selection, community connectivity, and interior environment, among other factors. As sustainable design becomes more connected to the type of high-quality design that increases property values, governments, and developers will find these rating systems increasingly helpful in both designing and marketing the buildings.

Numerous studies have been completed that compare American rental and sales price premiums, as well as occupancy rates, for buildings that have some form of sustainability certification compared to those without any certification (***Eichholtz et al., 2013; Fuerst and McAllister, 2011; Reichardt et al., 2012; and Wiley et al., 2010***). The studies' findings consistently show an increase in rental price of 2–9%, with occupancy rate increases of a similar scale. Fuerst and McAllister reported an increase in sales premium of 25% for LEED certified buildings.

ENERGY MODELING

Energy modeling uses computer-based programs to simulate a building's energy consumption over a defined period of time, typically the equivalent of one year or 8,760 hours. The model represents the geometry and materiality of a building and is populated with carefully considered assumptions that would impact the building's energy usage, such as occupancy, operation schedules, lighting and plug loads, and HVAC (Heating, Ventilation, and Air Conditioning) systems. Because energy models are usually an attempt to simulate the energy operation of a project that is being designed or otherwise not yet constructed, they must be populated with assumptions about its use.

Most simulation programs already include vast libraries of templates for commonly used constructions, activities, and schedules, which are helpful when creating a baseline model preforming a comparative study. Other resources, such as guidelines for building energy calculation and compliance with ASHRAE standards, provide loads, system descriptions, and minimum envelope performance values that can help guide the program inputs.

Energy modeling has become an indispensable tool in the design industry to help predict the energy consumption of a building before it is built, allowing the user to test different design variations through determining the effect on overall energy consumption. In this study, we compare building performance using energy models that were designed for each prototype, using the software program DesignBuilder.

Within DesignBuilder the EnergyPlus engine is used to undertake the simulations. This United States Department of Energy developed simulation engine facilitates "energy smart design" among architects and engineers. Another commonly referenced resource is the US Department of Energy's Commercial Reference Building Models of the National Building Stock, which describes a series of standard energy models developed by the National Renewable Energy Laboratory (NREL). The study depicts 16 building typologies in 16 US locations, which are estimated to represent two-thirds of the national building stock and were created to serve as base models for energy-efficient research. The models are a good reference to verify the results of specific simulations and were applied in this study. Figure 17 is an example of the energy breakdown for a mid-rise apartment building in Chicago.

Although no single comprehensive guide is available that describes and defines all these assumptions, many resources are available that have helped inform the input for the study models. These resources include the ASHRAE 90.1–2010 Manual, the US Department of Energy Commercial Reference Building Models, program defaults, professional experience, and peer reviews.

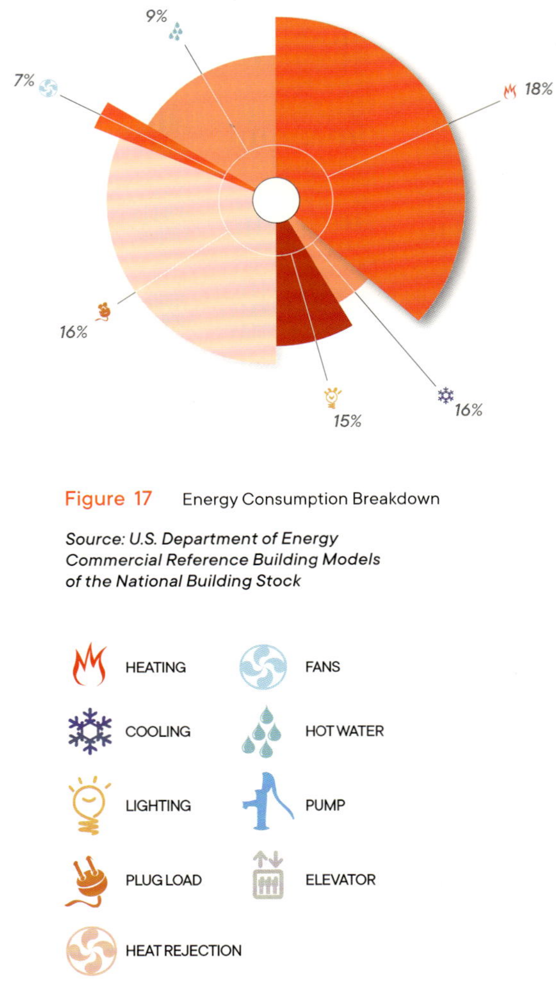

Figure 17 Energy Consumption Breakdown

Source: U.S. Department of Energy Commercial Reference Building Models of the National Building Stock

MODELING PARAMETERS

Human behavior is difficult to predict and building simulation tools do not always accurately reflect the energy consumption of a building. This is demonstrated in a study published in 2011 by RDH Group—in conjunction with local Vancouver government agencies and utility companies—in which energy model outputs of existing buildings were generated, and the results compared with actual metered data from the buildings (***Hanan et al., 2011***).

Results showed as much as 270% higher gas consumption and 100% more electrical consumption in the simulations, than in the actual metered data, with most of the differences attributed to occupants such as hot water use and thermostat set points. Most energy modeling specialists agree that the real value is in the comparison of the variations between different building types, rather than the absolute values—such as between a building with shading overhangs and one without—since the calculations are more likely to represent the effect of relative changes to the building design.

CLIMATE

The study assumes that all prototypes are within ASHRAE Climate Zone 5A. The US Department of Energy (DOE) Weather File for O'Hare International Airport was used in the evaluations of this study. The climate zone is characterized for being cold and humid with high climatic variations throughout the year. The climate also has four distinct seasons: a cold winter, a rainy spring, a hot and humid summer, and a temperate autumn. It is considered a heat-dominated climate, with space heating needed for about six months of the year to maintain comfortable indoor temperatures to reach comfortable levels.

ORIENTATION + CONTEXT

Building orientation can play an important role in how a building performs, impacting heating, cooling, and lighting. Strategically orienting a building or considering the glazing orientation in relation to the sun, can greatly influence indoor temperatures. In heating-dominated climates, solar heat gain is desired in colder months through south facing windows, while less exposure is advised on the west, where shading is more difficult. In some of the modeled prototypes, energy consumption variations were as high as 6% due to orientation alone. To adjust for this, each building was modeled in four orientations—facing north, south, east, and west—with the average overall energy demand calculated. This practice is standard when following the ASHRAE 90.1 Appendix G simulation modeling protocol.

Buildings in the study were modeled as part of a prototypical community. In reality, they would be overshadowed by other buildings of the same typology. This type of simulation, known as context modeling, provides a more realistic estimate on the overall energy demand of the building being investigated as they would rarely exist in a stand-alone condition.

The values in Figure 18 show the percentage of energy consumption in a certain prototype as it increases or decreases based on overshadowing by neighboring buildings. The studies were run for the four orientations with the most critical scenario—where the difference between the shaded and unshaded prototype was the greatest—is shown. A positive value indicates the energy consumption increased when there was no overshadowing. A negative value indicates a decrease when the building was completely exposed on all sides.

The results of the test reveal that most of the lower-density buildings are affected by the surrounding buildings, which do not allow for ample solar exposure and heat gain. Larger high-rise buildings, with higher glazing ratios, benefited from being in such a context because the neighboring towers helped block excessive radiation in the summer.

ZONING + ACTIVITIES

In an energy model, a building is partitioned into thermal zones to divide the building into areas of similar uses, such as occupant densities, schedules, HVAC equipment, lighting, and power loads. Another important factor in determining zoning is the envelope load, which is defined as the heat coming into a space that is directly exposed to the outdoors. The areas near the perimeter of the building should be zoned separately from those positioned closer to the core. Having fewer zones, yet still enough to generate accurate results, simplifies the modeling process and reduces simulation running times.

The prototypes developed for this study implement this strategy, with areas sharing the same orientation and use, such as all south-facing units on a floor, grouped into one zone. Large zones are divided into perimeter and interior zones, defined as those more than five meters from exterior glazing. Figure 19 shows a typical zoning layout for a residential floor in the High-Rise prototype.

Five different program uses were defined for the study: living units, circulation spaces, common areas, mechanical rooms, and parking. These uses were assigned to the corresponding zones and specific loads are associated with each. For an accurate comparison of the prototypes, these zones have the same characteristics throughout the buildings: the lighting power density assigned to the living unit zones in the Three-Flat prototype is the same as assigned to the High-Rise prototype.

BUILDING ENVELOPE

In energy simulation programs, construction assemblies are typically modeled by listing a series of material layers and their thicknesses, in a specific order, resulting in a building construction with thermal mass and a calculated U-value that represents the thermal properties of the construction. The prototypes in this study were modeled after typical building constructions and represent assemblies used in common practice, reflecting envelope efficiencies established by kncwn authorities.

Where available, professional experience and existing measured data are the most valuable resources when populating the energy model with data.

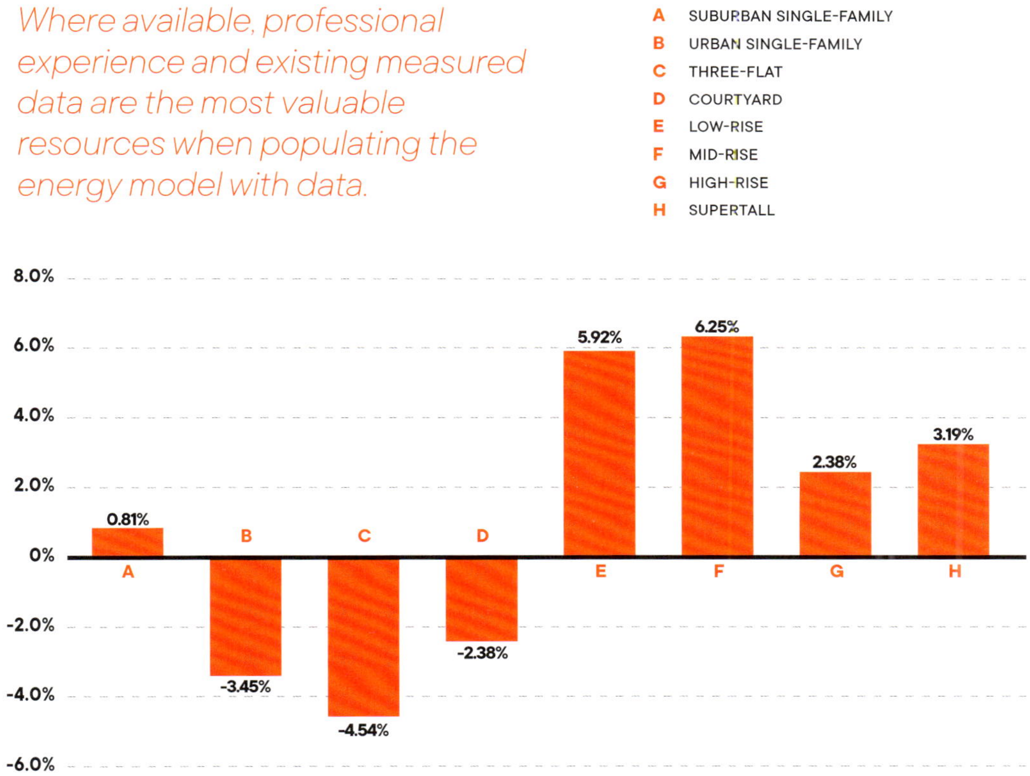

Figure 18 Effect of Overshadowing in Prototype Energy Consumption

Note: there was no over-shading of the Megatall Prototype

For the Low-Rise prototype, International Energy Conservation Code was used as a reference for minimum envelope U-values, with a low-rise defined as, "a building containing one or more dwelling units not exceeding four stories above grade where occupants are primarily permanent." In all applicable cases, these values were adhered to and represent the prototype building envelope U-values shown in Table 5. For the buildings in the study that are over four stories in height, ASHRAE 90.1–2010 Standard's Prescriptive Option Reference U-Values for Zone 5 were used as a benchmark, shown in Table 6.

These minimum requirements are meant for buildings that have a glazing area that does not exceed 40% of the window-to-wall ratio. When a prototype's ratio exceeded 40%, more efficient envelope constructions were used. These proposed constructions were tested in comparison with the ASHRAE minimum U-values in an energy modeling exercise to ensure that the higher glazing ratio did not negatively impact the building's energy consumption, and that a consistent level of envelope performance was maintained.

Another important aspect of a building envelope is infiltration, defined by the International Energy Conservation Code as the uncontrolled inward air leakage into a building caused by the pressure effects of wind, or the effect of differences in the indoor and outdoor air density, or both. Infiltration happens in most places where different materials meet in a building, such as window frames and doors, but can also occur from cracks and openings in the construction. This unwanted air movement between the interior and exterior environments can be detrimental to the effectiveness of the HVAC system, making it more difficult to maintain stable interior temperatures. For the prototypes, this value was set as part of building construction and differs between interior and perimeter zones.

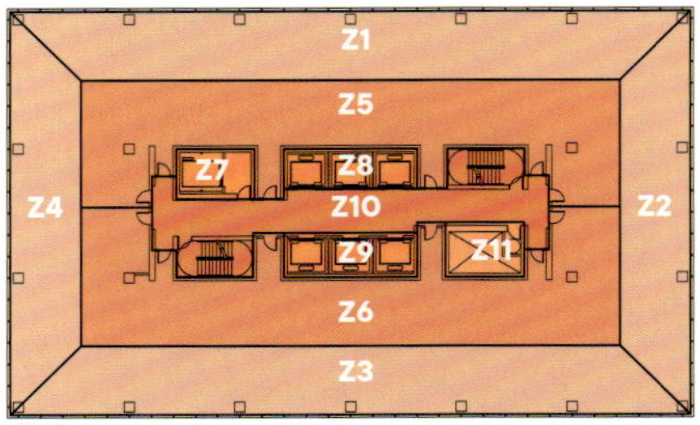

Figure 19

High-Rise Prototype
Typical Floor Thermal Zones

Z1-Z4	PERIMETER APARTMENTS
Z5-Z6	INTERIOR APARTMENTS
Z7-Z9	ELEVATOR SHAFTS
Z10	CIRCULATION CORRIDOR
Z11	MECHANICAL CLOSET

LIGHTING LOADS

Lighting interior spaces can be a major contributor to the energy consumption of a building; beyond power use, lighting can emit heat, increasing indoor temperatures. Different lighting loads were assigned to the different programs in each building prototype and remain consistent throughout the models, operating on a schedule that responds to the space type and frequency of use. The lighting power densities for the different zones were taken from the ASHRAE 90.1–2010 Lighting Power Allowances per Space Type table, which defines the lighting power allowance for the interior of a building. ASHRAE 90.1 does not stipulate lighting power for residential units and so we selected usage types for the tables that best match the residential spaces when modeled. (Table 7) The Lighting Power Density (LPD) is the maximum lighting power per unit area of a space function within a building.

PLUG LOADS

Plug loads are associated with typical service loads, including appliances and other equipment connected to power outlets. Plug loads are modified by a schedule that never reaches 0% use because some appliances are never turned off or consume power even when not in use. According to the United States Department of Energy's 2012 Buildings Energy Data Book, refrigerators alone accounted for 26% of all residential electrical equipment energy consumption in 2010. The prototype's plug loads values were taken from the energy modeling program defaults for each space type and are the same throughout all the prototypes.

OCCUPANCY

Occupancy relates to the number of people in a space and is modified by a schedule that responds to the operational pattern of the building type. Space occupancy is important for the energy model as occupants produce heat that contributes to space heating in colder months and must be removed by the HVAC system in warmer weather. Outside air ventilation rates are also affected by the occupancy if minimum fresh air per person is required.

Space occupancy for the prototypes was determined to be 2.61 people per residential unit, based on 2010 estimates from the Census Bureau for Chicago, which established average household size for owner-occupied units (46% of all units) at 2.78, while the average household size for renter-occupied units (54% of all units) is 2.47.

HVAC SYSTEMS

Modeling HVAC systems can be approached in different ways. When a system has been designed in detail, all of its parts can be modeled; when a system has been assigned, but not designed or sized, templates from the program can be used and an auto-sizing option can be selected. In this study, the program includes heating and cooling design calculations to determine the size of equipment required to meet the desired temperature set-points and ventilation rates, based on the most extreme weather conditions for a specific location.

Within the modeling environment, the user can specify system parameters, including efficiency, fuel type, heating system, and cooling system. The HVAC systems assigned to the prototypes were based on commonly used systems for their respective building types. Two systems were used: constant air volume with central gas heating and central electric cooling for the low-density prototypes, and central boilers and chillers with hot and cold-water distribution to four pipe fan-coil units for the higher density designs. Ventilation rates were set to comply with the minimum ventilation rates in breathing zones established in ASHRAE 62.1–2010 (Table 8).

COMPONENTS	MIN U-VALUE[A]	MODEL U-VALUE
Envelope Walls	0.34	0.342
Fenestration	1.99	1.786
Ceiling	0.15	0.153
Floors	0.19	0.191

Table 5 Envelope U-Values [W/(m²K)] for Low-Rise Constructions

Source: Chicago Energy Conservation Code 2008 Residential Energy Efficiency (Table 18-13-402.1.3, Article 4)

COMPONENTS	MIN U-VALUE[A]	MODEL U-VALUE
Envelope Walls	0.365	0.300
Fenestration	2.560	1.960
Ceiling	0.273	0.261
Floors	0.363	0.363

Table 6 Envelope U-Values [W/(m² x K)] for High-rise Constructions

Source: Building Envelope Requirements for Climate Zone 5 (TABLE 5.5-5 ASHRAE 90.1)

SPACE TYPE	LPD (W/M²)
Living Quarters	4.1
Corridors / Common Areas	7.1
Electrical / Mechanical	10.2

Table 7 Lighting Power Densities

Source: Lighting Power Densities using the Space-by-Space Method (TABLE 9.6.1 ASHRAE 90.1)

OCCUPANCY CATEGORY	L/S-PERSON	L/S-M²
Dwelling Unit	2.5	0.3
Common Corridor	-	0.3
Lobbies	2.5	0.3
Electrical Equip. Rooms	-	0.3
Elevator Machine Rooms	-	0.6

Table 8 Outside Air Definition Method

Source: Outside Air Definition Method (Min fresh air = sum per person + per area) based on TABLE 6-1 Minimum Ventilation Rates in Breathing Zone (ASHRAE 62.1 - 2010) Residential

HOT WATER CONSUMPTION

The US Energy Information Administration (EIA) identified domestic water heating as the second largest energy end-use in residential buildings in the nation, exceeded only by space heating. Residential water use has two major impacts in energy consumption: heating it for use and pumping it to high floors in taller buildings. According to the US Department of Energy's 2012 Buildings Energy Data Book, the average American consumes approximately 382 liters of water at home daily, with 70% of this consumed indoors. Indoor residential demands include water used for cooking, cleaning, and showering, with about 40% of the water volume being heated.

Hot-water demand values for the prototypes in this study were extracted from the 2011 ASHRAE Handbook, HVAC Applications. The daily average residential hot water consumption ranges from 132.7L/unit to 159.2L/unit, depending on the number of units in the building (Table 9). Dedicated natural gas hot-water boilers with a storage tank temperature of 60 C were also assumed for each prototype.

APARTMENT / HOUSE: # UNITS	AVERAGE DAILY
20 OR LESS	**159.2 L / unit**
50 UNITS	**151.6 L / unit**
75 UNITS	**144.0 L / unit**
100 UNITS	**140.2 L / unit**
200 OR MORE	**132.7 L / unit**

Table 9 Hot-Water Demand per Residential Unit

Source: Based on TABLE 7 Hot-Water Demands and Use for Various Types of Buildings (2011 ASHRAE Handbook - HVAC Applications)

ELEVATORS

Elevators were included in prototypes that are over four stories and the selection was based on standard practices; for more complex cases, referenced sample buildings, along with other input from consultants, were used. The energy consumption of an elevator is primarily affected by three factors: weight, speed, and frequency of use. The first two determine the horsepower (HP) capacity of the motor needed to move a cab at a desired speed. In most cases, it is correct to assume that the faster and larger the elevator, the more energy it will need to move. The frequency of use affects the elevator in terms of how much time it is in use versus how long it is in standby mode—an elevator in stand by mode consumes only about 3% of the power it uses when it is moving.

Currently, there is no standard method for including elevators in an energy model. Although an elevator travels through a building's full height, they typically only thermally impact the designated elevator room. Nevertheless, even if they are never occupied, mechanical rooms should be ventilated—and in some cases cooled—to avoid equipment overheating.

To calculate the maximum load associated with an elevator, the motor's horsepower and the amount of energy needed to operate the motor, was established. Horsepower was converted to watts using a conversion factor of one HP equals 746 W. The corresponding loads were assigned to the zones designated as elevator shafts in the energy models. A schedule was developed to represent elevator use.

LIMITATIONS TO THE MODELING PROCESS

Although energy modeling is still a relatively new field in computer analysis, and the available programs have limitations, the best available data was compiled for this study so that the most accurate results were reached. Variables may differ from reality in some aspects but the method allows for accurate comparisons between different prototypes, which is the main objective of the study.

One of the biggest challenges to modeling large buildings is the high number of zones and excessive input data needed to be calculated. This can translate into long running times—as much as 40 hours per prototype—or program errors due to lack of computing capacity. The modeling of HVAC systems, for high-rise buildings in particular, poses an important limitation. Although EnergyPlus has ample flexibility in describing the systems, certain elements cannot be modeled. In a high-rise building, for example, central air handling units located in mechanical zones condition the outdoor air, which is then distributed to a series of sub-loops on different floors. This translates to a more efficient system—due to economies of scale—but also adds to the fan energy load because the air needs to be distributed to different floors.

It was also challenging to model elevators because it was difficult to calculate elevator power use and then correlate it to a realistic schedule. While some schedules were available—such as DOE Commercial Reference Building Models and ASHRAE 90-1 User's Manual—conversations with elevator manufacturers shed light on how much elevator use varies, causing inaccuracy of these resources. For this study, available schedules were modified to reflect a more realistic elevator schedule, which was then applied to the models.

Additionally, the Megatall prototype is the only prototype that consists of one building. The other prototypes represented are comprised of multiple buildings and then in the modeling process, one building of each prototype is modeled and analyzed, with the results multiplied post-simulation.

Elevators in the United States take 18 billion passenger trips each year, moving people 1.36 billion miles according to the national elevator industry.

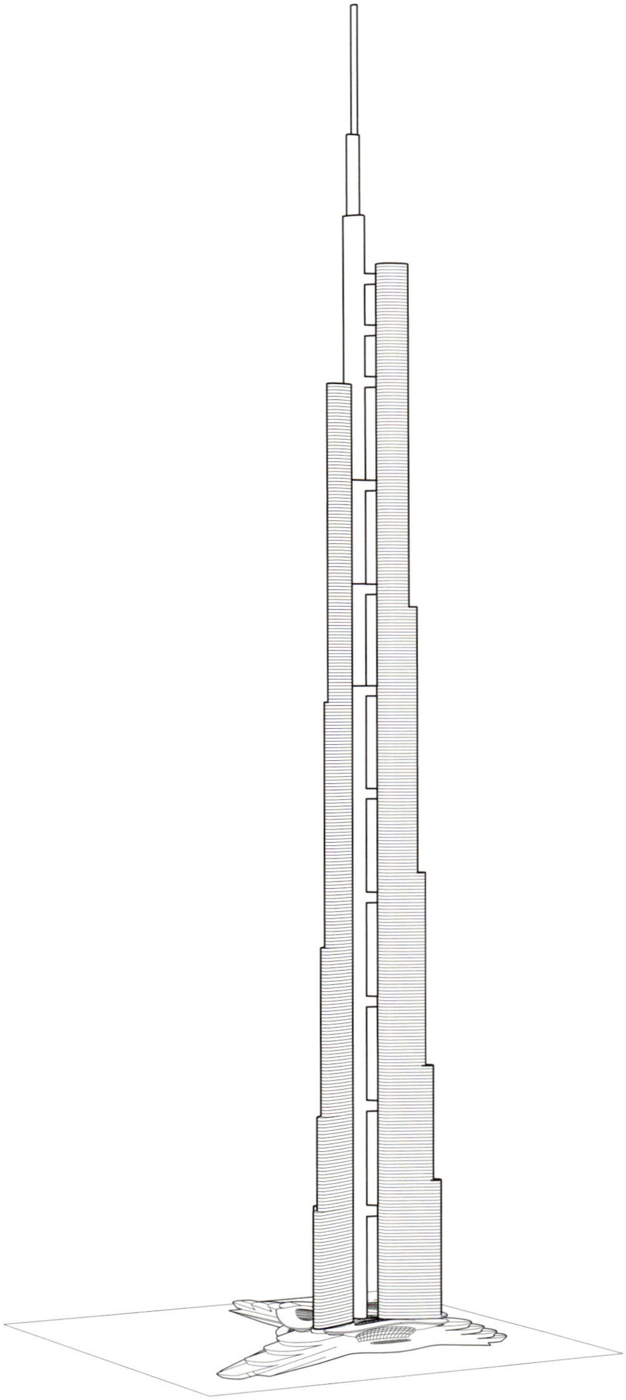

MEGATALL

The energy model for the Megatall prototype poses a challenge for even the most experienced simulation specialists, with obstacles including geometric complexities, large building scale, and intricate interior systems overloading analyses applications. To address these issues, simplifications were made to the prototype's energy model, including rationalizing the geometry, modeling curved walls as straight, and splitting the model into five smaller units with the results added outside of DesignBuilder.

The typical floors consist of a central core and circulation area, with large perimeter zones that represent living space. Residential units are zoned in groups based on orientation, with separate zones created for corner conditions. The Megatall prototype energy model also includes common areas, mechanical floors, and underground parking, and incorporates the concrete structure with a double-glazed curtain wall composed of 40% vision glazing and spandrel panels.

The results reveal that a large amount of energy is consumed to support such a tall structure. Systems such as pumps, fans, and elevators are not needed in a low-density development but are essential in taller buildings, and account for more than 25% of their energy consumption. The tower's energy consumption is also affected by the energy use of non-residential spaces including lobbies, corridors, and parking. Systems related to heating and cooling the building only account for 37% of the total energy consumption. High-glazing ratios and the lack of shading systems typically pose a problem in both summer and winter. In summer, sun exposure adds to the space temperature, whereas in winter, the glazing increases internal heat loss.

The elevator system in the Megatall prototype requires more cabs per unit than in smaller scale buildings because a convenient and efficient vertical transportation system is essential to the overall functioning of the tower.

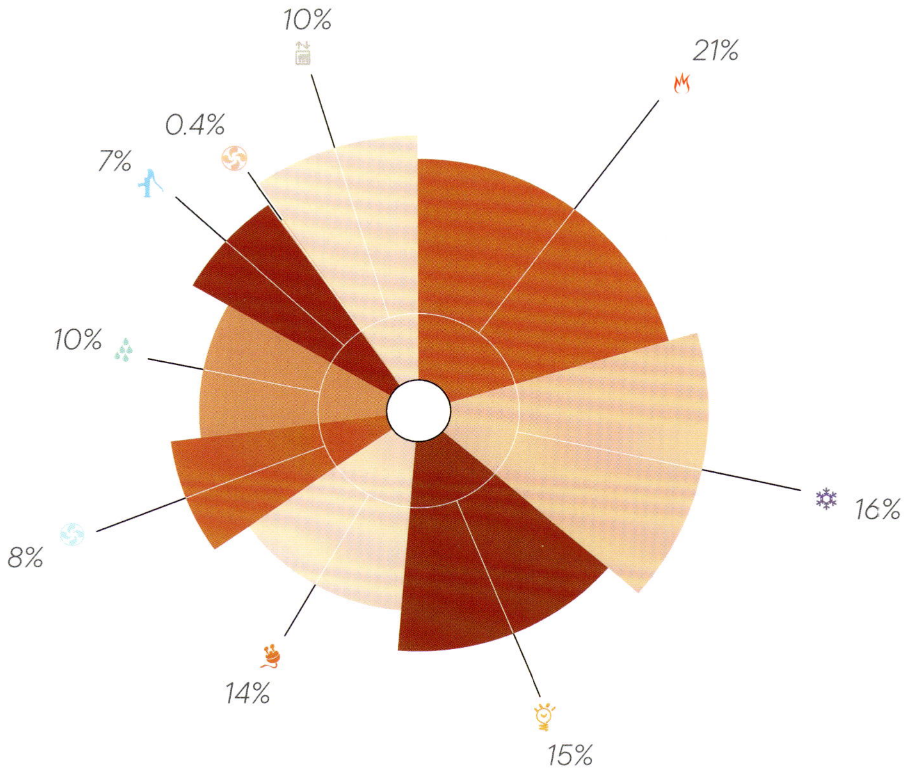

TOTAL BUILDING ENERGY CONSUMPTION BREAKDOWN (KWH/YEAR)

HEATING	21%	12,003,931
COOLING	16%	9,227,289
LIGHTING	15%	8,720,520
PLUG LOAD	14%	8,157,011
FANS	8%	4,514,844
HOT WATER	10%	5,968,086
PUMP	7%	3,992,628
HEAT REJECTION	0.4%	232,823
ELEVATOR	10%	5,612,268

MEGATALL ENERGY USE

NUMBER OF BUILDINGS	1
NUMBER OF UNITS / BUILDING	2,000
BUILDING AREA	451,480 m^2
CONDITIONED AREA	435,619 m^2
NET RESIDENTIAL AREA	299,991 m^2
TOTAL ENERGY USE	58,429,403 kWh
BUILDING ENERGY USE	58,429,403 kWh
UNIT ENERGY USE	29,215 kWh
ENERGY USE INTENSITY(EUI)	195 kWh/m^2
ENERGY USE PER PERSON	11,193 kWh

TOTAL ENERGY CONSUMPTION

SOUTH	58,203,806 kWh/year
EAST	58,599,228 kWh/year
NORTH	58,342,749 kWh/year
WEST	58,571,827 kWh/year
AVERAGE	58,429,403 kWh/year

SPACE ALLOCATION

LIVING AREA	69%
CIRCULATION	12%
COMMON AREAS	2%
PARKING	10%
MECHANICAL SYSTEMS	7%

SUPERTALL

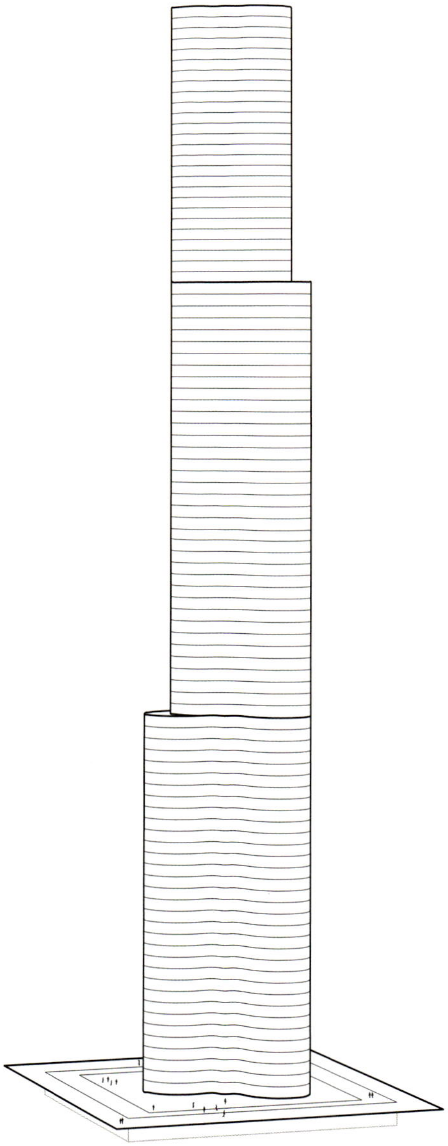

For the Supertall prototype, one tower was modeled with two overshadowing simulations to account for the shade differences of the two buildings. Like the Megatall prototype, the Supertall prototype energy model also simplifies the prototype's geometry and residential units are zoned in groups based on orientation, use, and loads. The simulation ran in four separate parts, with the results combined.

The Supertall prototype is slightly more efficient than the Megatall in terms of program and mechanical floor requirements; similarly, it has a sky lobby and two observation floors, with 71% of the total area allocated to units. Even though the Supertall is half the size and has fewer units than the Megatall, the amenity spaces are similar. The prototype's below-grade parking structure requires constant illumination and ventilation for safety and consequently contributed significantly to energy demand.

As a result of overshadowing on the south facade by the neighboring tower, the west facing model was the lower energy consumer. Southern exposure to the sun can be critical (at higher latitudes) for cooling loads, especially in buildings with high-glazing ratios. Sun obstruction can help alleviate these loads. Space heating, space cooling, and plug loads are the highest energy consumers in this prototype. Elevator loads are also extremely high, accounting for over 10% of the total energy consumption.

The Supertall prototype was the least energy efficient building of all prototypes, partially due to the supplementary spaces that are continuously conditioned throughout the tower to support the residences.

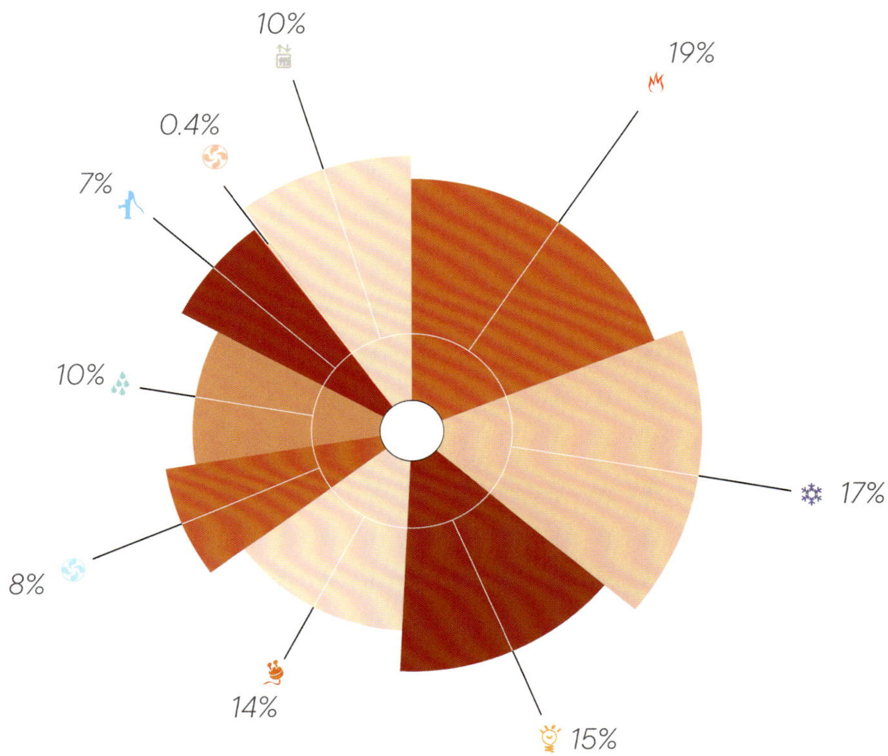

TOTAL BUILDING ENERGY CONSUMPTION BREAKDOWN (KWH/YEAR)

	HEATING	19%	5,848,265
	COOLING	17%	5,119,583
	LIGHTING	15%	4,461,165
	PLUG LOAD	14%	4,290,304
	FANS	8%	2,285,619
	HOT WATER	10%	3,109,858
	PUMP	7%	2,142,755
	HEAT REJECTION	0.4%	122,239
	ELEVATOR	10%	3,008,495

SUPERTALL ENERGY USE

NUMBER OF BUILDINGS	2
NUMBER OF UNITS / BUILDING	1,000
BUILDING AREA	231,869 m^2
CONDITIONED AREA	222,503m^2
NET RESIDENTIAL AREA	150,069 m^2
TOTAL ENERGY USE	60,776,568 kWh
BUILDING ENERGY USE	30,388,284 kWh
UNIT ENERGY USE	30,388 kWh
ENERGY USE INTENSITY(EUI)	203 kWh/m^2
ENERGY USE PER PERSON	11,643 kWh

TOTAL ENERGY CONSUMPTION

SOUTH	30,348,659 kWh/year
EAST	30,848,092 kWh/year
NORTH	29,830,051 kWh/year
WEST	30,526,334 kWh/year
AVERAGE	30,388,284 kWh/year

SPACE ALLOCATION

LIVING AREA	71%
CIRCULATION	10%
COMMON AREAS	3%
PARKING	8%
MECHANICAL SYSTEMS	8%

HIGH-RISE

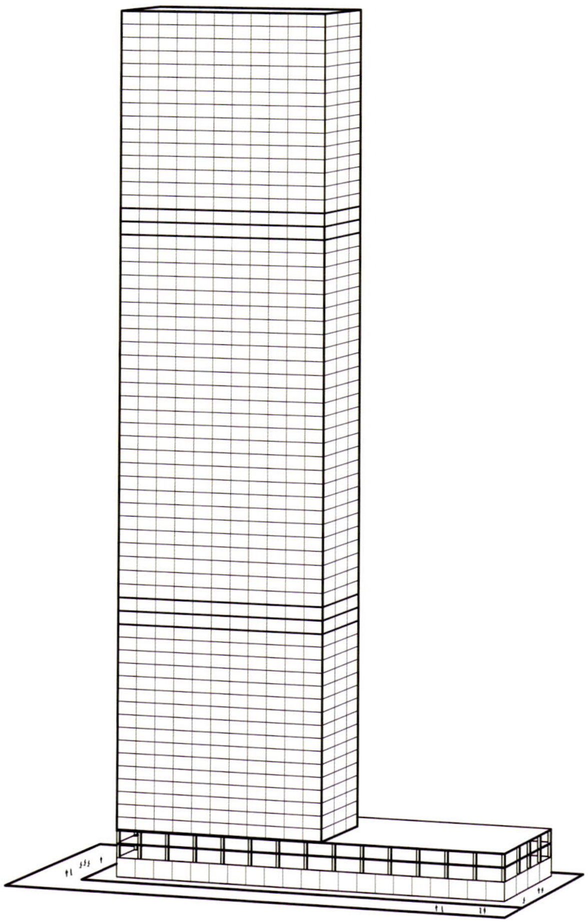

Although considered a tall building in most contexts, the High-Rise prototype differs from the Megatall and Supertall prototypes, not just in height but because it lacks sky lobbies to transfer between elevators. Observation floors are also unlikely, making the tower programmatically more efficient than the Megatall or the Supertall.

The High-Rise prototype has 65 residential stories, an entrance lobby, an amenities floor, and two mechanical zones at the lower and upper third of the building. Parking is elevated as part of the podium and is naturally ventilated. The tower's envelope is a double-glazed curtain wall, with vision glazing accounting for 40% of the facade on the four orientations.

The results from the energy model shows that the most energy-intensive loads are heating and cooling both of which account for 18% of the total energy consumption. The4 heating aspect is expected in a heating-dominated Zone 5 climate regions, and the cooling is explained by the unshaded high window-to-wall ratios. Elevators account for only 5% of the energy consumption, half of what it represents for the taller prototypes, because the elevator configuration in this system is simpler than the preceding prototypes.

This is a common configuration in many cities, where underground parking is avoided because of the cost of excavation and high water tables.

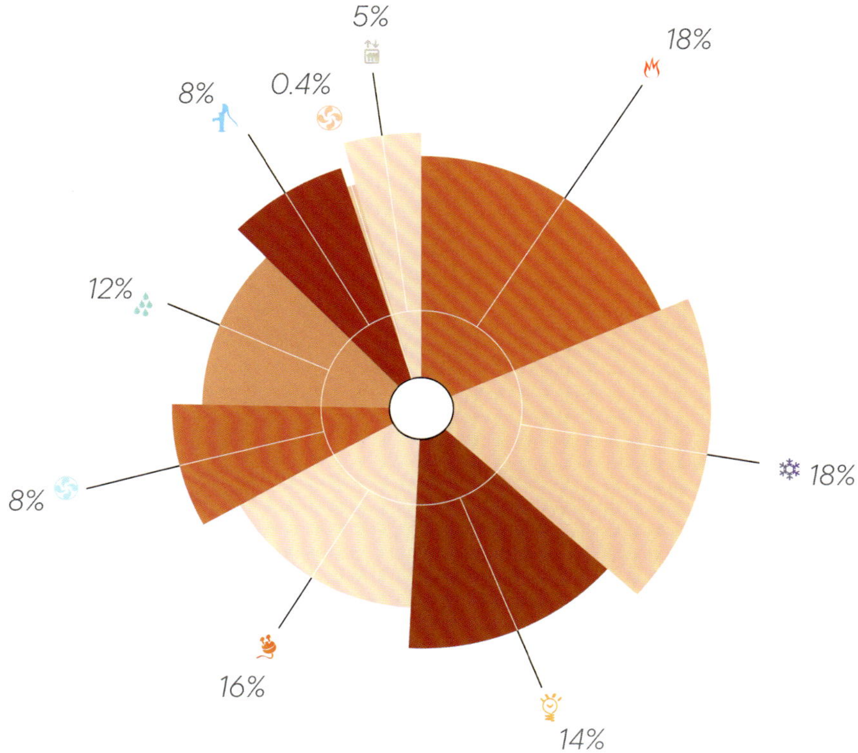

TOTAL BUILDING ENERGY CONSUMPTION BREAKDOWN (KWH/YEAR)

	HEATING	18%	2,194,782
	COOLING	18%	2,138,794
	LIGHTING	14%	1,691,286
	PLUG LOAD	16%	1,917,223
	FANS	8%	977,996
	HOT WATER	12%	1,466,050
	PUMP	8%	892,517
	HEAT REJECTION	0.4%	51,915
	ELEVATOR	5%	543,033

HIGH-RISE ENERGY USE

NUMBER OF BUILDINGS	4
NUMBER OF UNITS / BUILDING	500
BUILDING AREA	110,184 m^2
CONDITIONED AREA	98,393 m^2
NET RESIDENTIAL AREA	75,039 m^2
TOTAL ENERGY USE	47,494,382 kWh
BUILDING ENERGY USE	11,873,595 kWh
UNIT ENERGY USE	23,747 kWh
ENERGY USE INTENSITY(EUI)	158 kWh/m^2
ENERGY USE PER PERSON	9,099 kWh

TOTAL ENERGY CONSUMPTION

SOUTH	11,917,792 kWh/year
EAST	11,994,447 kWh/year
NORTH	11,389,875 kWh/year
WEST	12,192,268 kWh/year
AVERAGE	11,873,595 kWh/year

SPACE ALLOCATION

LIVING AREA	77%
CIRCULATION	7%
COMMON AREAS	4%
PARKING	8%
MECHANICAL SYSTEMS	4%

MID-RISE

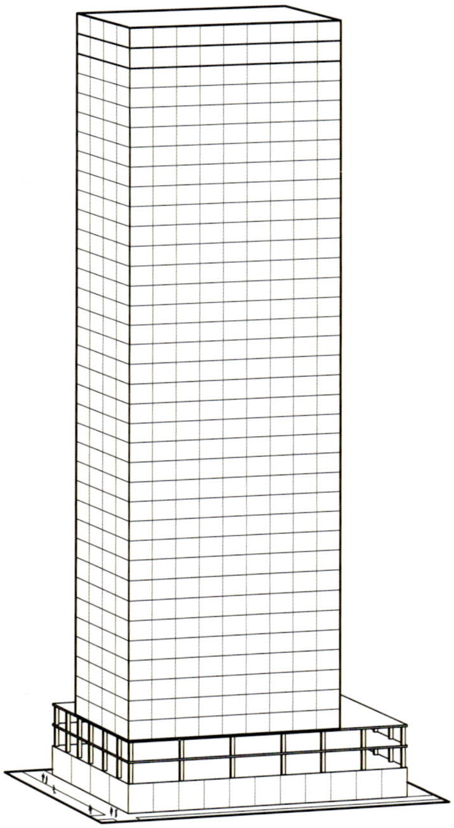

The Mid-Rise prototype is also considered a tall building in most contexts, but it does not require sky lobbies for elevator transfers or include an observation floor. Therefore, like the High-Rise prototype, the Mid-Rise prototype is more programmatically efficient than the Megatall or Supertall prototypes, with 76% of the total area allocated to residential units.

The Mid-Rise has an above-ground podium parking structure that is naturally ventilated, eliminating the need for energy-intensive systems of the Megatall and Supertall's below-grade parking. The envelope is a double-glazed curtain wall, with the vision glazing accounting for 40% of the facade on all four orientations, and was modeled in the prototypical context, surrounded by three other towers of the same scale.

The Mid-Rise energy model results indicate that the most energy-intensive load is space heating, accounting for 26% of the total energy consumption. And, like the High-Rise, this is expected for buildings with high window-to-wall ratios within a heating-dominated climate. Cooling demand is lower (16%) than with the High-Rise due to the effect of all-round shading. The elevator configuration is simpler than the Megatall and Supertall prototypes, so elevators only account for around 3% of the buildings' energy consumption.

Cooling is the second highest energy consumer for the Mid-Rise prototype. When the rectangular footprint model is orientated to the north, the cooling load is 25% lower than when oriented to the west.

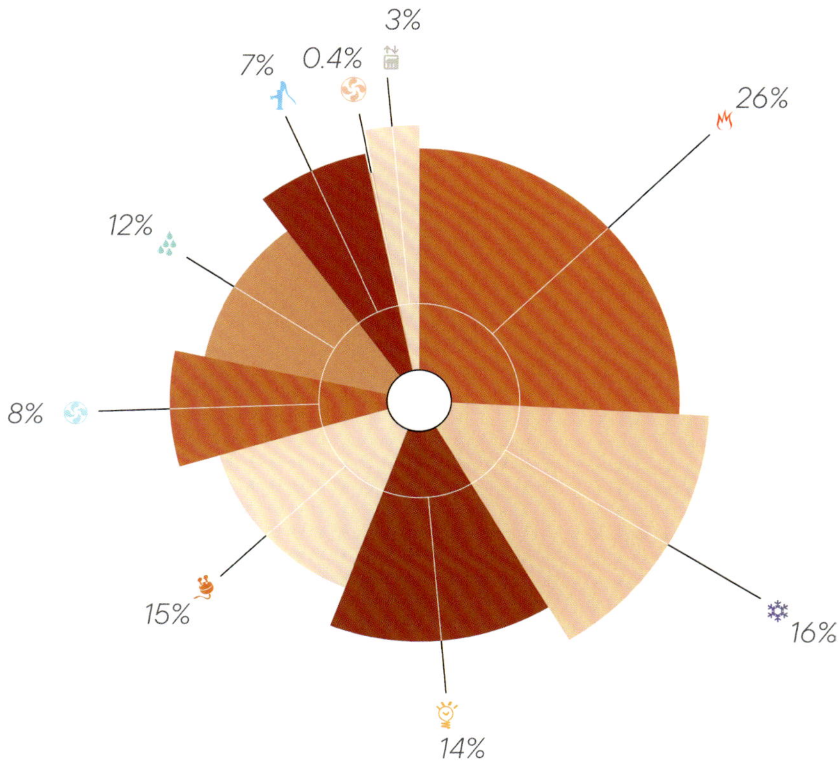

TOTAL BUILDING ENERGY CONSUMPTION BREAKDOWN (KWH/YEAR)		
HEATING	26%	1,282,832
COOLING	16%	768,155
LIGHTING	14%	711,643
PLUG LOAD	15%	732,962
FANS	8%	381,092
HOT WATER	12%	570,785
PUMP	7%	340,055
HEAT REJECTION	0.4%	19,600
ELEVATOR	3%	146,201

MID-RISE ENERGY USE	
NUMBER OF BUILDINGS	10
NUMBER OF UNITS / BUILDING	200
BUILDING AREA	42,896 m^2
CONDITIONED AREA	37,834 m^2
NET RESIDENTIAL AREA	30,077 m^2
TOTAL ENERGY USE	49,533,258 kWh
BUILDING ENERGY USE	4,953,326 kWh
UNIT ENERGY USE	24,767 kWh
ENERGY USE INTENSITY(EUI)	165 kWh/m^2
ENERGY USE PER PERSON	9,489 kWh

TOTAL ENERGY CONSUMPTION	
SOUTH	4,838,251 kWh/year
EAST	5,003,408 kWh/year
NORTH	4,864,428 kWh/year
WEST	5,107,216 kWh/year
AVERAGE	4,953,326 kWh/year

SPACE ALLOCATION	
LIVING AREA	76%
CIRCULATION	8%
COMMON AREAS	5%
PARKING	9%
MECHANICAL SYSTEMS	2%

LOW-RISE

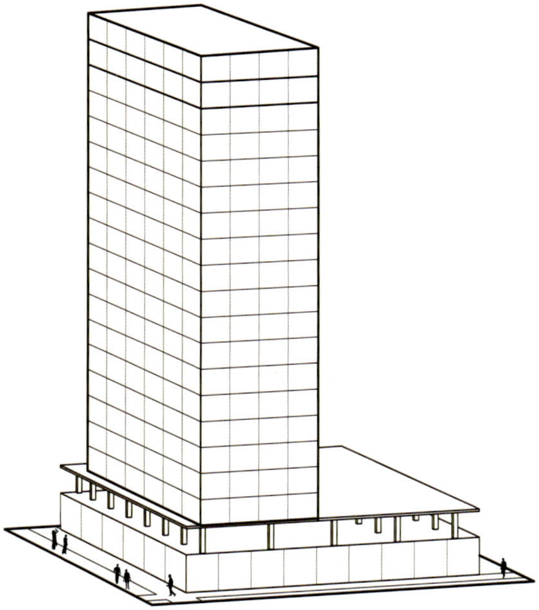

The Low-Rise prototype is a rectangular, 20-story tower. The main challenge with the energy model was that the orientation of the prototype can greatly impact the overall energy performance. Because of the standard rectangular massing, north-south facing prototypes perform better than the east-west facing ones.

The tower sits directly on top of a two-story podium, which consists of a lobby and an amenities floor. Parking and a mechanical zone are located on top of the podium. Glazing accounts for 40% of the building envelope, distributed evenly on all four facades.

The glazing on the facades allows for high heat gains through the windows for most of the units, reducing overall heating demand. Nevertheless, highly glazed facades also contribute to heat gain in summer, demanding higher cooling in the warmer seasons.

The low-rise building at just 20 stories is not tall enough to benefit from some of the efficiencies enjoyed by the Mid-Rise and High-Rise buildings. Consequently, it pays the price in increased energy demand for having a lower living area %.

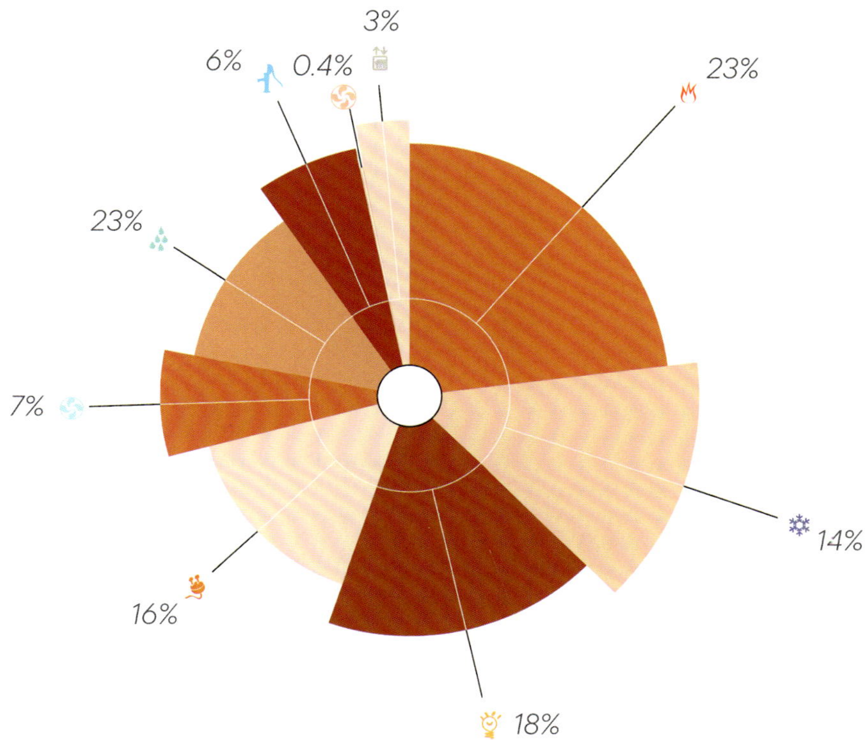

TOTAL BUILDING ENERGY CONSUMPTION BREAKDOWN (KWH/YEAR)

HEATING	23%	579,461
COOLING	14%	363,319
LIGHTING	18%	445,829
PLUG LOAD	16%	390,968
FANS	7%	185,550
HOT WATER	12%	306,106
PUMP	6%	159,814
HEAT REJECTION	0.4%	9,615
ELEVATOR	3%	81,223

LOW-RISE ENERGY USE

NUMBER OF BUILDINGS	20
NUMBER OF UNITS / BUILDING	100
BUILDING AREA	24,300 m^2
CONDITIONED AREA	21,000 m^2
NET RESIDENTIAL AREA	14,980 m^2
TOTAL ENERGY USE	50,437,705 kWh
BUILDING ENERGY USE	2,521,885 kWh
UNIT ENERGY USE	25,219 kWh
ENERGY USE INTENSITY(EUI)	168 kWh/m^2
ENERGY USE PER PERSON	9,662 kWh

TOTAL ENERGY CONSUMPTION

SOUTH	2,508,835 kWh/year
EAST	2,550,887 kWh/year
NORTH	2,485,474 kWh/year
WEST	2,542,345 kWh/year
AVERAGE	2,521,885 kWh/year

SPACE ALLOCATION

LIVING AREA	70%
CIRCULATION	7%
COMMON AREAS	9%
PARKING	9%
MECHANICAL SYSTEMS	4%

COURTYARD

The best performing prototype, The Courtyard, is commonly found in many cities' urban residential communities, consisting of four units stacked on top of each other and sharing circulation space with the neighboring units, similar to town homes. The layout minimizes the unit's exterior surface exposure to two or three walls, helping protect the indoor environment from exterior conditions. The geometry allows the units to extend throughout the length of the building and are effective for natural cross ventilation and daylighting on both sides of the building.

The Courtyard is made of a concrete block structure with an exterior brick finish and wooden beams that support interior wood floors. The zones in the building are divided into living space (which accounts for 81% of the area) and circulation space. The units are individually conditioned with packaged units, commonly used in buildings that are four stories or less; units with more people consume more water but not necessarily more heating or cooling. Emergency exit stairs are also shared by two unit blocks and are located outside, without need for mechanical ventilation. In heating-dominated climates, buildings of this shape with more solar exposure perform better than those with no solar heat gain.

The garage buildings were modeled separately. As external open structures they were assigned a lighting demand only. It is interesting to note that because the heating and cooling loads are lower than other prototypes, water heating becomes the second-most energy-intensive load in the building.

The courtyard building performs so well, due in part to the high density of units, with less exposed envelope per unit, and a scale that is dense but lacks the equipment, such as elevators, needed to operate taller buildings.

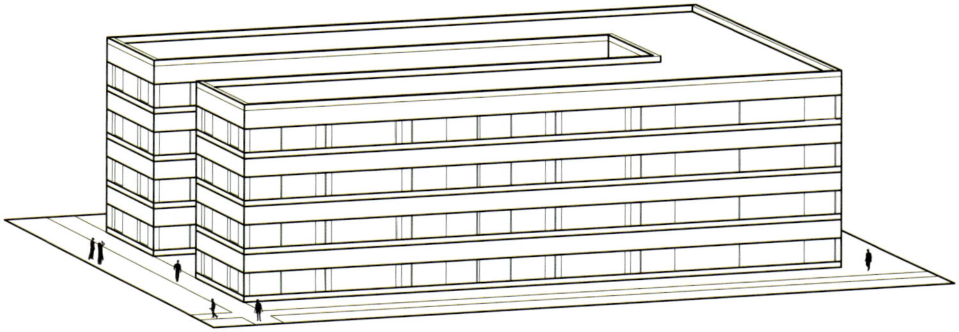

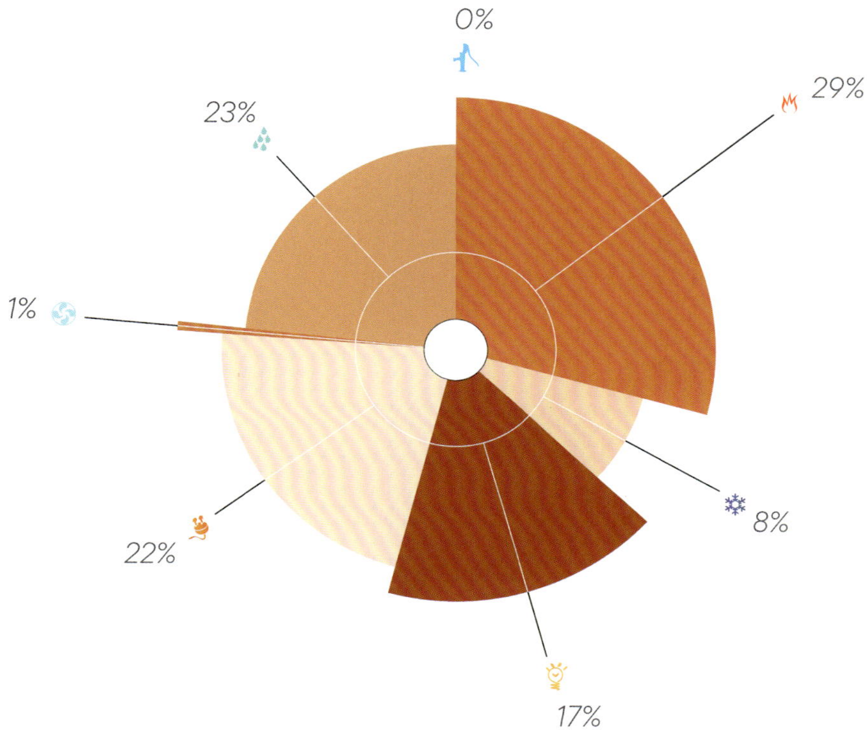

TOTAL BUILDING ENERGY CONSUMPTION BREAKDOWN (KWH/YEAR)

HEATING	29%	91,099
COOLING	8%	24,201
LIGHTING	17%	54,348
PLUG LOAD	22%	68,405
FANS	1%	1,775
HOT WATER	23%	73,385
PUMP	0%	42

COURTYARD ENERGY USE

NUMBER OF BUILDINGS	100
NUMBER OF UNITS / BUILDING	20
BUILDING AREA	3,756 m^2
CONDITIONED AREA	3,268 m^2
NET RESIDENTIAL AREA	2,995 m^2
TOTAL ENERGY USE	31,325,511 kWh
BUILDING ENERGY USE	313,255 kWh
UNIT ENERGY USE	15,663 kWh
ENERGY USE INTENSITY(EUI)	105 kWh/m^2
ENERGY USE PER PERSON	6,001 kWh

TOTAL ENERGY CONSUMPTION

SOUTH	310,667 kWh/year
EAST	312,323 kWh/year
NORTH	316,971 kWh/year
WEST	313,059 kWh/year
AVERAGE	313,255 kWh/year

SPACE ALLOCATION

LIVING AREA	81%
CIRCULATION	6%
PARKING	13%

THREE-FLAT

The Three-Flat prototype is also commonly found in many cities' urban-residential neighborhoods. It has two zones: living spaces and circulation. This prototype is typically detached with a front entrance leading to a small corridor and stairs that provide circulation to each of the three floors. The units are relatively compact, making them easier to cool and heat, and there is no attached interior parking.

The building is made from wood or brick, or constructed from a combination of both. Glazing ratio is higher at the front of the building, where windows are larger, while on the sides and at the back the windows are typically smaller, and the glazing ratio is lower. The overall glazing ratio can be as low as 11%.

The proximity to adjacent buildings allows little light into this prototype, helping it stay cool during summer. The energy model results indicate that energy consumption is dominated by space heating. Having effectively no solar exposure along the sides of the building, the front glazing in the south facing model contributes to passive solar gain, helping to reduce the overall energy consumption for this configuration.

The Three-Flat prototype has the highest percentage for lighting demand and heating demand of all the multi-unit buildings, resulting from its low glazing ratio and the high degree of shading from neighboring buildings.

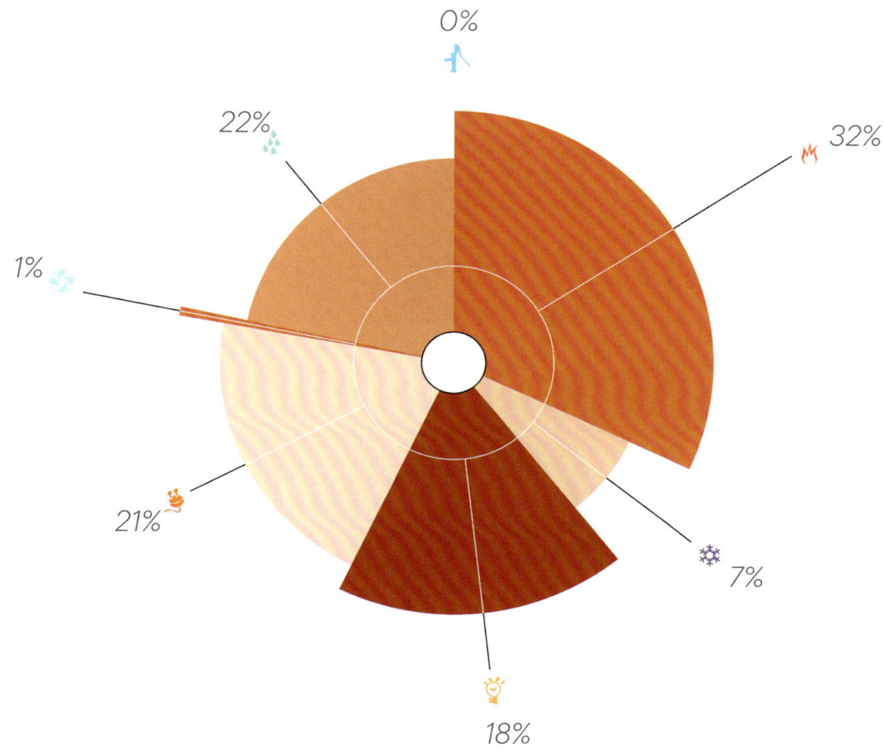

TOTAL BUILDING ENERGY CONSUMPTION BREAKDOWN (KWH/YEAR)

HEATING	32%	15,752
COOLING	7%	3,563
LIGHTING	18%	8,887
PLUG LOAD	21%	10,152
FANS	1%	287
HOT WATER	22%	10,869
PUMP	0%	7

COURTYARD ENERGY USE

NUMBER OF BUILDINGS	667
NUMBER OF UNITS / BUILDING	3
BUILDING AREA	554 m^2
CONDITIONED AREA	513 m^2
NET RESIDENTIAL AREA	450 m^2
TOTAL ENERGY USE	33,011,689 kWh
BUILDING ENERGY USE	49,518 kWh
UNIT ENERGY USE	16,506 kWh
ENERGY USE INTENSITY(EUI)	110 kWh/m^2
ENERGY USE PER PERSON	6,324 kWh

TOTAL ENERGY CONSUMPTION

SOUTH	47,752 kWh/year
EAST	50,405 kWh/year
NORTH	49,494 kWh/year
WEST	50,419 kWh/year
AVERAGE	49,518 kWh/year

SPACE ALLOCATION

LIVING AREA	83%
CIRCULATION	10%
PARKING	7%

URBAN SINGLE-FAMILY

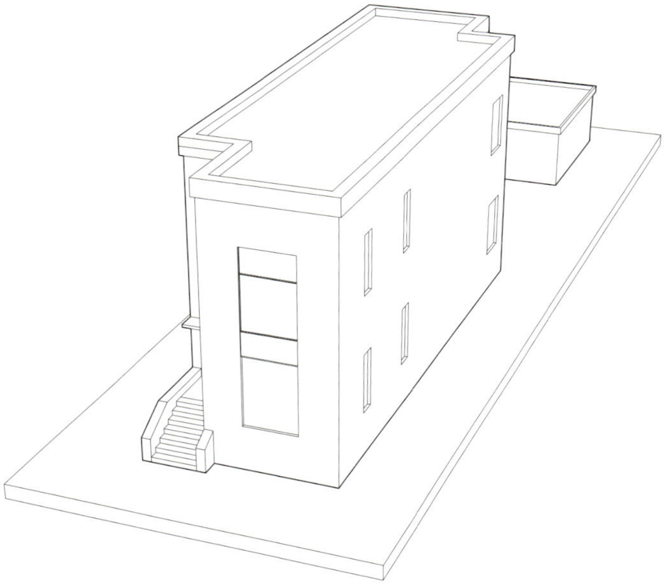

This prototype represents a typical urban single-family home. Because the plot sizes are so small, the houses tend to be small and close together, with barely any windows on the sides. This proximity blocks direct sunlight from penetrating the house from the sides, resulting in a very cool interior environment, even in summer months. This house is also a wood-framed house, with a brick veneer on the outside. Most of the houses have attics and basements, not considered occupied space for this study, and a detached garage. The garage, although frequently used, was considered unconditioned for the calculations.

Out of the four cardinal orientations, the best performing building was the one facing south. This is due to the fact that heating accounts for 48% of the energy used in the house—the highest percentage of energy use for heating of all prototypes. Although the south facing facade exposes the most glazing to the sun, allowing for solar heat gain and lower heating loads, the rectangular shape still leads to the majority of the wall area receiving no direct sunlight. Another factor that contributes to space heating is the attic void space, where much of the heat escapes to (unless the ceilings are heavily insulated). Although the sunlight blocked from the side walls proved to be detrimental in the winter months, it did result in very low cooling demands for the rest of the year (with only 3% of the energy use being attributed to space cooling).

The Urban Single-Family prototype has the lowest percentage for cooling demand and the highest percentage for heating demand of all the building prototypes, as a result of its low glazing ratio and the high degree of shading from neighboring buildings.

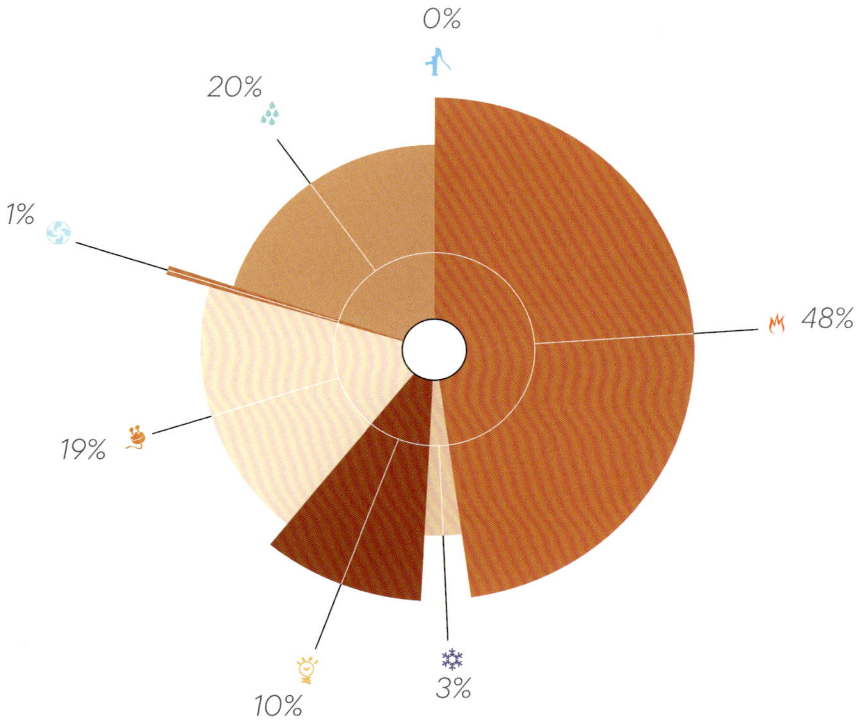

TOTAL BUILDING ENERGY CONSUMPTION BREAKDOWN (KWH/YEAR)

	HEATING	48%	8,703
	COOLING	3%	531
	LIGHTING	10%	1,822
	PLUG LOAD	19%	3,378
	FANS	1%	111
	HOT WATER	20%	3,624
	PUMP	0%	3

COURTYARD ENERGY USE

NUMBER OF BUILDINGS	2000
NUMBER OF UNITS / BUILDING	1
BUILDING AREA	216 m^2
CONDITIONED AREA	172 m^2
NET RESIDENTIAL AREA	150 m^2
TOTAL ENERGY USE	36,347,035 kWh
BUILDING ENERGY USE	18,174 kWh
UNIT ENERGY USE	18,174 kWh
ENERGY USE INTENSITY(EUI)	121 kWh/m^2
ENERGY USE PER PERSON	6,963 kWh

TOTAL ENERGY CONSUMPTION

SOUTH	17,994 kWh/year
EAST	18,221 kWh/year
NORTH	18,293 kWh/year
WEST	18,136 kWh/year
AVERAGE	18,174 kWh/year

SPACE ALLOCATION

LIVING AREA	79%
CIRCULATION	21%

SUBURBAN SINGLE-FAMILY

Water is distributed differently from the other prototypes because yards typically consume about 30% of a household's water consumption for irrigation.

The Suburban Single-Family prototype is a typical Zone 5, North American suburban house. It has two stories with a basement and attic, both of which are unconditioned for this study, with their areas not included in the energy totals calculations. The attached garage, also unconditioned, was considered part of the total area (but not the residential area) of the house because it is frequently used and illuminated. The larger volume of the space is more difficult to heat and cool than the other prototypes, and heat from humans and equipment do not contribute to the interior environment in a measurable way because of the larger air volumes.

This prctotype is a wood-framed construction, with insulation within the walls and an exterior layer of brick. The high quality of the building envelope and shading provided by trees on the lot help keep the house cool in summer. However, it has a low window-to-wall ratios at 12% and although it was modeled in a community, the suburban plots allow for larger separation between the houses, with little overshadowing from other residences occurring. While this is a positive aspect in the winter months, it means most of the walls and roofs are exposed to the sun, which can cause overheating in summer.

As with most single-family residential units in colder climates, the Suburban Single-Family's energy consumption is dominated by space heating, followed by plug loads, and water heating. This prototype also has the highest cooling load of all the low-density prototypes. Of the four orientations modeled, the north facing model has the lowest energy consumption, this is because in this orientation, the garage is on the east side and the exposed west wall receives all the hot afternoon sun, warming the building.

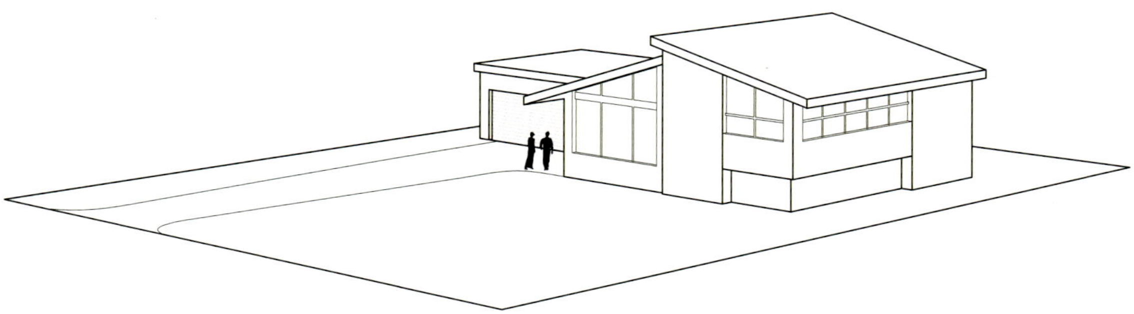

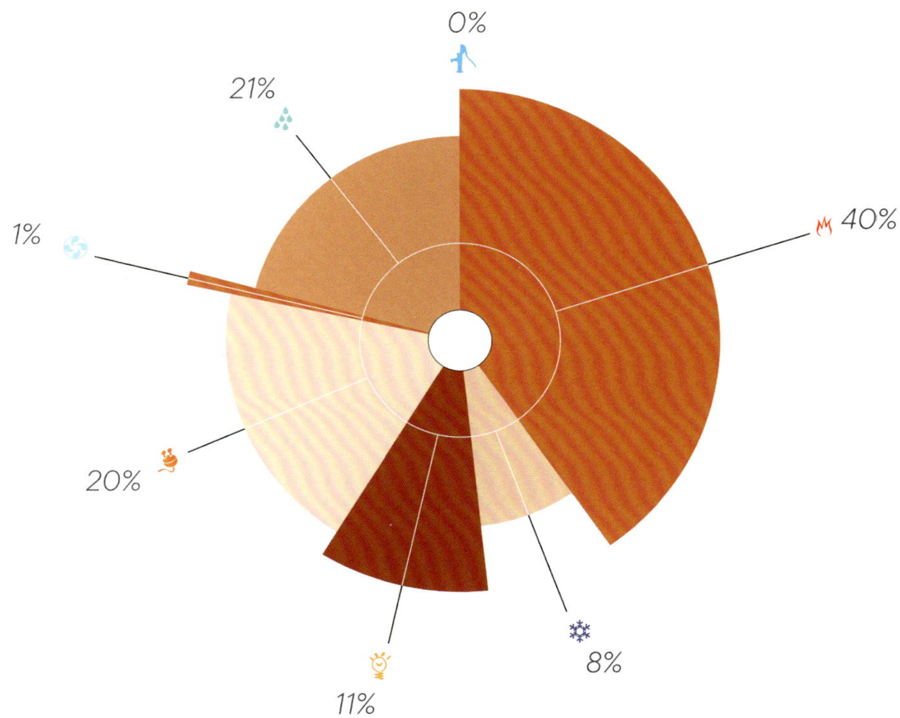

TOTAL BUILDING ENERGY CONSUMPTION BREAKDOWN (KWH/YEAR)

HEATING	40%	7,061
COOLING	8%	1,403
LIGHTING	11%	1,863
PLUG LOAD	20%	3,425
FANS	1%	124
HOT WATER	21%	3,674
PUMP	0%	3

COURTYARD ENERGY USE

NUMBER OF BUILDINGS	2000
NUMBER OF UNITS / BUILDING	1
BUILDING AREA	233 m^2
CONDITIONED AREA	176 m^2
NET RESIDENTIAL AREA	150 m^2
TOTAL ENERGY USE	35,104,156 kWh
BUILDING ENERGY USE	17,552 kWh
UNIT ENERGY USE	17,552 kWh
ENERGY USE INTENSITY(EUI)	117 kWh/m^2
ENERGY USE PER PERSON	6,725 kWh

TOTAL ENERGY CONSUMPTION

SOUTH	17,431 kWh/year
EAST	18,006 kWh/year
NORTH	16,833 kWh/year
WEST	17,839 kWh/year
AVERAGE	17,552 kWh/year

SPACE ALLOCATION

LIVING AREA	76%
CIRCULATION	24%

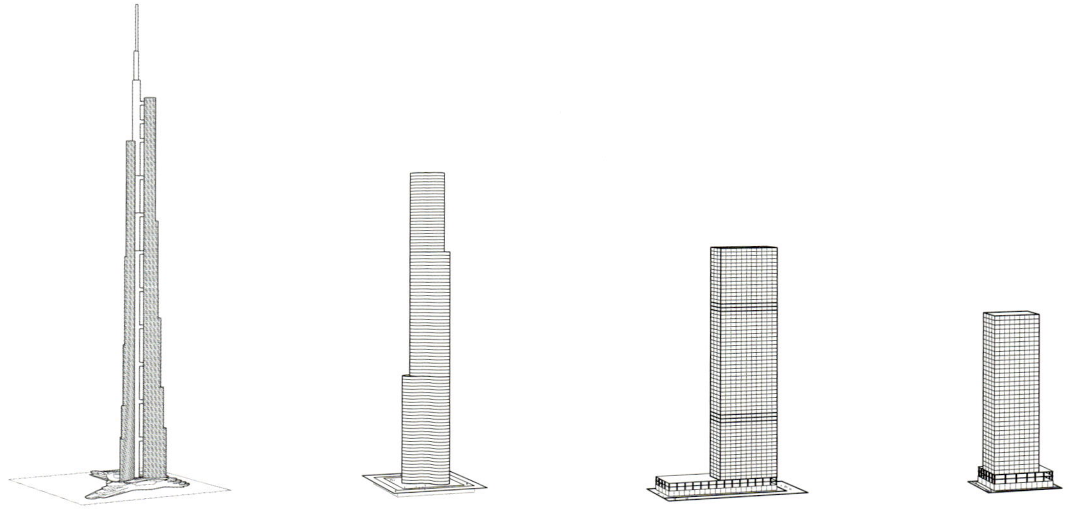

SUMMARY	MEGATALL	SUPERTALL	HIGH-RISE	MID-RISE
NUMBER OF BUILDINGS	1	2	4	10
NUMBER OF UNITS / BUILDING	2,000	1,000	500	200
ABOVE GRADE BUILDING FLOOR AREA (M^2)	451,480	231,869	110,184	42,896
CONDITIONED AREA (M^2)	435,619	222,502	98,392	37,834
NET RESIDENTIAL FLOOR AREA (M^2)	299,991	150,069	75,039	30,077
TOTAL ENERGY USE (KWH/YEAR)	58,429,403	60,776,568	47,494,382	49,533,258
BUILDING ENERGY USE (KWH/YEAR)	58,429,403	30,388,284	11,873,595	4,953,326
UNIT ENERGY USE (KWH/YEAR)	29,215	30,388	23,747	24,767
ENERGY USE INTENSITY (KWH/M^2)	195	203	158	165
ENERGY USE PER PERSON (KWH/YEAR)	11,193	11,643	9,099	9,489
ENERGY USE BREAKDOWN				
TOTAL HEATING ENERGY (KWH/YEAR)	12,003,931 (21%)	5,848,265 (19%)	2,194,782 (18%)	1,282,832 (26%)
TOTAL COOLING ENERGY (KWH/YEAR)	9,227,289 (16%)	5,119,583 (17%)	2,138,794 (18%)	768,155 (16%)
TOTAL LIGHTING ENERGY (KWH/YEAR)	8,720,520 (15%)	4,461,165 (15%)	1,691,286 (14%)	711,643 (14%)
TOTAL PLUG LOAD ENERGY (KWH/YEAR)	8,157,010 (14%)	4,290,304 (14%)	1,917,222 (16%)	732,962 (15%)
TOTAL FAN ENERGY (KWH/YEAR)	4,514,844 (8%)	2,285,619 (8%)	977,996 (8%)	381,092 (8%)
TOTAL HOT WATER ENERGY (KWH/YEAR)	5,968,087 (10%)	3,109,858 (10%)	1,466,049 (12%)	570,785 (12%)
TOTAL PUMP ENERGY (KWH/YEAR)	3,992,629 (7%)	2,142,755 (7%)	892,517 (8%)	340,055 (7%)
HEAT REJECTION ENERGY (KWH/YEAR)	232,823 (0.4%)	122,239 (0.4%)	51,915 (0.4%)	19,600 (0.4%)
ELEVATOR ENERGY (KWH/YEAR)	5,612,268 (10%)	3,008,495 (10%)	543,033 (5%)	146,201 (3%)

Table 10 Energy-use data

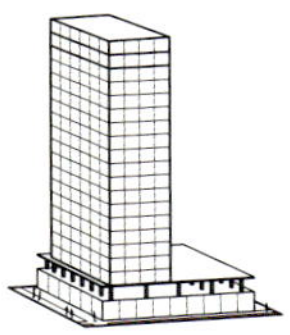 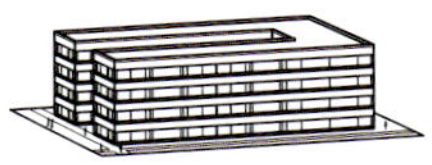  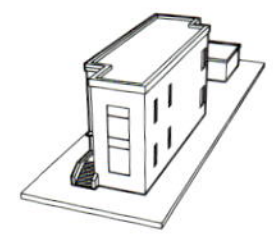 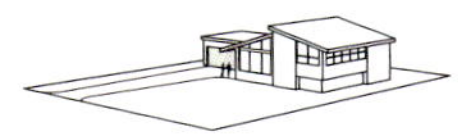

LOW-RISE	COURTYARD	THREE-FLAT	URBAN SINGLE FAMILY	SUBURBAN SINGLE FAMILY
20	100	667	2,000	2,000
100	20	3	1	1
24,300	3,756	554	216	233
21,000	3,696	560	172	177
14,980	2,995	450	150	150
50,437,705	31,325,511	33,011,689	36,347,035	35,104,156
2,521,885	313,255	49,518	18,174	17,552
25,219	15,663	16,506	18,174	17,552
168	104	110	121	117
9,662	6,001	6,324	6,963	6,725
579,461 (23%)	91,099 (29%)	15,752 (32%)	8,703 (48%)	7,061 (40%)
363,319 (14%)	24,201 (8%)	3,563 (7%)	531 (3%)	1,403 (8%)
445,829 (18%)	54,348 (17%)	8,887 (18%)	1,822 (10%)	1,863 (11%)
390,968 (16%)	68,405 (22%)	10,152 (21%)	3,378 (19%)	3,425 (20%)
185,550 (7%)	1,775 (1%)	287 (1%)	111 (1%)	124 (1%)
306,105 (12%)	73,385 (23%)	10,869 (22%)	3,624 (20%)	3,674 (21%)
159,814 (6%)	41.8 (0.01%)	6.8 (0.01%)	3.3 (0.02%)	2.8 (0.02%)
9,615 (0.4%)	N/A	N/A	N/A	N/A
81,223 (3%)	N/A	N/A	N/A	N/A

DISCUSSION

Figure 20, on the following page, shows the results of each of the energy models in the study (Table 10). On the previous pages, the individual results were described and discussed in detail, identifying the highest and lowest loads for each building type. The analysis and energy consumption breakdown graphs were developed from an average of the results of the models run in four orientations. Here, the averaged results have been extrapolated to represent 2,000 units, with their totals compared.

The bar graph shows the comparison of the energy consumption of each prototype, representing the total energy consumption of 2000 units. The prototypes are broken down into the sum of loads associated with their totals for a more in depth understanding of their behavior. As the graph indicates, the lower density prototypes have six significant loads that affect their overall consumption, compared with nine loads that the higher density prototypes, due to their more complex systems. Heating and water heating are the most energy-intensive loads in almost all prototypes. Cooling becomes more significant in buildings with higher glazing ratios, where overheating occurs in the summer.

The analysis shows that the Courtyard prototype is the most energy efficient, due to a series of factors, including a glazing ratio lower than 20% and a high density of units that have only two walls exposed to the exterior. These factors help reduce infiltration and contain heat in the winter, as well as minimize solar heat gain in summer, where cooling is a primary concern. Also important, is that although the Courtyard is a relatively dense prototype at 50 units per building, its low height allows it to operate with simple systems, without requiring elevators. The most significant energy load in this prototype is space heating but plug load, lighting, and water heating are all similar.

The High-Rise, Mid-Rise, and Low-Rise prototypes have similar energy consumptions that are around 50%–60% higher than the Courtyard prototype. They have added energy loads from pumps, elevators, and fans, and, when compared to the lower density prototypes, higher cooling, lighting and plug loads. These prototypes also perform similarly to the Suburban Single-Family, which is the least efficient of the lower-density prototypes. This prototype requires a large amount of energy for space heating and cooling, and has a higher equipment load per unit.

The Megatall and Supertall prototypes are the least efficient and consume the most energy, for numerous reasons. A major factor in this conclusion, is that 30% of the total area is used for non-residential functions such as mechanical floors, lobbies, corridors, cores, and parking garages, and are continuously illuminated and conditioned, yet not always occupied. These prototypes also have higher glazing ratios that perform poorly when compared to the high-mass envelopes of the other prototypes, translating into higher infiltration rates and heat losses in the winter and unwanted heat gain in the summer.

Another factor contributing to high energy use in Megatall and Supertall is the extensive elevator use. An efficient vertical transportation system is critical for their operation and accounts for around 10% of the total energy consumption, compared to only 4–5% the High-Rise, Mid-Rise, and Low-Rise prototypes. Sky lobbies, elevator transfers, and in most cases double-decker elevators all contribute to the energy consumption yet are necessary for the proper functioning of the building. Water for domestic use and systems operations also increases the energy consumption because it needs to be pumped to higher elevations and requires more power.

It should be noted that auxiliary energy has not been considered. Auxiliary energy is additional energy necessary for the operation of the building that is not consumed within the building, such as water distributed from a utility company that requires electricity. Therefore, the potable water network in a suburban neighborhood of 2,000 single-family homes is over 100 times longer than the one needed to supply one supertall building, accounting for significantly more energy use and losses. The energy consumption calculations for the study used the building site as the boundary for the analysis, and so these loads are not accounted for in the overall results.

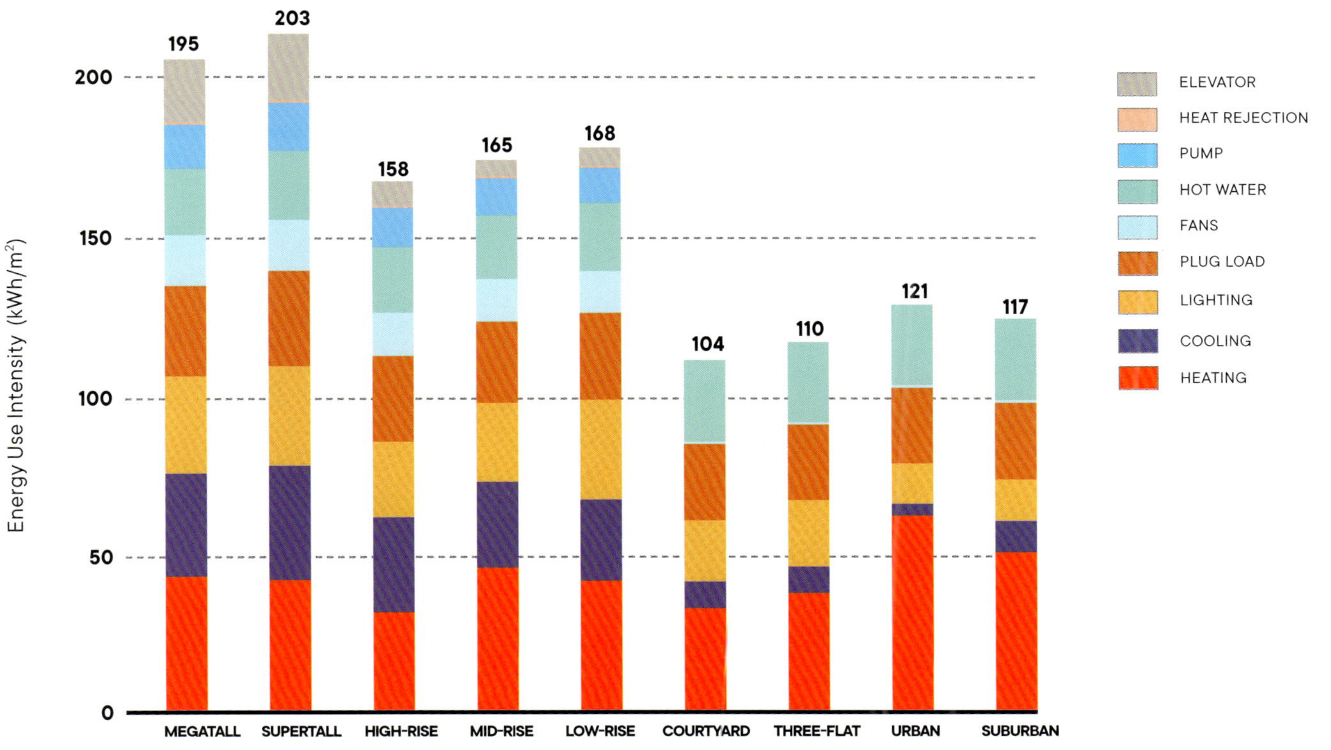

Figure 20 Energy Use Intensity for Each Prototype

TRANSPORT

This chapter is a detailed discussion of different types of transportation networks as they correlate to the different density prototypes that are included in the study, along with the benefits and challenges related to each. Transportation is the second largest contributor of carbon emissions in the United States, at 28.5% of total emissions (***EPA, 2018***), and in Europe at 33% with 72% of that being from road transportation ***(Papadimitriou et al., 2013)***. A building or community can be highly energy efficient but can still have a significant negative environmental impact because of the lack of an adequate transportation network. A development can be planned and designed as the ideal live-work community, but if it lacks connectivity, the benefits of living there are minimal.

Some of the world's most daunting problems are linked to transportation patterns and excess car use, in terms of travel times, congestion, and accessibility to affordable and convenient transportation. When an urban population reaches a certain density threshold, a well-operated mass transit system is not just convenient, it is necessary to avoid traffic congestion and consequently excessive commute times. But in many urban environments, it can be viewed as an inefficient option that is expensive to operate and maintain or a mode of transportation only used by those who either don't own or are unable to drive a car.

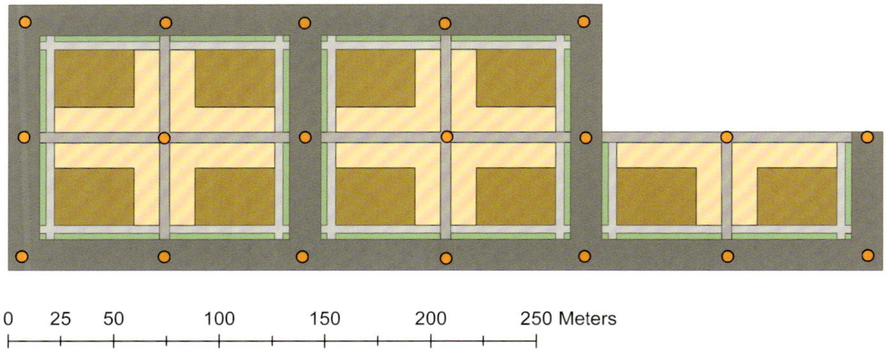

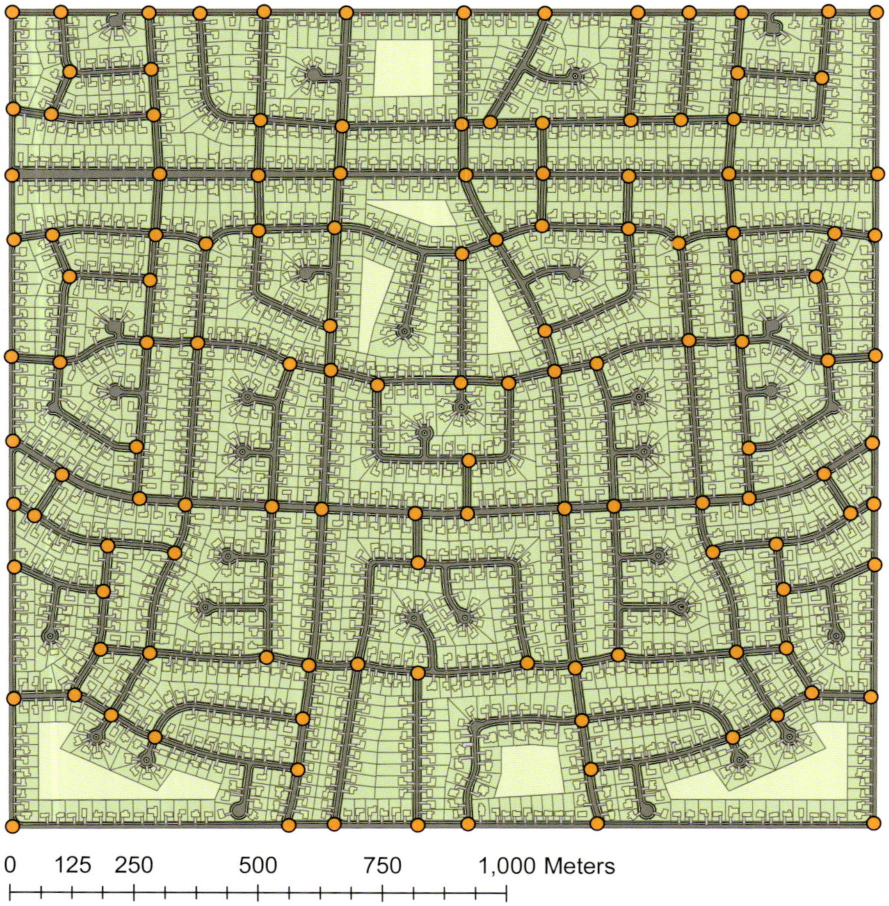

Figure 21 Intersection density of Mid-Rise prototype community compared with Suburban Single-Family neighborhood

WALKING AND BICYCLING

In a local community, whether urban or suburban, the mode of transportation that has the lowest energy impact—and is the least expensive—is walking. Adequate lighting, thoughtful streetscapes, and a variety of accessible local amenities all contribute to encourage walking. Connectivity is one of the most widely considered attributes for defining the livability of a neighborhood. When block sizes are smaller and streets have fewer cul-de-sacs with frequent direction changes at intersections walking and cycling to a destination becomes more convenient.

Local mass transit networks that provide additional capacity at peak times help reduce overall commute times—as compared to sitting in traffic—and help relieve highway congestion.

A growing number of urban design rating systems say increased connectivity is one of the most important factors for promoting pedestrian travel. Improving a neighborhood's walkability is directly associated with fewer vehicle miles traveled, leading to reduced carbon emissions, less road congestion, and improved local air quality. Intersection density is typically reported as road or sidewalk intersections per square kilometer. Cul-de-sac entrances with driveways are not included.

Intersection density is lowest in suburban areas and highest in urban areas (Figure 21). The Suburban Single-Family prototype is less connected, so walking from one place to another will take longer because of less convenient routes. In contrast, the Mid-Rise prototype has 9.5 times more intersections per square kilometer (Table 11). USGBC's LEED Neighborhood Development rating scheme rewards intersection densities as seen in Table 12 below.

	MEGATALL	SUPERTALL	HIGH-RISE	MID-RISE	LOW-RISE	COURTYARD	THREE-FLAT	URBAN	SUBURBAN
INTERSECTIONS	4	6	9	19	31	54	79	162	132
AREA (km^2)	0.027	0.036	0.036	0.045	0.086	0.323	0.49	1.28	2.97
INTERSECTION DENSITY	148*	167	250	417	360	167	161	126	44.4

Table 11 USGBC's LEED Neighborhood Development rating scheme

78-96	INTERSECTIONS PER km^2	1 POINT
97-115	INTERSECTIONS PER km^2	2 POINTS
116-134	INTERSECTIONS PER km^2	3 POINTS
135-153	INTERSECTIONS PER km^2	4 POINTS
≥ 154	INTERSECTIONS PER km^2	5 POINTS

Table 12 Intersection densities

Walking is only convenient when traveling short distances; environmental conditions can significantly impact walking and bicycling choices. Children or the elderly who need to be accompanied, may not be able to walk or ride long distances– if at all–and consequently, when they need to travel they will use a form of motorized transport.

Access to safe, dedicated bike lanes is a challenge for cyclists, especially in denser areas where heavy traffic volumes can lead to competition for road space. People are more likely to ride a bike as their primary form of daily transit when they do not share lanes with cars. Protected bike lanes and specific bicycle routes remain the best solution and research indicates that the number of cyclists increases when these designations are in place ***(Buehler and Pucher, 2011)***. When a community where people primarily walk or use bicycles, it is still necessary for transportation to have access to the community, such as municipal collection and delivery vehicles, emergency services, and school buses.

Studies have found that better transportation access improves property values, access to jobs, and reduces crime. Often the most blighted parts of the city are those that lack mixed-use amenities or have an excessive commute time to the urban core, due to poor access to public transit.

PUBLIC TRANSPORT

When it is not possible or practical to walk or bike, or for traveling longer distances, public transit at peak times is generally the most carbon efficient mode of transportation (Table 13). Buses are the most common form of public transit, although most larger cities also have a form of light rail to increase the efficiency of traveling long distances and minimize traffic volumes. A light rail system avoids traffic congestion and is widely considered the fastest and most convenient way to move large amounts of people during peak periods. Although commute times vary from city to city, so does the convenience of a local transportation network.

MODE OF TRANSPORT	GCO2 PER PASSENGER KM	REFERENCE
High Speed Rail	17	International Union of Railways (UIC) (2011)
New York City Subway	41	US DOT (2010)
	63	US DOT (2010)
US National Average Light Rail	103	US DOT (2010)
US National Average Bus	181	US DOT (2010)
Saloon car 2.0l Gasoline	108[1]	https://www.nextgreencar.com/tools/emissions-calculator
Saloon Car 2.0l Diesel	124[1]	https://www.nextgreencar.com/tools/emissions-calculator
Plug-In Hybrid Car	28[1,2]	https://www.nextgreencar.com/tools/emissions-calculator
Electric Saloon Car	0	https://www.nextgreencar.com/tools/emissions-calculator

Table 13 Mode of transport per passenger

[1] Assumes one person per car

[2] Electric car emissions do not include the emissions from producing electricity

It is beyond the scope of this study to make a comparative analysis on the merits of various modes of transport based on their emissions. Manipulating parameters, such as the number of occupants in the car, ridership percentage of the public transport network, and emissions factor of the electricity being used to operate the transit network or to charge the hybrid/electric cars, can change the relative performance of the different modes of transport.

Finding the balance between providing frequent, reliable transportation and the related costs when ridership is down is a major challenge to the efficiency of a local transportation system. Local transportation networks are inefficient when they run at lower levels of ridership or when the transportation provided is too unreliable to be efficient for maximum ridership. The distance from dwelling and destination to transportation hubs is also an important measurement when establishing both the type, convenience, and cost of a local transit system, along with the frequency of use and the population served.

For example, in low-density areas, such as the Suburban Single-Family prototype, the population is more dispersed and may not support any mass transit beyond a simple bus system and so for most people, cars may be the preferred mode of transportation. But for communities that have a higher density, such as in the highly compact conditions of the Three-Flat prototype, multiple bus systems, light rails, or subway systems are viable alternatives to a personal vehicle.

Even when a transportation network is satisfactory, it may still lack connectivity in the first or last mile of a commute. If a commuter has a long walk to reach a station or their destination, they may choose to drive a car instead. Therefore, bike-sharing, local buses, and shuttles connecting to a light rail system are important to a successful integrated transportation network.

Extensive research has been undertaken to study whether there is a correlation between density and distance driven. In a meta-analysis of the existing built environment travel literature that existed up until 2009, it was found ***(Ewing and Cervero, 2010)*** that only a weak correlation exists between population density and driving behavior, this supported earlier findings that there exists a statistically significant but quantitatively small impact of residential density on vehicle use behavior ***(Brownstone and Golob, 2009)***. A more recent study by Canada's Victoria Transport Policy Institute (***Litman, 2018***) looked at the transportation impacts of a number of land use factors. The conclusions support earlier findings adding that each land use factor, such as regional accessibility, density, and land use mix, only affects vehicle travel by a few percent. The figures are cumulative and synergistic, therefore an integrated approach to community and transport planning could lead to 20–40% less vehicle miles traveled, as well as other benefits like increased walking and cycling and lower levels of car ownership.

FUTURE TRANSPORTATION TRENDS

Over the past decade there has been a significant shift in consumer behavior patterns, with the emergence of online shopping giants, such as Amazon and Alibaba, coupled with a desire for on-demand delivery services. We are also seeing the maturation of rideshare technology like Uber and Lyft, the continued evolution of bike share systems with a transition toward dockless systems, and the potential for disruptive transport technologies such as autonomous cars and drone delivery that will change the way we design cities and the buildings within them. The landscape of transit and mobility is changing rapidly and cities will learn to adapt. The merits of density in relation to current and emerging transit systems is something that requires research in its own right.

CARBON

This chapter examines the lifecycle carbon dioxide emissions of each prototypical community. Lifecycle emissions are associated with the embodied carbon of the materials that are used in the construction of the building, the associated infrastructure of the building, and the operation of the building. Only the major components of the buildings are factored in the embodied carbon calculations, including reinforcement and structural steel, concrete, exterior wall materials, windows, and insulation. It does not include any maintenance or end of life deconstruction or demolition factors.

Each 2,000 unit community has a utilities and infrastructure network that was designed to service the needs of all the units, including roads, sidewalks, roadside green areas, driveways, and utilities pipes networks, which includes domestic fresh water, fire services hydrant networks, waste water, and storm water. Electrical and telecommunications infrastructure was not included in the calculations.

To calculate operational emissions, a grid emissions factor of 0.564 kg CO_2/kWh was used for electricity, as reported in the US EPA eGrid database. 5.31 kg CO_2/therm was used for natural gas, as established by the EPA. Materials emissions factors were obtained from a number of different sources including the University of Bath ICE (Inventory of Carbon & Energy) and various manufacturing societies and associations. In the calculations, no consideration was given to sourcing materials locally, the emissions associated with delivering materials from factory to site, or for the construction process.

Our study is not intended to be the definitive lifecycle carbon study for each typology, as that would require detailed design, product selection, and site-specific product Life Cycle Analysis. It is intended to provide a relative comparison between the prototypical communities while identifying components or aspects of the 2,000-unit communities that should be focused on to reduce the overall carbon footprint.

INTRODUCTION

Carbon dioxide is a naturally occurring gas that, prior to the advent of the industrial revolution, had an atmospheric concentration of approximately 280 parts per million (***Etheridge et al., 1996***). Following this period, the concentration has risen sharply and is currently at a level of 407 parts per million with rises predicted to continue (***NOAA, 2018***).

NAME	FORMULA	LIFETIME (YEARS)	GWP (20 YEARS)	GWP (100 YEARS)
Carbon Dioxide	CO_2	-	1	1
Methane	CH_4	12	72	25
Nitrous Oxide	N_2O	114	289	298
CFC-12 (Freon-12)*	CCl_2F_2	100	11,000	10,900
HCFC-22 (R-22)**	$CHClF_2$	12	5,160	1,810
Tetrafluoromethane	CF_4	50,000	5,210	7,390
Hexafluoroethane	C_2F_6	10,000	8,630	12,200
Sulfur Hexafluoride	SF_6	3,200	16,300	22,800
Nitrogen Trifluoride	NF_3	740	12,300	17,200

Table 14 Greenhouse Gases

Source: Data from the United Nations Framework Convention on Climate Change (UNFCC)

**CFC-12 has largely been phased out*

***R-22 is being phased out in many countries*

Carbon dioxide levels are naturally managed globally as part of the carbon cycle—a balancing relationship between the atmosphere, oceans, biosphere, sediments, and the geological carbon cycle. This overall cycle has been disrupted through the anthropogenic liberation of CO2 sequestered in fossil fuels, through the liberation of CO2 locked up in limestone (clinker production for cement), and through deforestation and agriculture with the consequent decomposition of organic matter.

Anthropogenic carbon dioxide emissions are measured and reported by various Governmental and International Agencies. According to the World Resources Institute 2012 data, China was the world's largest emitter of greenhouse gases, producing 10,975 million tons of CO2 equivalent in 2011 (***CAIT, 2015***). However, as with many topics associated with the carbon dioxide debate, things are not as clear as they may appear. According to the Global Carbon Project, 1,369 million tons of China's CO2 emissions in 2014 resulted from the combustion of fossil fuels directly or indirectly associated with the manufacture of products that are exported to other countries (***Carbon Brief, 2017***). Technically, when calculating the carbon footprint of country, the emissions of carbon dioxide associated with the manufacture of those products becomes the (accounting) responsibility of the importing country. These emissions—along with the transportation of those products from the factory to the point of use—contribute to the embodied carbon of the product.

GREENHOUSE GASES AND GLOBAL WARMING

Carbon dioxide is a greenhouse gas, meaning that it can absorb and trap infrared radiation (heat) that would otherwise reflect off the earth's surface and out of the atmosphere. There is still some denial regarding the global warming phenomenon and whether it is caused by CO2 levels. Indeed, global carbon dioxide levels have fluctuated over the past millennia with an apparent cycle. Much debate stems from the fact that we are currently experiencing a rise in CO2 levels as part of a natural cycle; however, the current peak is significantly higher than any previously recorded in the past 400,000 years.

The fact remains that carbon dioxide is a greenhouse gas and anthropogenic carbon dioxide levels in the atmosphere are increasing, as shown in Figure 22. Carbon dioxide is not the only greenhouse gas. There are several other gases that are significant, in relation to climate science. This s gnificance is measured relative to carbon dioxide using a unit known as Global Warming Potential (GWP), which is a function of how the gas behaves as a greenhouse gas and how long it lasts in the atmosphere. The main greenhouse gases are described in Table 14.

LIFECYCLE EMISSIONS

Lifecycle emissions are the combined GHG (CO2e) emissions associated with the construction, operation, maintenance, and demolition of a building. Lifecycle emissions are the most representative way of quantifying a building's environmental impact on the environment. The ratio of the various aspects of the building's lifecycle emissions are an important performative design decision making factor. For example, an energy-saving feature that has a limited life expectancy and a high-embodied carbon may not save enough energy to offset the overall energy that was required to manufacture, install, and maintain it over the building's lifetime.

Several studies have been undertaken which compare lifecycle emissions of buildings and communities. However, these studies examine existing scenarios and do not look at buildings that have been constructed to the same standard—and to the same building code. This is fundamental difference between this study and others that are published.

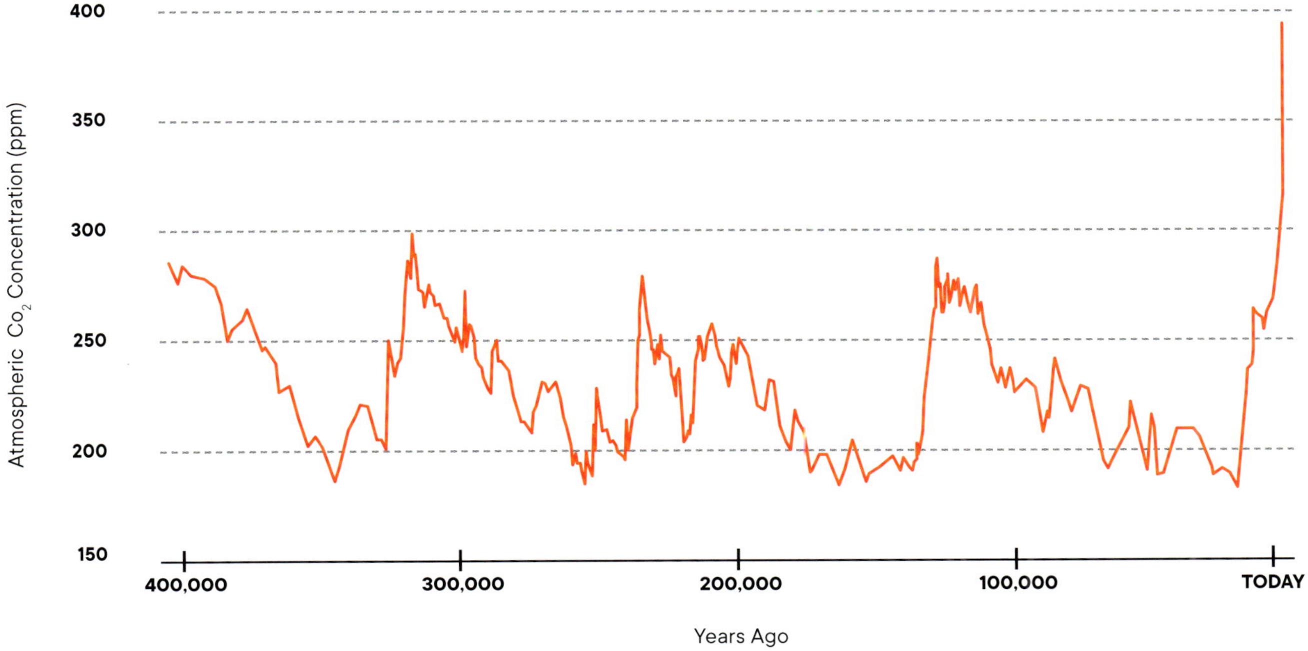

Figure 22 Measured CO_2 concentration in Antarctic Ice Cores
Source: Vostok Ice Core data from the U.S. National Oceanic and Atmospheric Administration (NOAA)

Figure 23 Building lifecycle carbon emissions

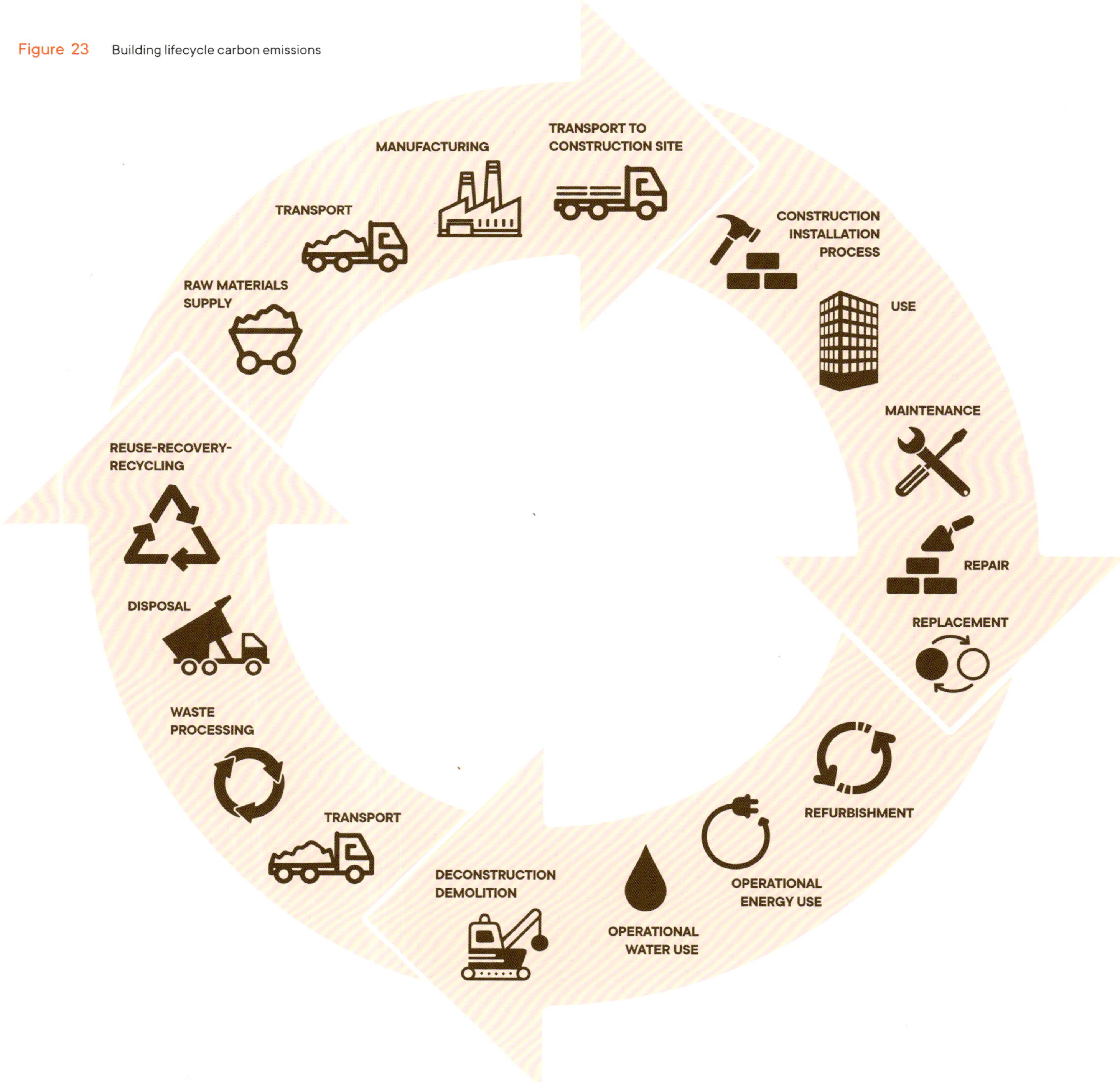

LIFECYCLE CARBON EMISSIONS

According to the World Resources Institute, residential buildings account for more than 10% of the world's greenhouse gas emissions. This overall percentage does not include the emissions associated with the manufacture and transportation of materials for use in construction, with the clearance of land for residential properties, with the construction process, or with maintenance and demolition If these figures were included, the number would likely increase to 15–17%.

The impact from residential buildings on Greenhouse Gas emissions is unequivocally significant and it is worth illustrating. The carbon flow diagram shows the lifecycle of a building, to help understand where emissions come from (Figure 23). Understanding this is the first step toward reducing a building's carbon emissions.

The lifecycle carbon emissions of a building are the sum of the CO_2 emissions that are accumulated from the construction, operation, maintenance, and demolition of a building. Defining the precise boundaries of this lifecycle accurately can be both controversial and complex, and acquiring all the data necessary to undertake a precise assessment is almost impossible and inevitably relies on a substantial number of assumptions being made.

The embodied carbon of a material can be defined as all of the carbon dioxide that was released into the atmosphere over the material's life, excluding any operational use. Ideally, all processes needed to produce the product—from the extraction of raw materials to the end of the product's life—should be considered in an analysis known as "cradle-to-grave." The most common type of analysis, "cradle-to-gate," includes the energy needed for the production of the material until the product leaves the factory, including extraction, manufacturing, and transportation. If no real products have been specified, then it is more difficult to predict where materials came from or how they will travel to the site.

Nevertheless, there are some clear points in the lifecycle where stakeholders can have an influence on the total emissions and can bring about significant improvements, through reduction in the total emission profile of the building. This chapter aims to study some of the aspects of the lifecycle of a building. Additionally, this study uses 2,000 single family units as its overall common denominator, therefore we include the emissions associated with the utilities and infrastructure required to support the lifecycle calculations. Further information is provided under the individual section headings dedicated to each component of the lifecycle.

The intent of our study is to make a relative assessment of the lifecycle carbon emissions for each building prototype. We define the boundaries to include the items that were likely to be the most significant.

Although this may lead to a debate on what is significant or not, we have tried to be as pragmatic as possible. The operational emissions, as output by the energy models in Chapter 3, include the major materials used to construct the buildings: concrete, steel, timber, bricks, glass, and insulation. We also include the infrastructure required to support the 2,000-unit prototypical communities: potable water, waste water, stormwater pipes, sidewalks, roads, and driveways, if applicable.

We exclude electricity and communications infrastructure because the number of variables involved were too high, such as the number of sub-stations, the proportion of recycled content within the copper cable, whether copper cable or optical fiber was used, or the level of redundancy. We also excluded the effect of construction, maintenance and demolition.

We also do not include commuting, as this would involve making significant assumptions regarding the proximity of places of employment, availability of public transport, and ridership ratios, leading to further boundary issues such as whether to include the embodied carbon of bus stops, bus shelters, railways stations, and railway lines in the study. We did however, include transport emissions associated with providing typical expected services to the units. Garbage collection services and mail deliveries were the two services selected for inclusion.

METHODS

We calculate carbon emissions by putting several pieces of information together, similar to the way a quantity surveyor might estimate building cost:

1. Quantity of materials or energy used, including waste.
2. Emissions factor of the materials or energy; cradle to factory gate.
3. Emissions associated with delivering the material to site.
4. Emissions associated with constructing the relevant building component with the material.

We only consider the first two aspects in this study because it was not intended to be a definitive assessment of lifecycle carbon emissions but instead was developed to facilitate a relative assessment of the nine prototypes and their communities.

OPERATIONAL EMISSIONS

The means of calculating the total energy demand of the building prototypes is detailed in the earlier chapter, Energy, where the annual energy consumption of the nine prototypes are compared using energy models designed in DesignBuilder. These models represent the geometry and materiality of the building, with the program simulating the energy use of a building over a period of time. To compare performance in a similar way, similar loads and construction assemblies were assigned and it was assumed that all the buildings were constructed to city codes equivalent to Chicago, Illinois. The total annual energy consumption was calculated and then extrapolated for each 2,000-unit prototypical community.

We were able to calculate annual carbon dioxide emissions because the energy modeling software analyzes how much natural gas and electricity is used by each prototype annually. For the Megatall prototype to the Low-Rise prototype, electricity is used for elevators, heat rejections, pumps, fans, plug loads, interior lighting, and cooling. Natural gas is used for heating and water heating. For the Courtyard through the Suburban Single-Family electricity is used for water heating, plug loads, interior lighting, and cooling. Natural gas is used for heating and water heating.

We used the total kWh per year and total therms per year for the 2,000 units from the energy modeling analysis and multiplied them by the corresponding emission factors for electricity and natural gas. Emission factors for electricity were 0.564kg CO2/kWh and 0.185 kgCO2/kWh for gas. Figure 24 illustrates the annual carbon dioxide emissions for the 2,000 units of each prototypical community. The results of the total operational carbon dioxide emissions mimic those of the total annual energy use. The Megatall through the Low-Rise prototypes have similar operational emissions, with the Supertall emitting the most carbon. Although the Urban Single Family has the lowest annual carbon dioxide emissions, all the low-rise buildings have similarly low CO2 emissions.

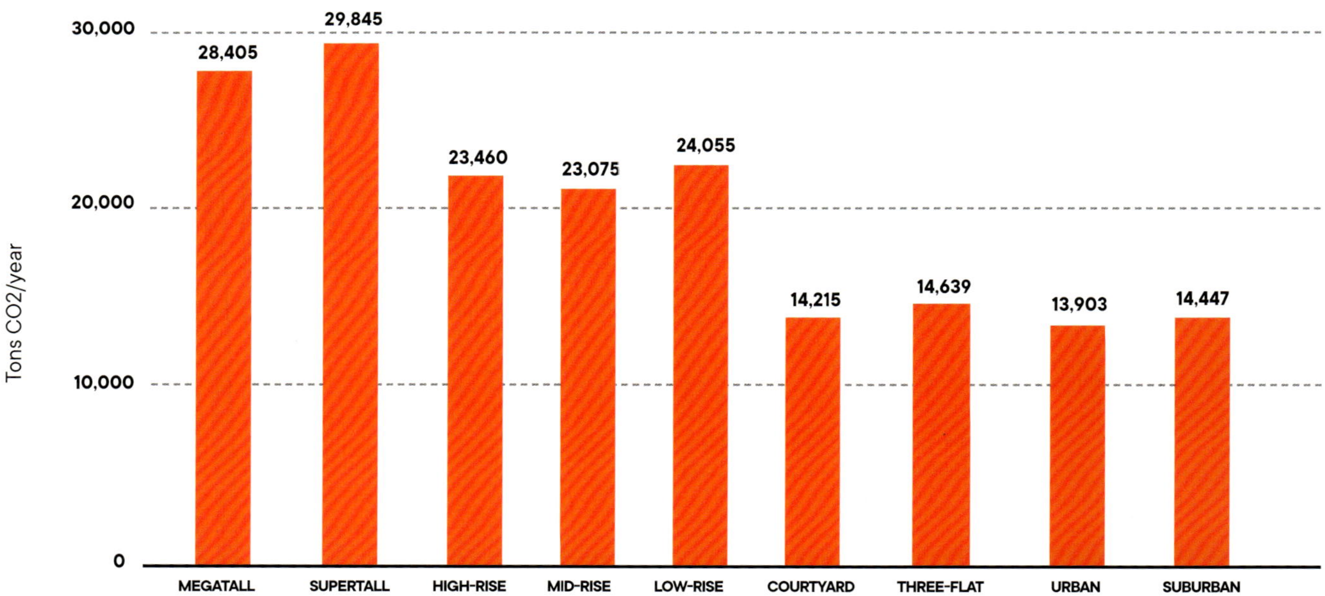

Figure 24 Annual operational carbon emissions for the nine prototypes designed for this study.

Note: Data quantified using total annual energy consumption simulated for each prototypical building for 2,000 units.

INFRASTRUCTURE

During the planning phase of this study, we learned that the amount of infrastructure required to support a community of 2,000 individual buildings was different than that required to support a single building, albeit a very large building. We considered carefully what should be included in the comparative study. By breaking the subject up into two areas—above grade infrastructure and utilities infrastructure—we were able to rationalize the components.

ABOVE-GRADE INFRASTRUCTURE

Above grade infrastructure includes roads, alleys, driveways, sidewalks, and footpath that were designed to serve each prototypical community based on standards established in the United States and on international construction best practices.

Roads. Road design varies depending on expected carrying capacity (volume and type of traffic) and soil bearing capacity. The design supports heavy traffic volumes on the perimeter roads and is strong enough to provide protection to pipework buried beneath the road. The design has 150mm sub-base, 150mm granular base, 90mm Hot Mix Asphalt (HMA) binder, and 50mm HMA running surface. Emissions factors for these components were derived from the Bath ICE database.

Alleys. Alleys provide off street access to the rear of each prototype except for the Megatall, Supertall, and Urban Single Family. For the purposes of this study, the alleys were designed with the same specifications as the roads.

Driveways. Driveways were only included in the Suburban Single Family. In suburban areas, driveway construction is either interlocking concrete block pavers, cast in-place reinforced concrete slab, and asphalt cement. Our study uses machine laid concrete block pavers, as this material is more likely used on newer properties. The design profile for the driveways is 150mm sub-base; 40mm fine aggregate, and 60mm concrete blocks. Embodied carbon figures for the materials were taken from the Bath ICE database and a paving block manufacturer's carbon calculator.

Sidewalks and Footpaths. Sidewalks offer safe pedestrian access along the roads and footpaths are walking routes within the property line, like the connection between a front door and the sidewalk. For this study, sidewalks and footpaths were considered to be constructed in an identical manner. They are typically constructed using pour in place unreinforced concrete slabs. A typical design profile is an average of 200mm sub-base and 100mm C30 concrete. Embodied carbon values were taken from the Bath ICE database.

BELOW-GRADE INFRASTRUCTURE

For each utility—potable water, waste water and stormwater—we created a prototypical distribution map using GIS that allowed us to create a network of pipes of varying dimensions and material types. These networks are typical of something that would be constructed on a greenfield site using modern materials. Specific pipe types and dimensions may vary, ranging from cost and local availability to individual preferences of the permitting authority or principal engineering consultant, as well as ground and climatic conditions. The designs that were established for this study were reviewed by civil engineers and deemed appropriate for conditions found in Zone 5.

Potable Water Network. We created potable water and fire hydrant utilities network maps for each prototypical community. The geographic boundary was designated from the edge of the site to the point of entry, therefore the Urban Single-Family and the Suburban Single-Family include pipework up to the foundation wall and pipework in the risers of the other prototypes. We did not include any pipework within the individual buildings. The external pipes used in the design were made of steel and internal pipes were made of PVC. The emissions factors for each pipe type are shown in Table 15. The study included only the pipes used for provision of water to the buildings and to fire hydrants. Pipeline components such as joints and gaskets, stop taps, booster pumps etc. were not included in the study.

Waste Water Network. Waste water is defined as sewage water. For the purposes of this study, sewage water and stormwater was collected in discrete networks. In Chicago, as in many cities with relatively old infrastructure, sewage water and stormwater are collected into a combined waste water treatment network. There are numerous disadvantages of such systems, which are highlighted to serve as a justification for selecting a separate collection system. The primary disadvantage is that the network has to be sized for the worst possible scenario, and depending on local code, this could be as much as 1 in 50 or 1 in 100-year storm event. Should the stormwater system fail and end up flooding, there is a high risk of raw sewage being discharged into areas that are typically used or accessible to the general public, including building basements, streets, and water bodies.

The second disadvantage is environmental. Rainwater can be discharged directly into water bodies, such as lakes and rivers, with minimal, simple treatment like interceptors and sediment traps, where it then re-enters the fresh water cycle. When combined, the entire water volume must pass through a waste water treatment plant that uses land, chemicals, and/or energy and is then discharged into water bodies that are not used as part of the fresh water cycle, which then connects to the ocean, as it does in Chicago.

The distribution network for waste water includes PVC pipes for the internal riser and for the smallest diameter pipes (<200mm) and concrete for the larger sized pipes (up to 600mm). Emissions factors are presented in Table 15 and include granular fill bedding material that is typically used to support and protect pipes. Other pipeline components, such as joints and gaskets, manholes, and covers, and lift pumps were not included within the boundaries of this study.

Stormwater Networks. The stormwater collection network was designed as a separate system to the sewage network. The boundary for rainwater collection covers the entire site, including the building footprints. It does not include the rainwater collection system on buildings. Green areas in the prototypes do not have sub-surface collection drains and Suburban Single-Family assumes that rainwater discharge is collected from the roofs into the front and back yards. The pipe types used were made from concrete and ranged from 225mm to 1500mm diameter.

Emissions factors are presented in Table 15 and include granular fill bedding material typically used to support and protect the pipes. Pipeline components such as road grids, manholes and covers, and booster pumps were not included within the boundaries of this study.

BUILDING MATERIALS

For the embodied carbon calculations of the building materials, the most important components of the constructions were analyzed: structures, (including foundations), building envelopes, insulation, and interior partitions. Other components, such as mechanical systems, wires, pipes, and elevators were not included in the calculations. The components analyzed represent the basic structure of all prototypes—core and shell—and amount to most of the material volume of the buildings.

The following analysis was based on the embodied carbon of the construction materials themselves, meaning that the emissions associated with the construction process of the building were not included, similar to a "cradle-to-gate" analysis. We compared the amount of materials needed to build the prototypes and the intensity of carbon needed to produce the materials and not a complete carbon analysis. Energy needed for the construction, transportation, and demolition of the building, for example, was not evaluated.

QUANTITIES ANALYSIS

The material quantities for the embodied carbon calculations were taken from the building models described in the Prototypes chapter. The dimensions of the structural components and foundations were reviewed by structural engineers, who provided material quantities for structural mats and piles, as well as concrete strengths and reinforcement steel quantities.

EMISSIONS FACTORS

The University of Bath's Sustainable Energy Research Team (SERT) from the Department of Mechanical Engineering, along with several other partners, developed the Inventory of Carbon & Energy (ICE). The second—and most recent—version of this database was released in January 2011 and contains calculations for the embodied energy and carbon of over 200 materials. Most emission factors used for the building materials in the study were extracted from this database, in conjunction with data provided by a series of manufacturing societies and associations. The emission factors of building assemblies, such as spandrel panels and brick walls, were calculated using data from these sources and based on the constructions specified in the prototypes chapter. The emission factors for all building materials and assemblies analyzed, as well as their source, are described in Table 15.

INFRASTRUCTURE MATERIALS

MATERIAL	DENSITY	EMISSION FACTOR	UNIT	SOURCE
PVC Pipe	1,400.00	3.23	$kgCO_2/kg$	BATH ICE v2.0
HDPE Pipe	kg/m3	2.52	$kgCO_2/kg$	BATH ICE v2.0
Concrete Pipe 225mm Diameter	941.00 kg/	26.93	$kgCO_2/m$	CPSA Pipeline Systems Comparison Report, carbonclear, www.carbon-clear.com
Concrete Pipe 300mm Diameter	m3	37.89	$kgCO_2/m$	CPSA Pipeline Systems Comparison Report, carbonclear, www.carbon-clear.com
Concrete Pipe 450mm Diameter	N/A	62.53	$kgCO_2/m$	CPSA Pipeline Systems Comparison Report, carbonclear, www.carbon-clear.com
Concrete Pipe 600mm Diameter	N/A	199.93	$kgCO_2/m$	CPSA Pipeline Systems Comparison Report, carbonclear, www.carbon-clear.com
Concrete Pipe 750mm Diameter	N/A	143.82	$kgCO_2/m$	CPSA Pipeline Systems Comparison Report, carbonclear, www.carbon-clear.com
Concrete Pipe 900mm Diameter	N/A	177.16	$kgCO_2/m$	CPSA Pipeline Systems Comparison Report, carbonclear, www.carbon-clear.com
Concrete Pipe 1.2m Diameter	N/A	290.74	$kgCO_2/m$	CPSA Pipeline Systems Comparison Report, carbonclear, www.carbon-clear.com
Concrete Pipe 1.5m Diameter	N/A	440.48	$kgCO_2/m$	CPSA Pipeline Systems Comparison Report, carbonclear, www.carbon-clear.com
Road Hot Mix Asphalt	N/A	142.00	$kgCO_2/m^3$	BATH ICE v2.0
Road Granular Base	N/A	16.20	$kgCO_2/m^3$	BATH ICE v2.0
Road Sub-Base	N/A	13.40	$kgCO_2/m^3$	BATH ICE v2.0
Sidewalk C30 Concrete	N/A	262.00	$kgCO_2/m^3$	BATH ICE v2.0
Sidewalk Sub-Base	N/A	13.40	$kgCO_2/m^3$	BATH ICE v2.0m
Driveway Pavers	N/A	26.0	$kgCO_2/m^2$	https://www.marshalls.co.uk/

BUILDING MATERIALS

MATERIAL	DENSITY	EMISSION FACTOR	UNIT	SOURCE
Dimensional Wood	563.00 kg/m^3	0.19fos+0.39bio*	$kgCO_2/kg$	BATH ICE v2.0
Oriented Strand Board (OSB)	650.00 kg/m^3	0.42fos+0.54bio*	$kgCO_2/kg$	BATH ICE v2.0 and http://www.osb-info.org/technical.html
Aluminum - Extruded	2,700.00 kg/m^3	8.16	$kgCO_2/m$	BATH ICE v2.0
Aluminum - Rolled	2,700.00 kg/m^3	8.26	$kgCO_2/m$	BATH ICE v2.0
Brick (100mm)	n/a	33.84	$kgCO_2/m$	BATH ICE v2.0 and UK Brick association
CMU Blocks (200 x 200 x 400mm)	n/a	27.24	$kgCO_2/m$	Portland Cement Association + assumption of 25mm mortar
Fiberglass mat (Densglass)	12.00 kg/m^3	1.35	$kgCO_2/m$	BATH ICE v2.0
Insulation (Fiber Glass Batts)	12.00 kg/m^3	1.35	$kgCO_2/m$	BATH ICE v2.0
Gypsum Board	800.00 kg/m^3	0.38	$kgCO_2/m$	BATH ICE v2.0
Double-Glazed IGU (Supertall)	N/A	51.26	$kgCO_2/m$	Assembly EC calculated based on Bath ICE v2.0 values
Double-Glazed IGU (High-Rise)	N/A	32.23	$kgCO_2/m^3$	Assembly EC calculated based on Bath ICE v2.0 values
Double-Glazed IGU (Low-Rise)	N/A	18.42	$kgCO_2/m^3$	Assembly EC calculated based on Bath ICE v2.0 values
Spandrel Panel	N/A	20.62	$kgCO_2/m^3$	Assembly EC calculated based on Bath ICE v2.0 values
Concrete C40	N/A	303.60	$kgCO_2/m^3$	Data extrapolated from Bath ICE v2.0
Concrete C60	N/A	416.30	$kgCO_2/m^3$	Data extrapolated from Bath ICE v2.0
Concrete C70	N/A	485.30	$kgCO_2/m^3$	Data extrapolated from Bath ICE v2.0
Concrete C80	N/A	563.50	$kgCO_2/m^3$	Data extrapolated from Bath ICE v2.0
Rebar (Steel)	7,800.00 kg/m^3	1.31	$kgCO_2/kg$	BATH ICE v2.0

Table 15 Materials emission factors for embodied carbon analysis

Notes: The sum of these values give the total CO2 emissions derived from fossil fuels and from biomass, if the biomass cannot be considered to be carbon neutral. For the study, the timber is assumed not to come from a sustainably managed forest.

SERVICE VEHICLES

Urban density affects the logistics of service vehicles and operations. The population density determines the frequency and routes of travel of service vehicles. For example, mail delivery vehicles have one stop per Megatall prototype to deliver to 2,000 househclds. But the mail delivery vehicle needs to drive 142 km to deliver to each household in the Single-Family Suburban prototypical development. This influences both vehicle emissions and economics and this holds true for many service vehicle types including delivery vehicles, garbage collection trucks, and maintenance vehicles.

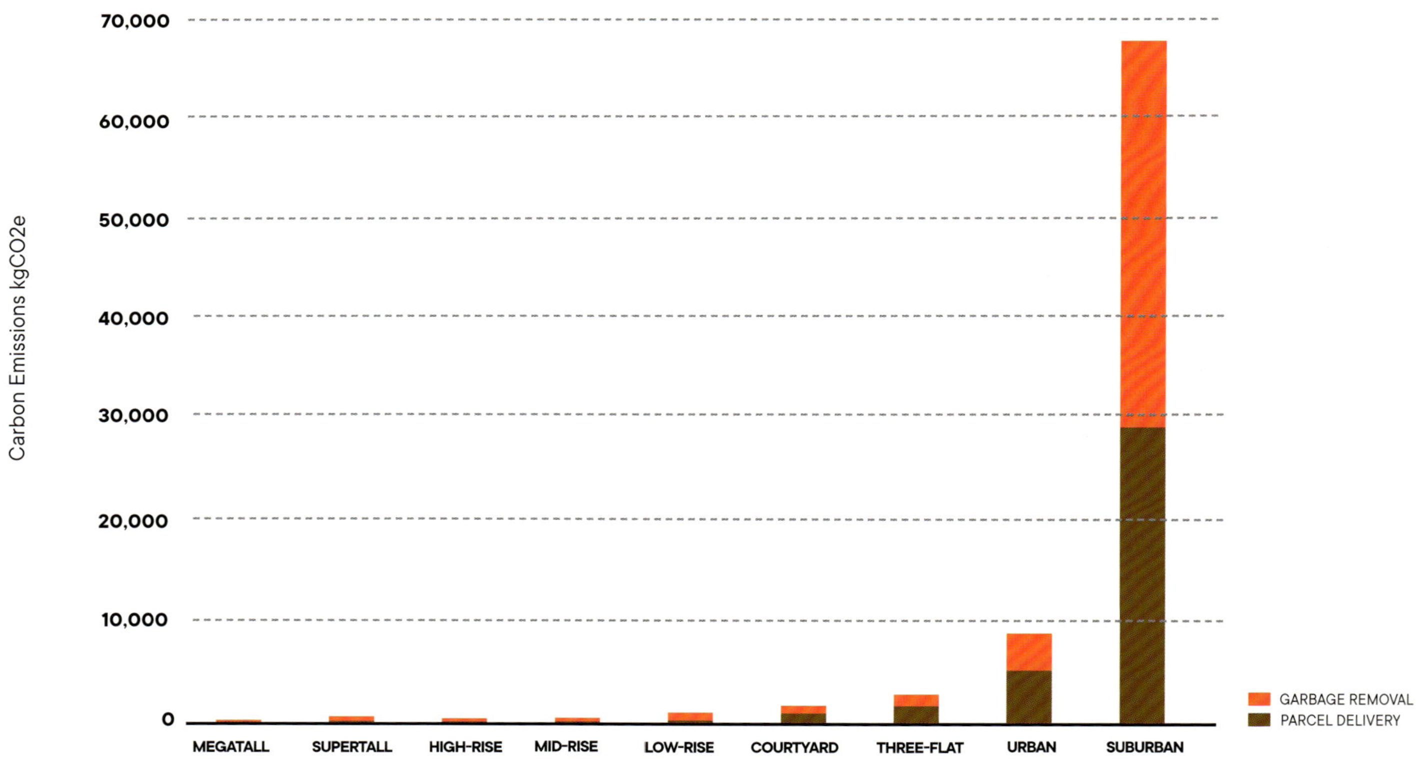

Figure 25 Comparison of annual service vehicle emissions for each prototype

Population density also affects road maintenance. Plowing and salting roads is more intensive for the Single-Family Suburban prototype because of the amount of roads per capita. And while salting of roads is necessary, it is both costly and bad for the environment. The increased emissions, as well as the increased amount of salt used, has negative effects on the surrounding environments. In Chicago, salt applied to roads gets into groundwater supplies and also changes the chemical makeup of water ecosystems.

The study analyzes the emissions of mail delivery and garbage collection for each prototype by measuring the total vehicle miles traveled for a service vehicle within each prototype, and then calculating the emissions. Total road lengths were taken from the GIS analysis of each prototype. It was assumed that each postal vehicle had an emissions factor of 0.63 kgCO2/km, based on a fuel efficiency of 23.5 liters / 100 km (USPS, 2010) and each garbage truck had an emission factor of 2.4 kgCO2/km, based on a fuel efficiency of 90.5 liters / 100 km (estimated from various sources).

It was assumed that mail delivery happens 302 days a year; six days a week minus ten postal service holidays. Garbage collection is assumed to be once a week for both recyclable and non-recyclable waste for all communities up to and including the Courtyard prototype with garbage collection being increased to 3 times a week for the Low-Rise and higher. Using these assumptions, we calculated the yearly emissions of mail delivery and garbage collection for each prototype.

Figure 25 summarizes the results from this study, showing the annual emissions from mail delivery and garbage collection for each prototypical community. Because the emissions were calculated using vehicle miles traveled, they mimic the same trend as total road length for the prototypes.

The annual emissions for the service vehicles of the Megatall prototype was 0.3% of the Single-Family Suburban prototype's annual emissions. Emissions for the respective prototypes follow an exponential decreasing curve from the Single-Family Suburban community to the Supertall community. There is a clear breaking point after the Urban Single-Family prototype, which has emissions that are 38% of the Suburban Single Family.

This study is just a brief look at how population density affects service vehicles and the emissions and environmental factors associated with them. We used the postal service and garbage collection as examples because of the consistency of delivery between all the prototypes. Although, it is just one example, it opens a discussion into the effects of density on servicing and logistics in a community. The dramatic difference in driving time and fuel used by postal deliveries between a megatall development and a suburban development highlights the extent to which service vehicles are impacted by residential density.

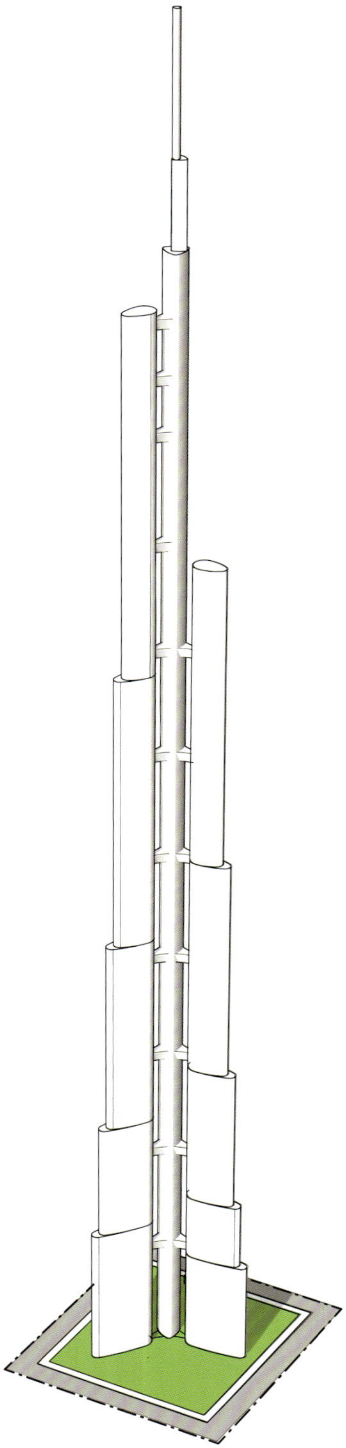

MEGATALL

ROADS + ALLEYS

8,672 m^2
436 tons CO_2

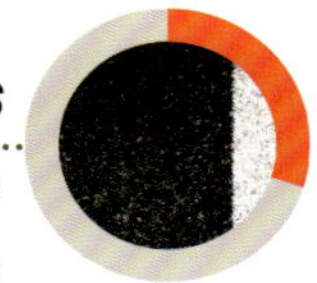

30%

SIDEWALKS

3,584 m^2
104 tons CO_2

7%

STORMWATER PIPES

1,004 m
55 tons CO_2

4%

POTABLE WATER PIPES

36,798 m
415 tons CO_2

28%

SANITARY SEWER PIPES

17,002 m
452 tons CO_2

31%

MEGATALL

NUMBER OF BUILDINGS	1
NUMBER OF UNITS / BUILDING	2,000
BUILDING EMBODIED CARBON (CO2)	238,971 tons
EMBODIED CARBON PER UNIT (CO2)	119 tons
EC / 2,000 UNITS	238,971
INFRASTRUCTURE EMBODIED CARBON (CO2)	1,462 tons
TOTAL EMBODIED CARBON (CO2)	240,433 tons

Note: Due to rounding, values might not add up to 100%

FOUNDATION REBAR
3,000,000 kg
3,930 tons CO_2

1.6%

SPANDREL PANELS
83,463 m^2
3,464 tons CO_2

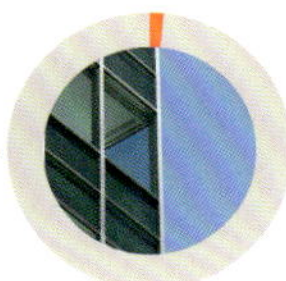

1.5%

CMU BLOCKS
448,357 kg
47 tons CO_2

0.02%

INSULATED GLAZING UNITS
68,633 m^2
2,029 tons CO_2

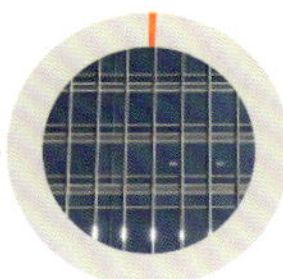

0.9%

STEEL REBAR
45,689,554 kg
57,922 tons CO_2

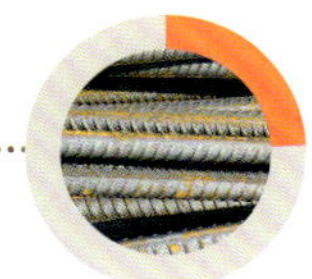

24.2%

ALUMINUM
824,694 kg
9,975 tons CO_2

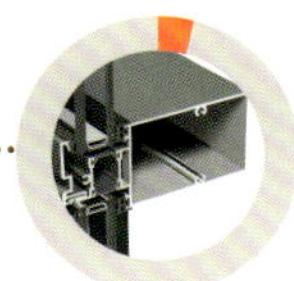

4.2%

INSULATION
50,078 kg
103 tons CO_2

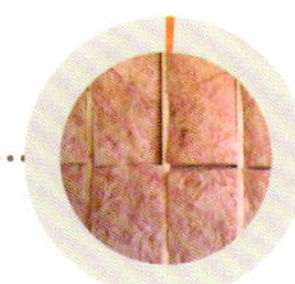

0.04%

FOUNDATION CONCRETE
65,160,000 kg
10,805 tons CO_2

4.5%

CONCRETE
759,871,158 kg
150,696 tons CO_2

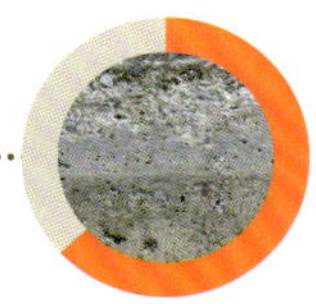

63.1%

SUPERTALL

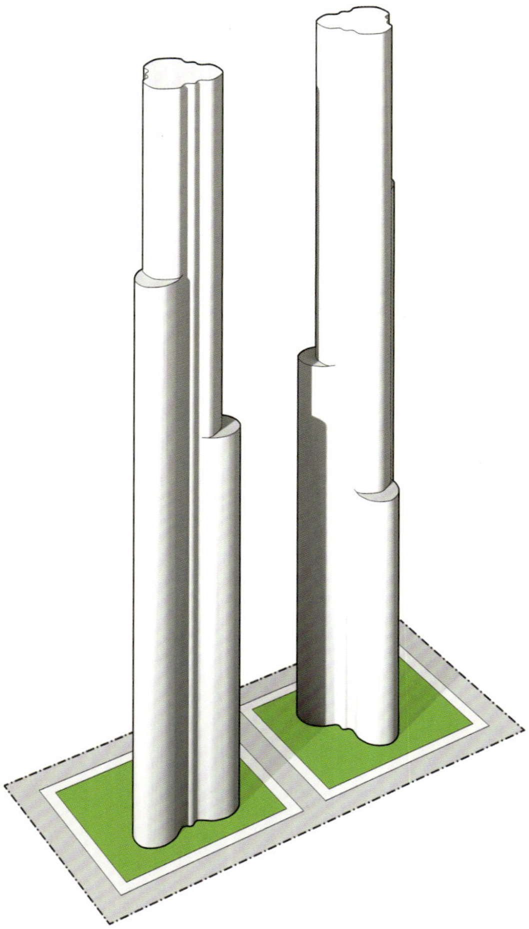

ROADS + ALLEYS

12,930 m^2
650 tons CO_2

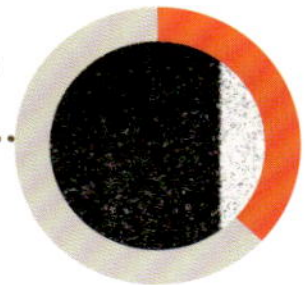

37%

SIDEWALKS

5,712 m^2
165 tons CO_2

9%

STORMWATER PIPES

1,283 m
77 tons CO_2

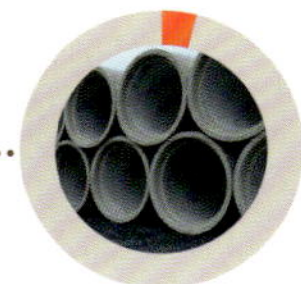

4%

POTABLE WATER PIPES

38,428 m
379 tons CO_2

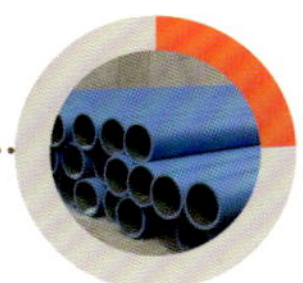

22%

SANITARY SEWER PIPES

17,675 m
491 tons CO_2

28%

SUPERTALL

NUMBER OF BUILDINGS	2
NUMBER OF UNITS / BUILDING	1,000
BUILDING EMBODIED CARBON (CO2)	110,597 tons
EMBODIED CARBON PER UNIT (CO2)	111 tons
EC / 2,000 UNITS	221,195
INFRASTRUCTURE EMBODIED CARBON (CO2)	1,762 tons
TOTAL EMBODIED CARBON (CO2)	222,957 tons

Note: Due to rounding, values might not add up to 100%

FOUNDATION REBAR

1,562,500 kg
2,047 tons CO_2

1.9%

SPANDREL PANELS

45,130 m^2
1,873 tons CO_2

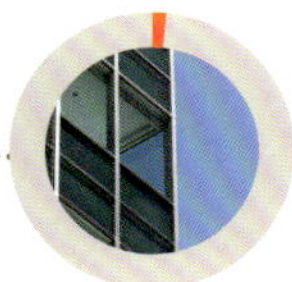

1.7%

INSULATED GLAZING UNITS

36,483 m^2
1,079 tons CO_2

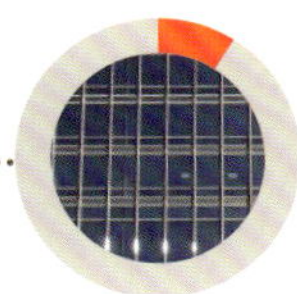

10%

ALUMINUM

420,252 kg
5,083 tons CO_2

4.6%

FOUNDATION CONCRETE

31,494,000 kg
4,970 tons CO_2

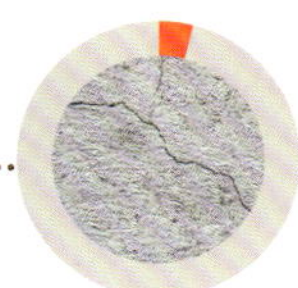

4.5%

CMU BLOCKS

294,907 kg
31 tons CO_2

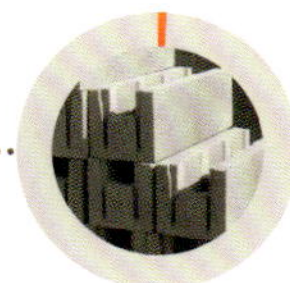

0.03%

STEEL REBAR

16,645,312 kg
21,102 tons CO_2

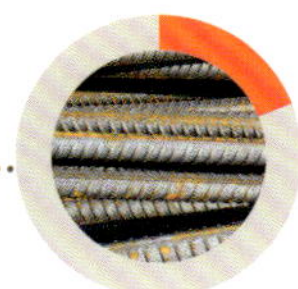

19.1%

INSULATION

27,078 kg
56 tons CO_2

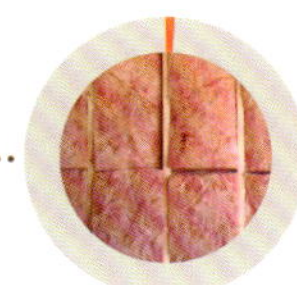

0.05%

CONCRETE

374,686,343 kg
74,358 tons CO_2

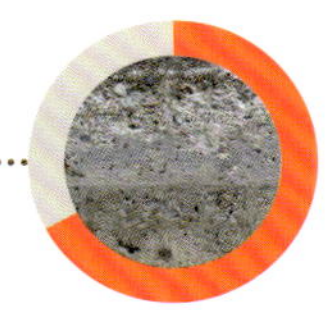

67.2%

HIGH-RISE

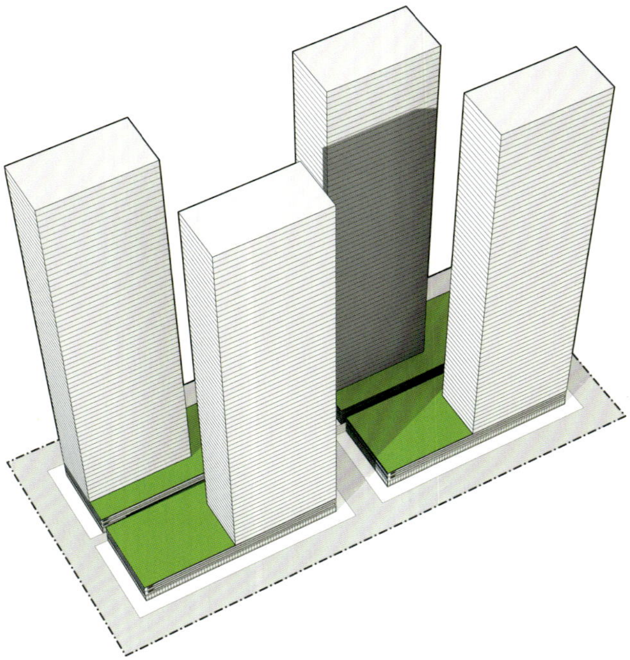

ROADS + ALLEYS

4,110 m^2
492 tons CO_2

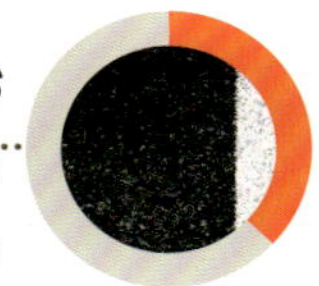

37%

SIDEWALKS

5,573 m^2
161 tons CO_2

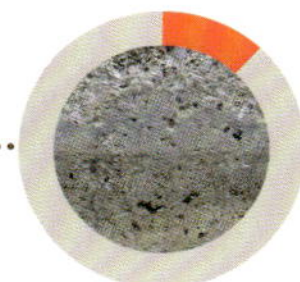

12%

STORMWATER PIPES

736 m
47 tons CO_2

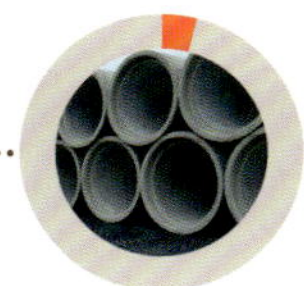

4%

POTABLE WATER PIPES

34,311 m
163 tons CO_2

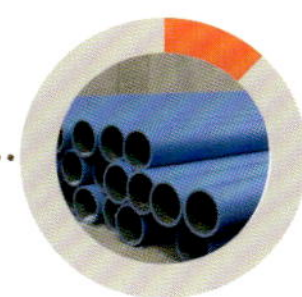

12%

SANITARY SEWER PIPES

17,077 m
460 tons CO_2

35%

HIGH-RISE

NUMBER OF BUILDINGS	4
NUMBER OF UNITS / BUILDING	500
BUILDING EMBODIED CARBON (CO2)	26,048 tons
EMBODIED CARBON PER UNIT (CO2)	52 tons
EC / 2,000 UNITS	104,191
INFRASTRUCTURE EMBODIED CARBON (CO2)	1,322 tons
TOTAL EMBODIED CARBON (CO2)	105,513 tons

Note: Due to rounding, values might not add up to 100%

FOUNDATION REBAR

737,500 kg
966 tons CO_2

3.7%

SPANDREL PANELS

17,794 m^2
738 tons CO_2

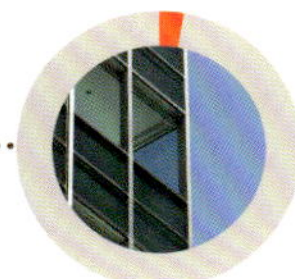

2.8%

CMU BLOCKS

222,689 kg
23 tons CO_2

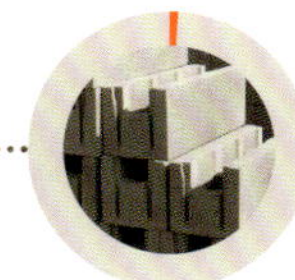

0.1%

INSULATED GLAZING UNITS

14,113 m^2
417 tons CO_2

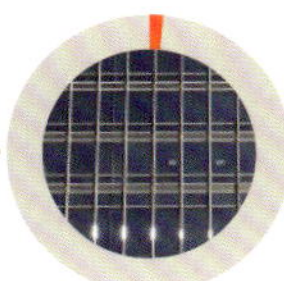

1.6%

STEEL REBAR

2,269,839 kg
2,878 tons CO_2

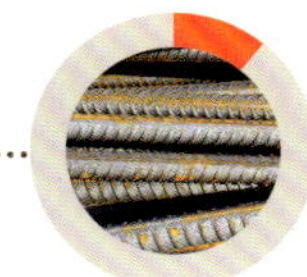

11%

ALUMINUM

235,242 kg
2,845 tons CO_2

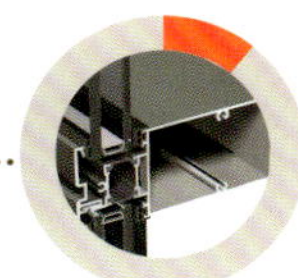

10.9%

INSULATION

860 kg
2 tons CO_2

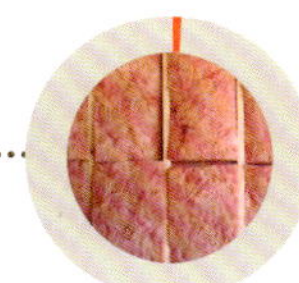

0.01%

FOUNDATION CONCRETE

14,118,000 kg
2,144 tons CO_2

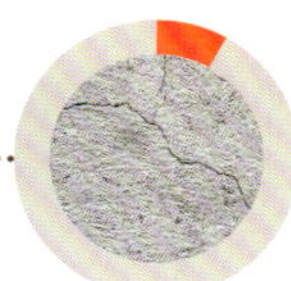

8.2%

CONCRETE

96,662,802 kg
16,033tons CO_2

61.6%

MID-RISE

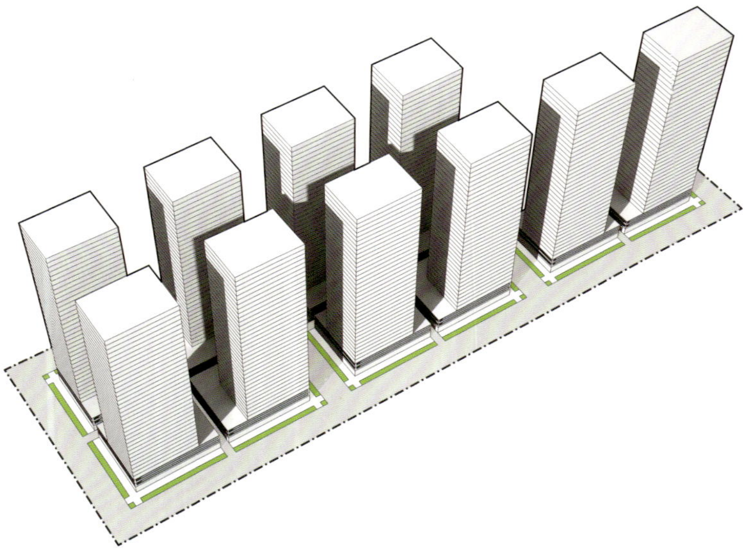

ROADS + ALLEYS
18,671 m^2
634 tons CO_2

35%

SIDEWALKS
4,004 m^2
161 tons CO_2

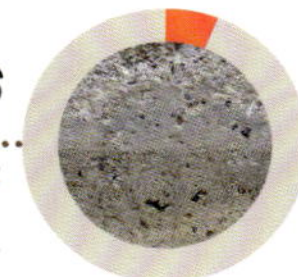

6%

STORMWATER PIPES
1,474 m
98 tons CO_2

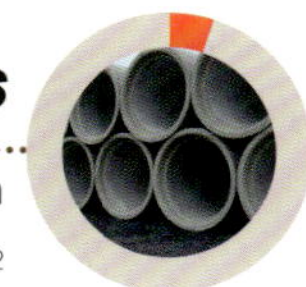

5%

POTABLE WATER PIPES
37,797 m
368 tons CO_2

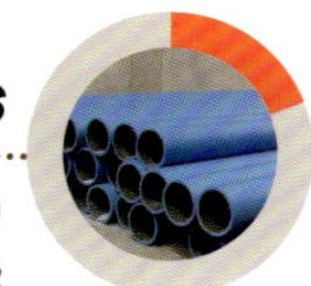

20%

SANITARY SEWER PIPES
24,687 m
628 tons CO_2

34%

MID-RISE

NUMBER OF BUILDINGS	10
NUMBER OF UNITS / BUILDING	200
BUILDING EMBODIED CARBON (CO2)	10,904 tons
EMBODIED CARBON PER UNIT (CO2)	55 tons
EC / 2,000 UNITS	109,038
INFRASTRUCTURE EMBODIED CARBON (CO2)	1,844 tons
TOTAL EMBODIED CARBON (CO2)	110,882 tons

Note: Due to rounding, values might not add up to 100%

FOUNDATION REBAR

375,000 kg
491 tons CO_2

4.5%

SPANDREL PANELS

8,019 m^2
333 tons CO_2

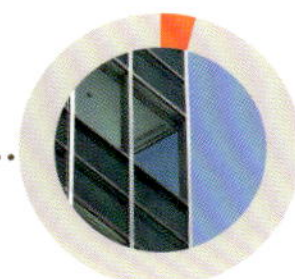

3.1%

INSULATED GLAZING UNITS

6,279 m^2
186 tons CO_2

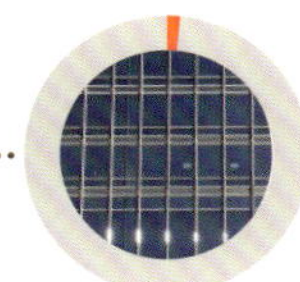

1.7%

ALUMINUM

102,392 kg
1,239 tons CO_2

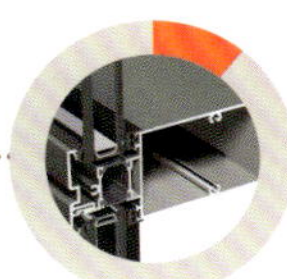

11.4%

FOUNDATION CONCRETE

6,979,200 kg
1,029 tons CO_2

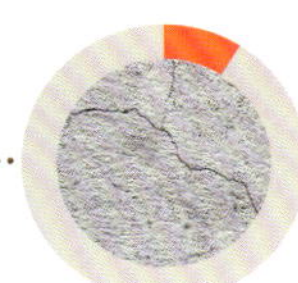

9.4%

CMU BLOCKS

138,529 kg
15 tons CO_2

0.1%

STEEL REBAR

883,220 kg
1,120 tons CO_2

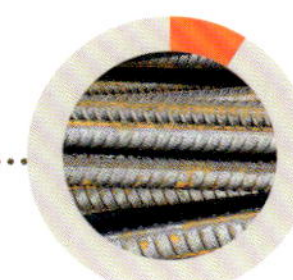

10.3%

INSULATION

336 kg
1 tons CO_2

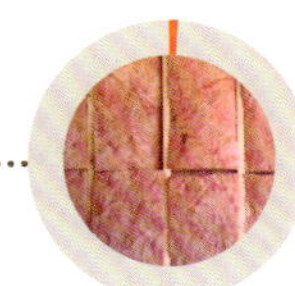

0.01%

CONCRETE

39,092,737 kg
6,492 tons CO_2

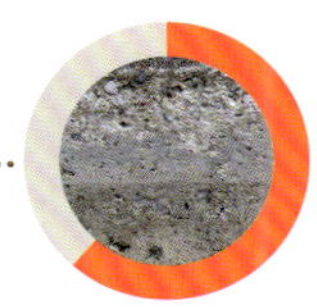

59.5%

LOW-RISE

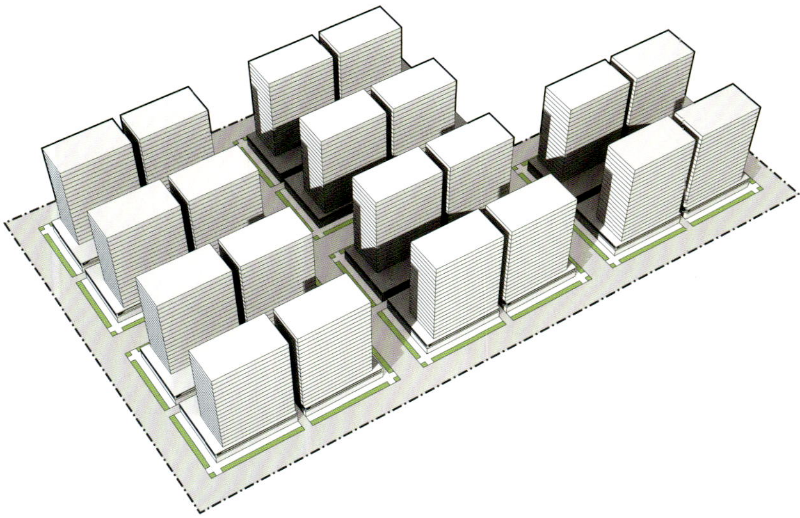

ROADS + ALLEYS
32,460 m^2
1,101 tons CO_2

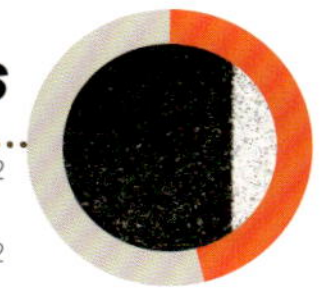

46%

SIDEWALKS
8,000 m^2
231 tons CO_2

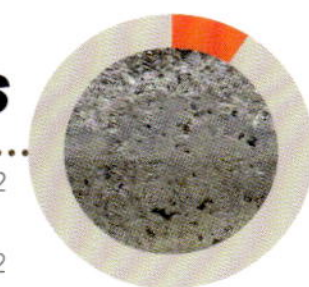

10%

STORMWATER PIPES
2,372 m
157 tons CO_2

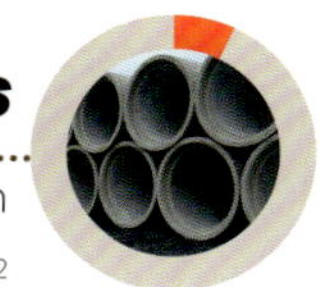

7%

POTABLE WATER PIPES
52,458 m
631 tons CO_2

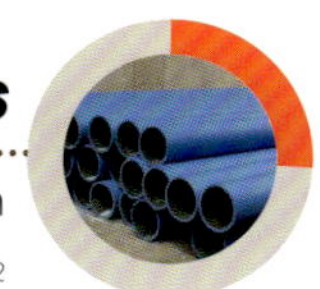

26%

SANITARY SEWER PIPES
24,270 m
263 tons CO_2

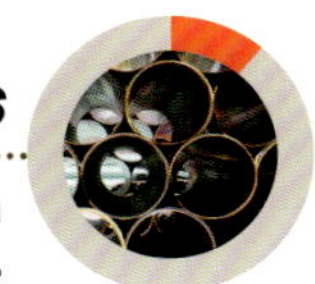

11%

LOW-RISE

NUMBER OF BUILDINGS	20
NUMBER OF UNITS / BUILDING	100
BUILDING EMBODIED CARBON (CO2)	6,945 tons
EMBODIED CARBON PER UNIT (CO2)	69 tons
EC / 2,000 UNITS	138,891
INFRASTRUCTURE EMBODIED CARBON (CO2)	2,383 tons
TOTAL EMBODIED CARBON (CO2)	141,274 tons

Note: Due to rounding, values might not add up to 100%

FOUNDATION REBAR
270,625 kg
355 tons CO_2

5.1%

SPANDREL PANELS
3,019 m^2
125 tons CO_2

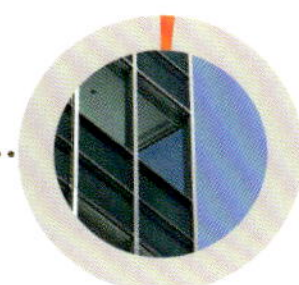

1.8%

CMU BLOCKS
109,695 kg
12 tons CO_2

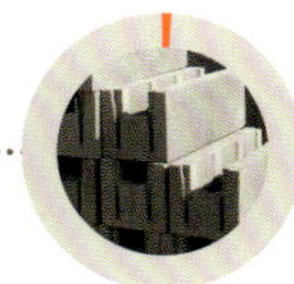

0.2%

INSULATED GLAZING UNITS
2,427 m^2
72 tons CO_2

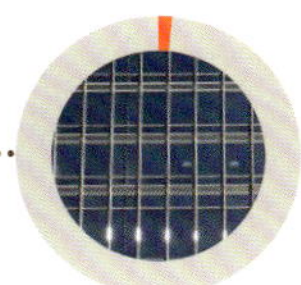

1%

STEEL REBAR
621,570 kg
788 tons CO_2

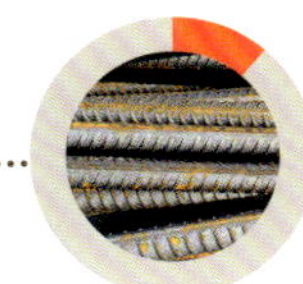

11.3%

ALUMINUM
40,197 kg
486 tons CO_2

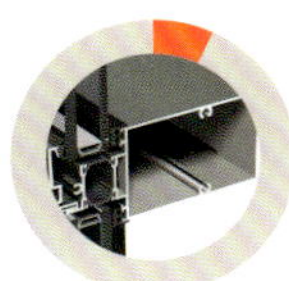

7%

INSULATION
2,200 kg
6 tons CO_2

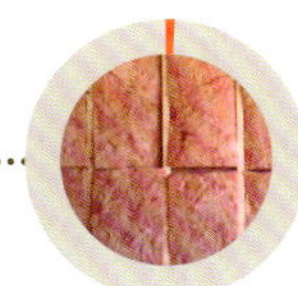

0.1%

FOUNDATION CONCRETE
4,961,775 kg
722 tons CO_2

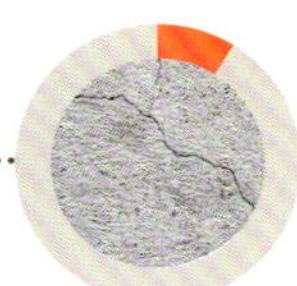

10.4%

CONCRETE
26,416,495 kg
4,368 tons CO_2

62.9%

COURTYARD

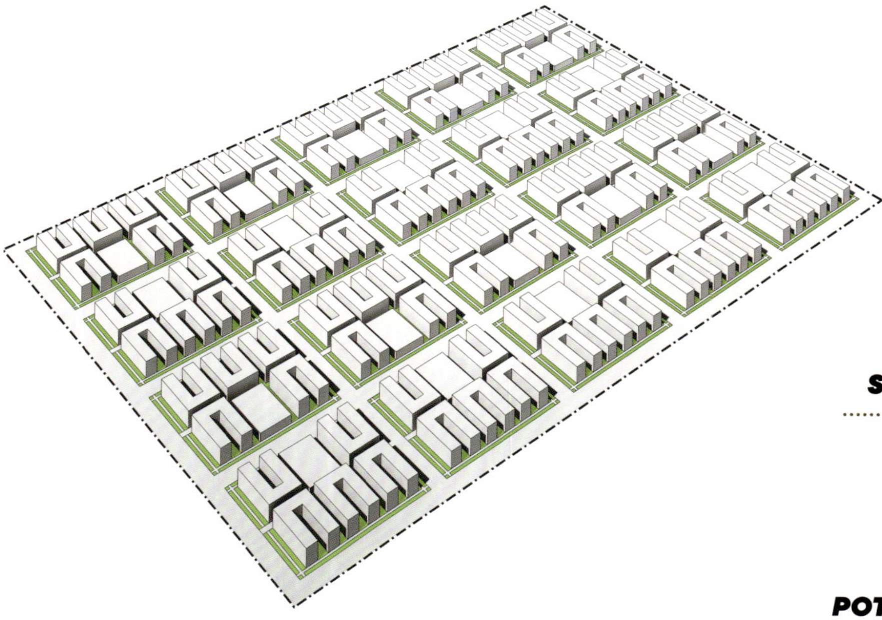

ROADS + ALLEYS

98,790 m^2

2,526 tons CO_2

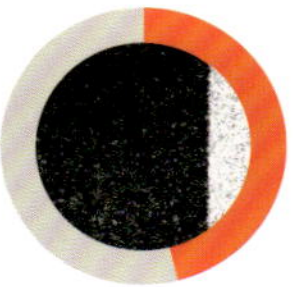

45%

SIDEWALKS

16,720 m^2

483 tons CO_2

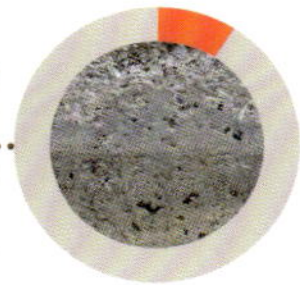

9%

STORMWATER PIPES

10,888 m

537 tons CO_2

10%

POTABLE WATER PIPES

15,902 m

1,748 tons CO_2

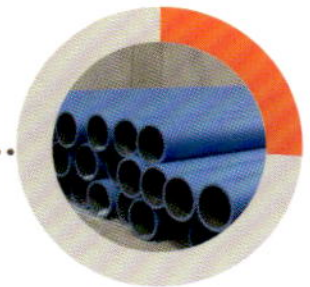

26%

SANITARY SEWER PIPES

12,054 m

268 tons CO_2

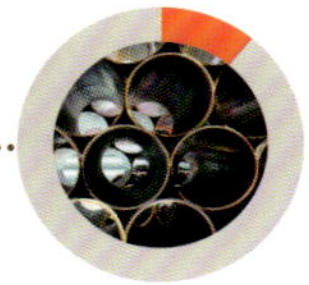

11%

COURTYARD

COURTYARD	
NUMBER OF BUILDINGS	100
NUMBER OF UNITS / BUILDING	20
BUILDING EMBODIED CARBON (CO2)	1,360 tons
EMBODIED CARBON PER UNIT (CO2)	68 tons
EC / 2,000 UNITS	135,934
INFRASTRUCTURE EMBODIED CARBON (CO2)	5,562 tons
TOTAL EMBODIED CARBON (CO2)	141,496 tons

Note: Due to rounding, values might not add up to 100%

FOUNDATION REBAR

81,250 kg
106 tons CO_2

7.8%

BRICKS

533,884 kg
138 tons CO_2

10.2%

GYPSUM BOARD

21,078 m^2
5 tons CO_2

0.4%

CMU BLOCKS

364,111 kg
39 tons CO_2

2.9%

INSULATED GLAZING UNITS

523 m^2
15 tons CO_2

1.1%

STEEL REBAR

83,089 kg
105 tons CO_2

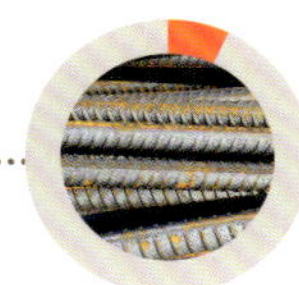

7.8%

ALUMINUM

5,067 kg
61 tons CO_2

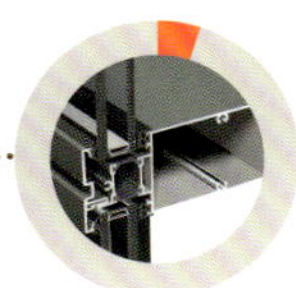

4.5%

INSULATION

632 kg
1 tons CO_2

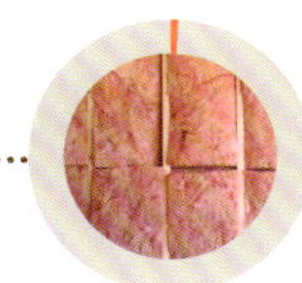

0.1%

FOUNDATION CONCRETE

1,417,650 kg
198 tons CO_2

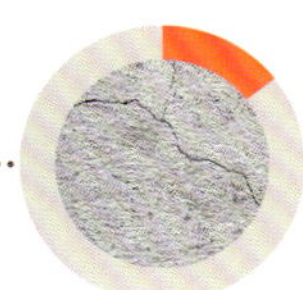

14.5%

CONCRETE

3,903,669 kg
689 tons CO_2

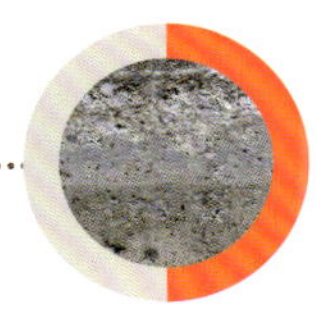

50.7%

THREE-FLAT

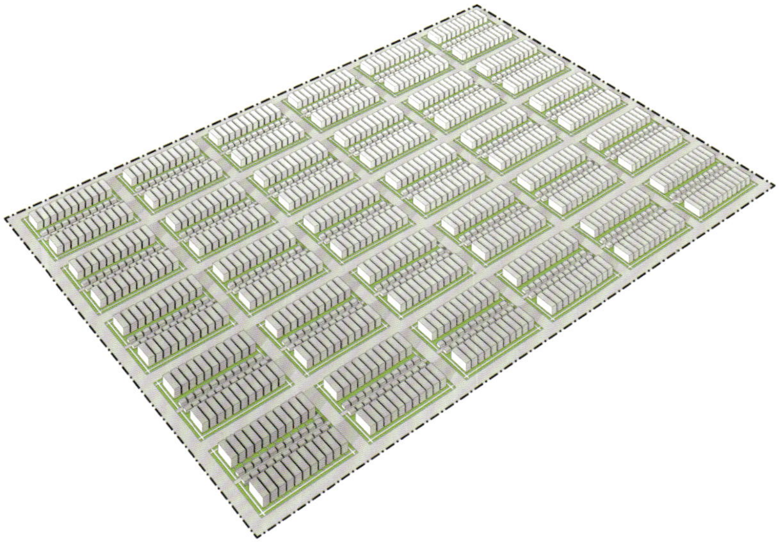

ROADS + ALLEYS

165,192 m^2
4,288 tons CO_2

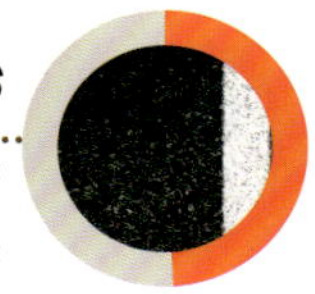

49%

SIDEWALKS

25,498 m^2
737 tons CO_2

8%

STORMWATER PIPES

23,140 m
971 tons CO_2

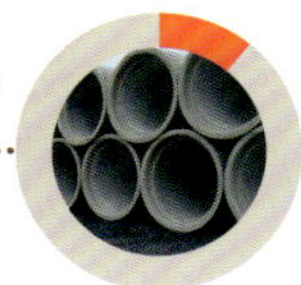

11%

POTABLE WATER PIPES

25,139 m
2,313 tons CO_2

26%

SANITARY SEWER PIPES

22,726 m
433 tons CO_2

5%

THREE-FLAT

NUMBER OF BUILDINGS	667
NUMBER OF UNITS / BUILDING	3
BUILDING EMBODIED CARBON (CO2)	218 tons
EMBODIED CARBON PER UNIT (CO2)	73 tons
EC / 2,000 UNITS	145,274
INFRASTRUCTURE EMBODIED CARBON (CO2)	8,742 tons
TOTAL EMBODIED CARBON (CO2)	154,016 tons

Note: Due to rounding, values might not add up to 100%

FOUNDATION REBAR

8,750 kg
11.5 tons CO_2

5.3%

GYPSUM BOARD

5,440 m^2
1.3 tons CO_2

0.6%

INSULATED GLAZING UNITS

64 m^2
2 tons CO_2

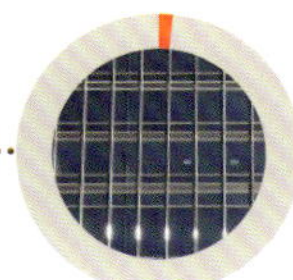

0.9%

ALUMINUM

811 kg
1.9 tons CO_2

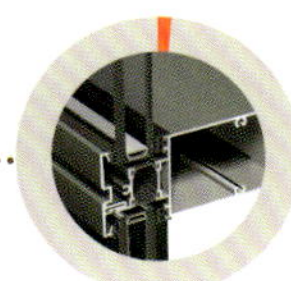

0.9%

FOUNDATION CONCRETE

152,670 kg
21.28 tons CO_2

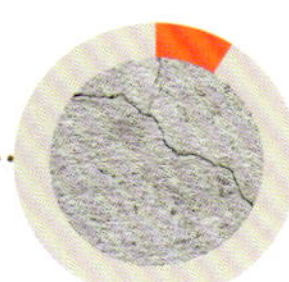

9.8%

BRICKS

130,735 kg
33.9 tons CO_2

15.5%

CMU BLOCKS

88,350 kg
9.3 tons CO_2

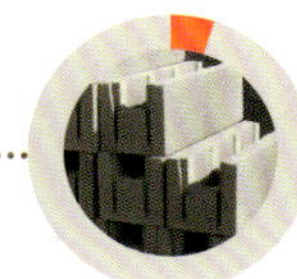

4.2%

STEEL REBAR

25,040 kg
31.7 tons CO_2

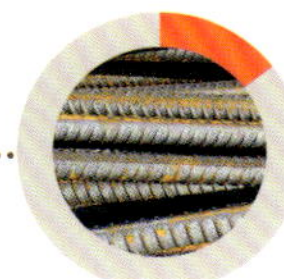

14.6%

INSULATION

163.22 kg
.34 tons CO_2

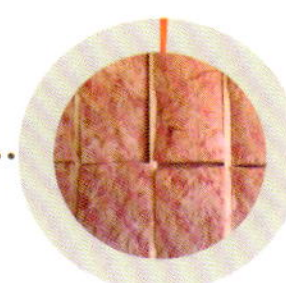

0.2%

CONCRETE

610,926 kg
105 tons CO_2

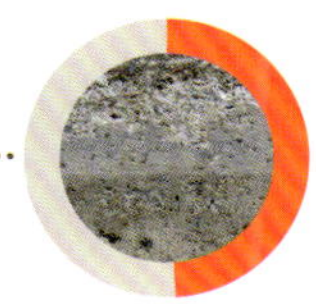

48%

URBAN SINGLE-FAMILY

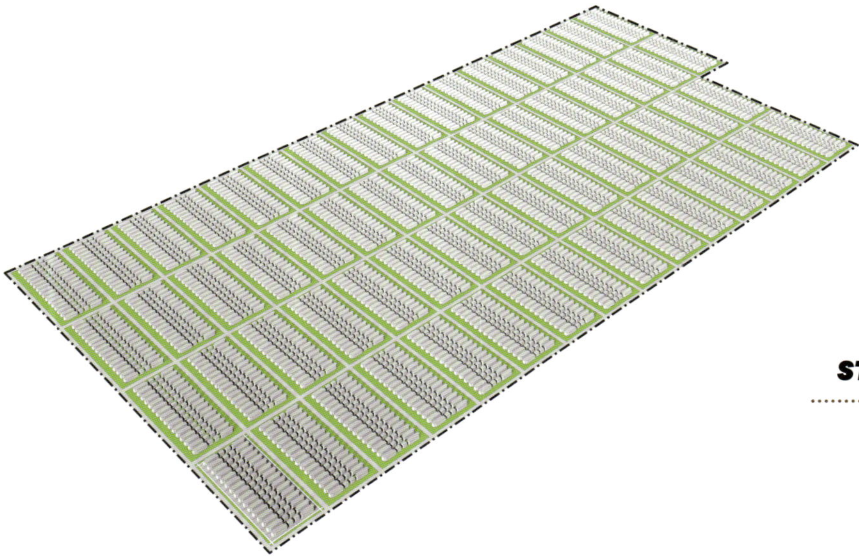

ROADS, ALLEYS + DRIVEWAYS

252,474 m^2
6,554 tons CO_2

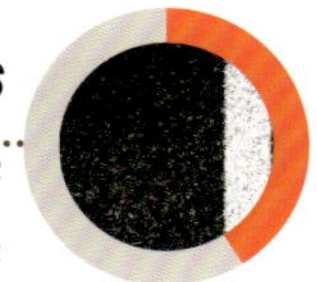

41%

SIDEWALKS

69,500 m^2
2,008 tons CO_2

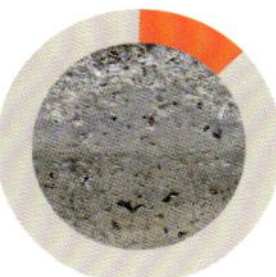

13%

STORMWATER PIPES

49,106 m
1,981 tons CO_2

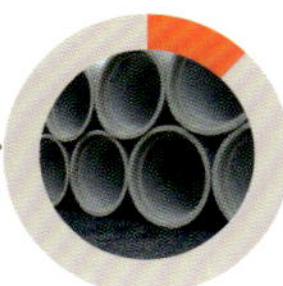

12%

POTABLE WATER PIPES

47,242 m
4,632 tons CO_2

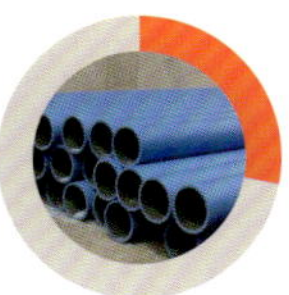

29%

SANITARY SEWER PIPES

42,954 m
848 tons CO_2

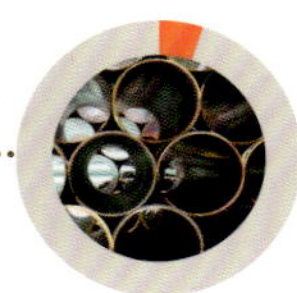

5%

URBAN SINGLE FAMILY

NUMBER OF BUILDINGS	2,000
NUMBER OF UNITS / BUILDING	1
BUILDING EMBODIED CARBON (CO2)	74 tons
EMBODIED CARBON PER UNIT (CO2)	74 tons
EC / 2,000 UNITS	148,800
INFRASTRUCTURE EMBODIED CARBON (CO2)	16,023 tons
TOTAL EMBODIED CARBON (CO2)	164,823 tons

Note: Due to rounding, values might not add up to 100%

FOUNDATION REBAR

5,625 kg
11.5 tons CO_2

9.9%

BRICKS

61,203 kg
16.2 tons CO_2

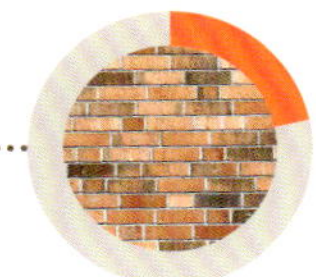

21.8%

WOOD

20,696 m^2
16.1 tons CO_2

21.6%

CMU BLOCKS

23,132 kg
2.4 tons CO_2

3.3%

INSULATED GLAZING UNITS

19 m^2
0.6 tons CO_2

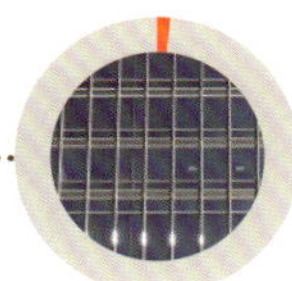

0.8%

STEEL REBAR

1,714 kg
2.2 tons CO_2

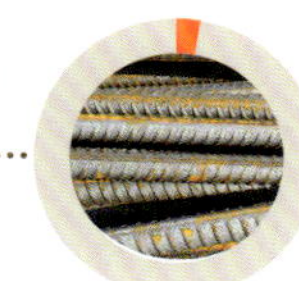

2.9%

ALUMINUM

90 kg
1.2 tons CO_2

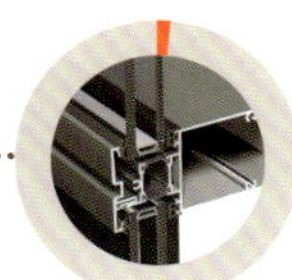

1.6%

INSULATION

730.2 kg
1.5 tons CO_2

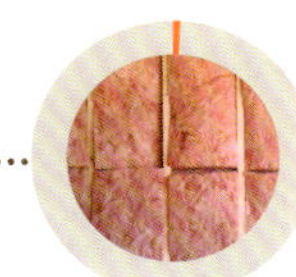

0.2%

FOUNDATION CONCRETE

98,145 kg
13.7 tons CO_2

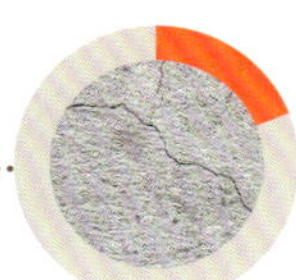

18.4%

CONCRETE

70,389 kg
12.06 tons CO_2

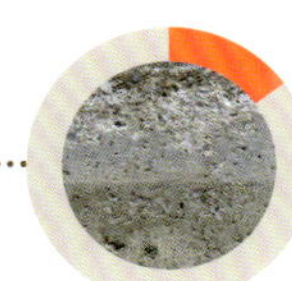

16.2%

SUBURBAN SINGLE-FAMILY

ROADS, ALLEYS + DRIVEWAYS

516,493 m^2
13,771 tons CO_2

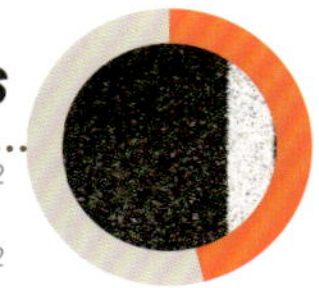

45%

SIDEWALKS

106,493 m^2
3,077 tons CO_2

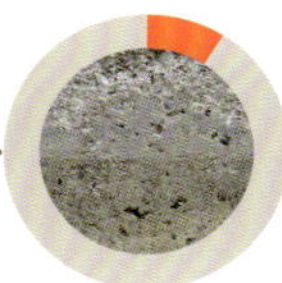

10%

STORMWATER PIPES

38,937 m
2,165 tons CO_2

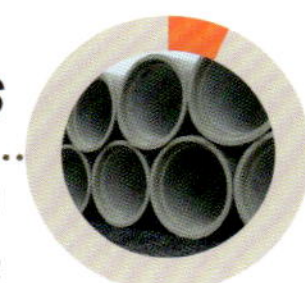

7%

POTABLE WATER PIPES

81,769 m
9,467 tons CO_2

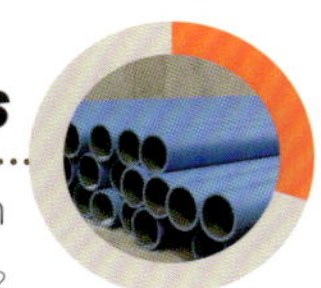

31%

SANITARY SEWER PIPES

81,634 m
2,049 tons CO_2

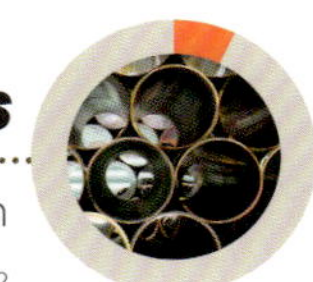

7%

SUBURBAN SINGLE FAMILY

NUMBER OF BUILDINGS	2,000
NUMBER OF UNITS / BUILDING	1
BUILDING EMBODIED CARBON (CO2)	71 tons
EMBODIED CARBON PER UNIT (CO2)	71 tons
EC / 2,000 UNITS	142,403
INFRASTRUCTURE EMBODIED CARBON (CO2)	30,529 tons
TOTAL EMBODIED CARBON (CO2)	172,932 tons

Note: Due to rounding, values might not add up to 100%

FOUNDATION REBAR

5,383 kg
7.1 tons CO_2

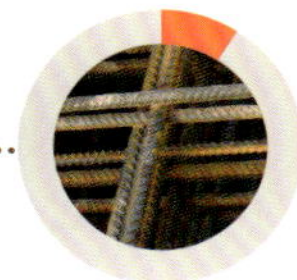

9.9%

WOOD

19,534 m^2
13.7 tons CO_2

19.2%

INSULATED GLAZING UNITS

24.5 m^2
0.7 tons CO_2

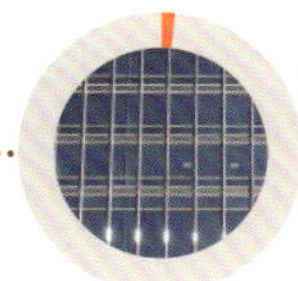

0.8%

ALUMINUM

106 kg
1.4 tons CO_2

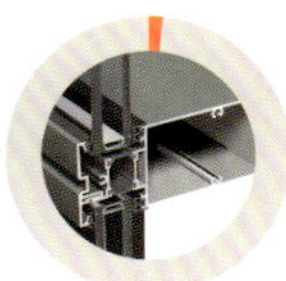

1.6%

FOUNDATION CONCRETE

93,925 kg
13.1 tons CO_2

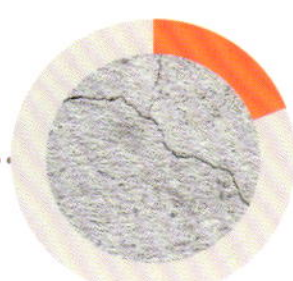

18.4%

BRICKS

55,624 kg
14.7 tons CO_2

20.7%

CMU BLOCKS

12,405 kg
1.3 tons CO_2

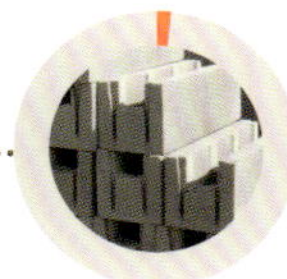

1.8%

STEEL REBAR

2,052 kg
2.6 tons CO_2

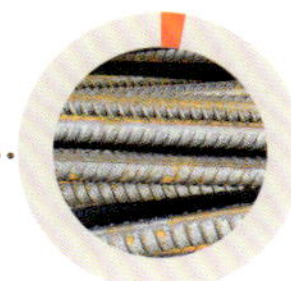

3.7%

INSULATION

499 kg
1 ton CO_2

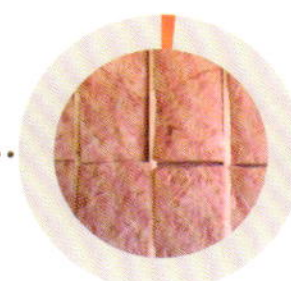

1.4%

CONCRETE

86,123 kg
14.8 tons CO_2

20.7%

SUMMARY	MEGATALL	SUPERTALL	HIGH-RISE	MID-RISE
NUMBER OF BUILDINGS	1	2	4	10
NUMBER OF UNITS / BUILDING	2,000	1,000	500	200
NUMBER OF STORIES (ABOVE GRADE)	213	121	65	38
BUILDING HEIGHT (M)	766	435	229	134.5
BUILDING FLOOR AREA (M^2)	495,880	231,869	110,184	42,896
BUILDING EMBODIED CARBON (TONS CO2)	238,971	110,597	26,048	10,904
EMBODIED CARBON PER UNIT (TONS CO2)	119	111	52	55
INFRASTRUCTURE EMBODIED CARBON (TONS CO2)	1,462	1,762	1,322	1,844
TOTAL EMBODIED CARBON (TONS CO2)	240,433	222,957	105,513	110,882
STRUCTURE (%)	93%	93%	85%	84%
WINDOW/WALL RATIO (%)	40%	40%	40%	40%

Table 16 Building carbon use data

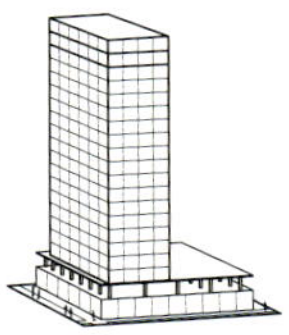
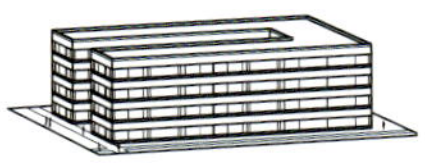

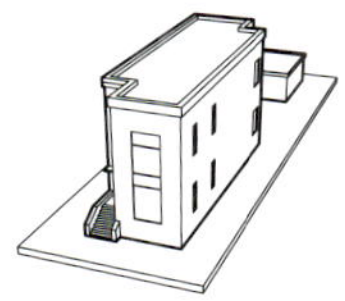
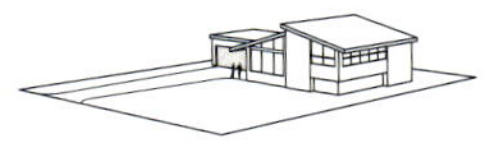

LOW-RISE	COURTYARD	THREE-FLAT	URBAN SINGLE FAMILY	SUBURBAN SINGLE FAMILY
20	100	667	2,000	2,000
100	20	3	1	1
20	4	3	2	2
71.5	14	10.5	5.6	8.6
24,300	3,756	554	216	233
6,945	1,360	218	74	71
69	68	73	74	71
2,383	5,562	8,742	16,023	30,529
141,274	141,496	154,016	164,823	172,932
90%	73%	78%	47%	53%
40%	14.6%	9.6%	8.9%	10.9%

EMBODIED CARBON DISCUSSION

The results for embodied carbon of infrastructure is summarized for each prototype is summarized in Table 16 and illustrated in Figure 26. The Suburban Single-Family prototype has the highest amount of embodied carbon, when compared with the other communities. This can be explained because the supporting infrastructure needs to support a community that is distributed across a much greater area of land. The embodied carbon of buildings is summarized in Figure 27, with the highest embodied emissions arising from construction of the Megatall prototype, followed by the Supertall prototype, and then followed by the Urban Single-Family prototypes.

The results are highly influenced by the amount of concrete, steel and masonry used in the construction of these prototypes, most significantly in the Megatall and Supertall prototypes because of their extensive cores and foundations. It is interesting to note that the Megatall's embodied carbon is 130% higher than the High-Rise prototype because both the Megatall and Supertall prototype needs more concrete, of a higher strength, a higher density of steel reinforcement, and are significantly less efficient, in terms of leasable area compared to constructed area.

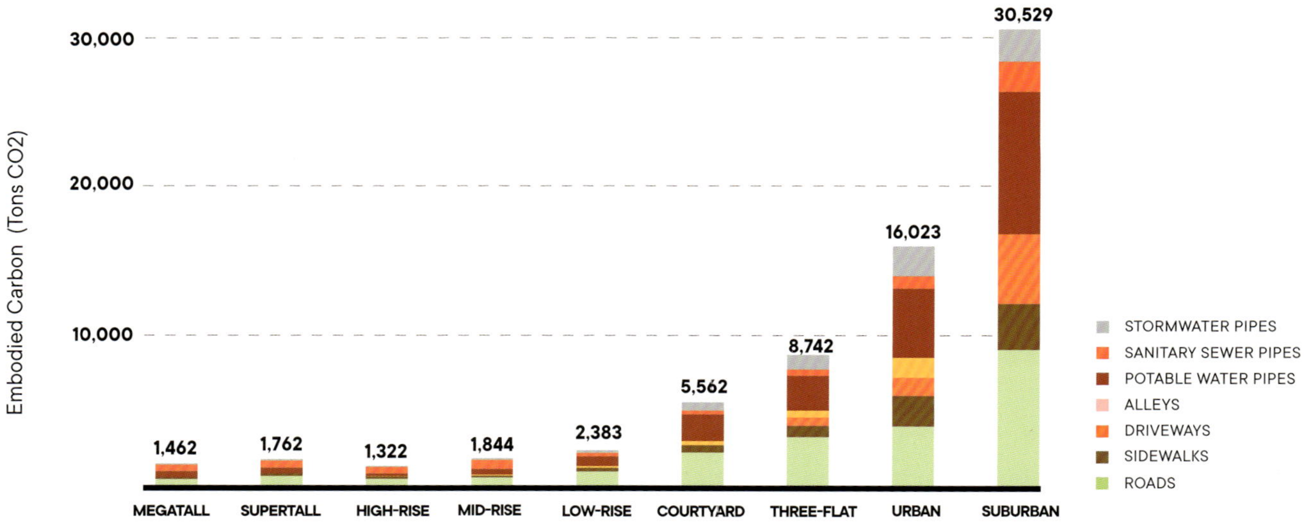

Figure 26 Breakdown of infrastructure embodied carbon for prototypical communities

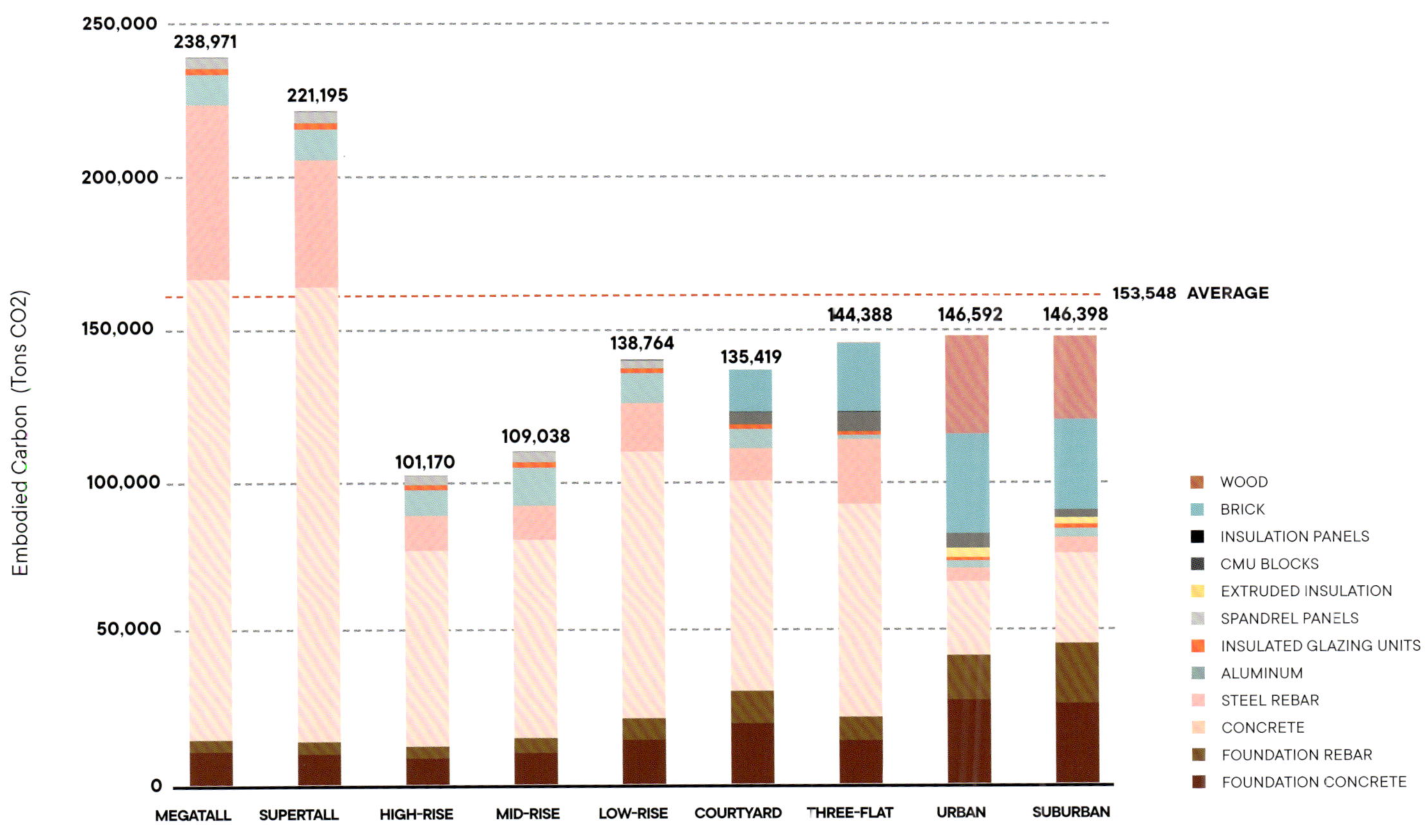

Figure 27 Breakdown of building embodied carbon for building prototypes

THE RELATIVE IMPACT OF INFRASTRUCTURE

In making a direct comparison of the embodied carbon of buildings and embodied carbon of infrastructure—the embodied carbon of the buildings has the largest impact on the results, seen in Figure 28 and Table 17. The impact of infrastructure on embodied carbon of the overall development is highly variable. In the most extreme case—the Suburban Single-Family prototype, the embodied carbon of infrastructure accounts for almost 18%. In the least extreme case—the Megatall—it accounts for only 0.6%. When infrastructure is added to the overall carbon footprint of the development, the relative performance of the prototypes becomes progressively worse with respect to embodied carbon as density decreases from the High-Rise prototype onwards.

Utilities infrastructure is buried directly beneath roads or sidewalks and consequently is subject to damage from above. Maintaining or replacing a leaking potable water pipe for example, has an impact on other infrastructural elements. Durability and minimizing or easing maintenance requirements is a high priority in reducing the overall lifecycle emissions of utility infrastructure. Road surfaces in high-traffic areas are likely to be replaced far more frequently than the lower traffic roads found within residential developments. Still, roads and sidewalks in residential developments require maintenance for repair work and climatic conditions such as freeze fracture. The consequence is that the impact of utilities infrastructure in the lower density neighborhoods will be significantly higher when considering maintenance and replacement.

There is an opportunity to reduce the lifecycle emissions of roads. Asphalt surfaces, for example, can incorporate a high volume of recycled aggregate such as recycled asphalt pavement, and can incorporate other waste material such as mixed-color glass cullet, fly ash, and recycled tires—this last example has the added benefit of reducing road noise. Concrete road surfaces and sidewalks can incorporate fly ash or ground granulated blast furnace slag (GGBFS) as low carbon replacements for ordinary Portland cement.

	MEGATALL	SUPERTALL	HIGH-RISE	MID-RISE	LOW-RISE	COURTYARD	THREE-FLAT	URBAN	SUBURBAN
TOTAL INFRASTRUCTURE (TONS CO2)	1,462	1,762	1,322	1,844	2,383	5,562	8,742	16,023	30,529
TOTAL BUILDING (TONS CO2)	238,971	221,195	104,191	109,038	138,891	135,934	145,276	148,800	162,403
% FROM INFRASTRUCTURE	0.6%	0.8%	1.3%	1.7%	1.7%	3.9%	5.7%	9.7%	17.7%

Table 17 Relative impact of infrastructure as a percentage of total embodied carbon

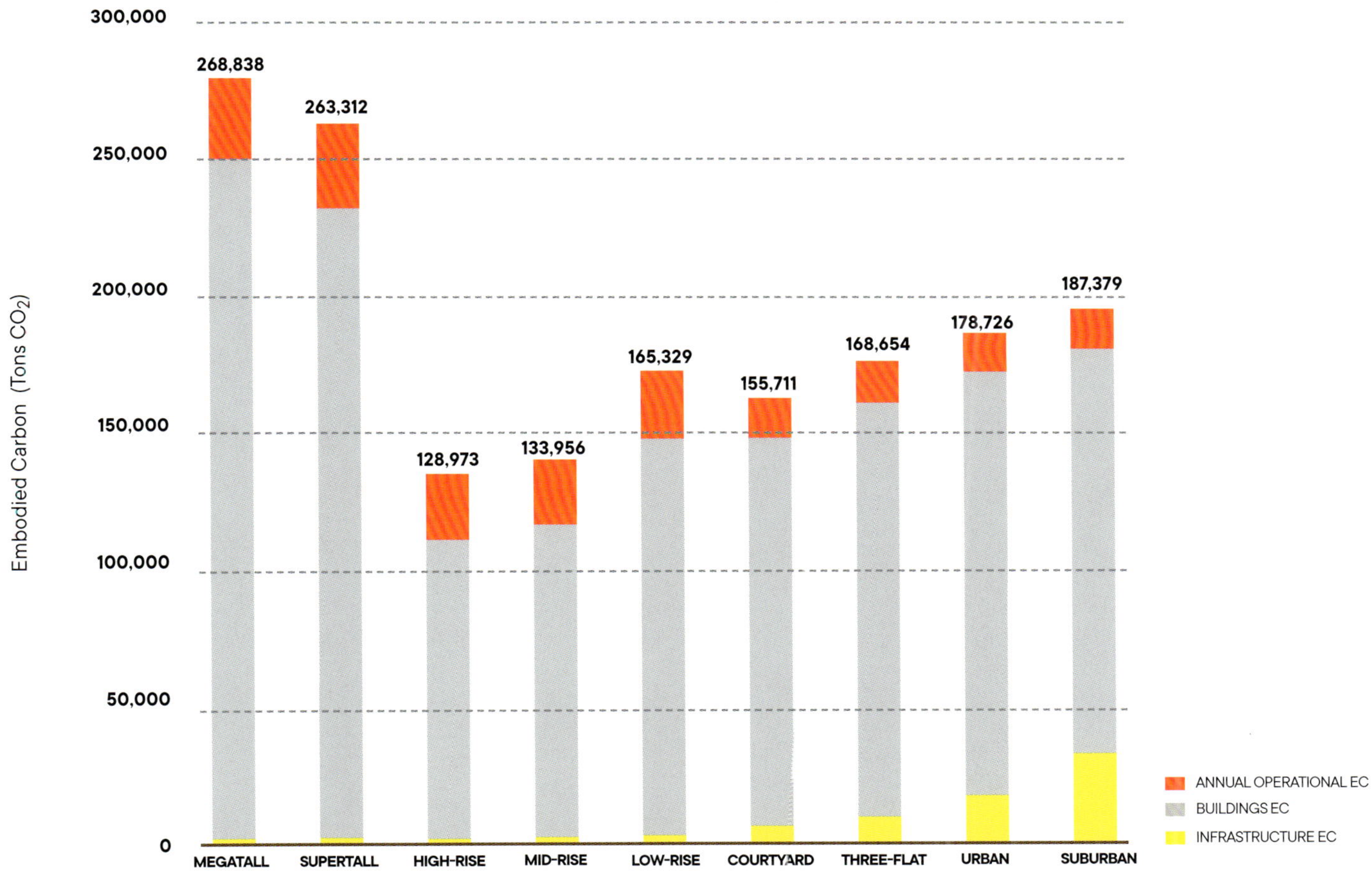

Figure 28 Carbon dioxide emissions summary for the nine community prototypes including: one-year operational emissions, embodied carbon for building materials, and embodied carbon for infrastructure.

LIFECYCLE CARBON EMISSIONS

The embodied carbon of the infrastructure and buildings was combined with operational emissions to produce an overall carbon emissions value for each prototype, as seen in Figure 28. Emissions from service vehicles were excluded from the lifecycle analysis. It is a statistically challenging task to compare the relative importance of embodied carbon versus operational emissions, one that requires a number of assumptions: What time frame should be considered for operational emissions? Is it the entire life of the building? Is it the period of time between major retrofits or renovations? Is it some other time length, perhaps determined by typically tenancy periods or some other factors? Once an operational time frame is decided, does it become standard between building prototypes or do we vary it for each type?

The lifecycle analysis uses an operational period of 40 years because it was a realistic compromise between the time period of when a megatall tower may need a facade and/or MEP systems retrofit—after which time a spike in embodied carbon and a reduction in operational emissions may be seen—and when a suburban single family home may require new wiring, new glazing, and/or new insulation. The study acknowledges the period is subjective and that would be impossible to satisfy every point of view.

Another important parameter is the grid emissions factor to use when calculating operational CO2 emissions. In Chicago, the grid emissions factor is 0.564 tonsCO2e/MWh (EPA eGRID 2018), which is higher than the United States average of 0.453 tonsCO2e/MWh. However, as the utilities companies continue to phase out older coal-fired power stations and replace them with newer more efficient designs fossil fuel powered plants or with renewable energy, the emissions factor will steadily fall and therefore realistically the grid emission factor at 40 years of operations will almost certainly be lower than in the first year of operations. We explore sensitivity to different grid emissions factors later in this chapter.

Table 18 shows embodied carbon data and operational emissions for each prototype over a 40-year period. This data is also shown graphically in Figure 29. Figure 30 presents the percentage of embodied carbon to operational carbon emissions. The proportion of embodied carbon emissions to operational emissions is not constant throughout the prototypes. It is significantly higher in the Megatall and Suburban Single-Family prototypes, where it is greater than 28% in both cases. The middle range in the other prototypes is approximately 12% to 17%.

This finding is perhaps better illustrated, also in Figure 30, by looking at the number of years it takes before the cumulative operation emission exceeds the embodied carbon emissions. Evaluating emissions in this way is an interesting approach. A designer strives to reduce energy demand, even if it is just from a cost saving perspective, however there is a tipping point where the cost (construction) of saving energy exceeds the actual savings over the lifetime of the building and this should be determined during design through a combination of lifecycle carbon analysis and lifecycle cost analysis. The analysis in this study introduces a second, less subtle tipping point that is more environmentally significant.

If a developer has a certain percentage of their construction cost uplift that they are prepared to accept, in order to reduce CO_2 emissions, then they may consider purchasing low-carbon materials, like rebar with a high-recycled content or concrete with a high percentage of cement replacement materials, instead of investing in energy-saving initiatives. This tipping point may be determined through a combination of the anticipated building lifetime, grid emissions factors, and product lifecycle analyses.

	MEGATALL	SUPERTALL	HIGH-RISE	MID-RISE	LOW-RISE	COURTYARD	THREE-FLAT	URBAN	SUBURBAN
EMBODIED CARBON (TONS CO2)	240,433	222,957	105,513	110,882	141.274	141,496	154,016	164,823	172,932
ANNUAL EMISSIONS ILLINOIS (TONS CO2)	28,405	29,845	23,460	23,075	24,055	14,215	14,639	13,903	14,447
40-YEAR OPERATION (TONS CO2)	1,136,188	1,193,800	938,382	922,993	962,182	568,598	585,546	556,107	577,871
% EMBODIED TO OPERATIONAL	17.5%	15.7%	10.1%	10.7%	12.8%	19.9%	20.8%	22.9%	23.0%
TIME FOR OPERATIONAL TO EXCEED EMBODIED (YEARS)	8.5	7.5	4.5	4.8	5.9	10.0	10.5	11.9	12.0

Table 18 Ratio of embodied carbon to 40-year operational emissions

SENSITIVITY TO GRID EMISSIONS FACTORS

When preparing a carbon-reduction strategy for a building or a master plan, it is important to understand the influence of grid-emissions factors, often referred to as carbon intensity of electricity. As national energy grids improve (in terms of carbon intensity) the relationship between embodied carbon and 40-year operational emissions alters, with the share of embodied carbon increasing.

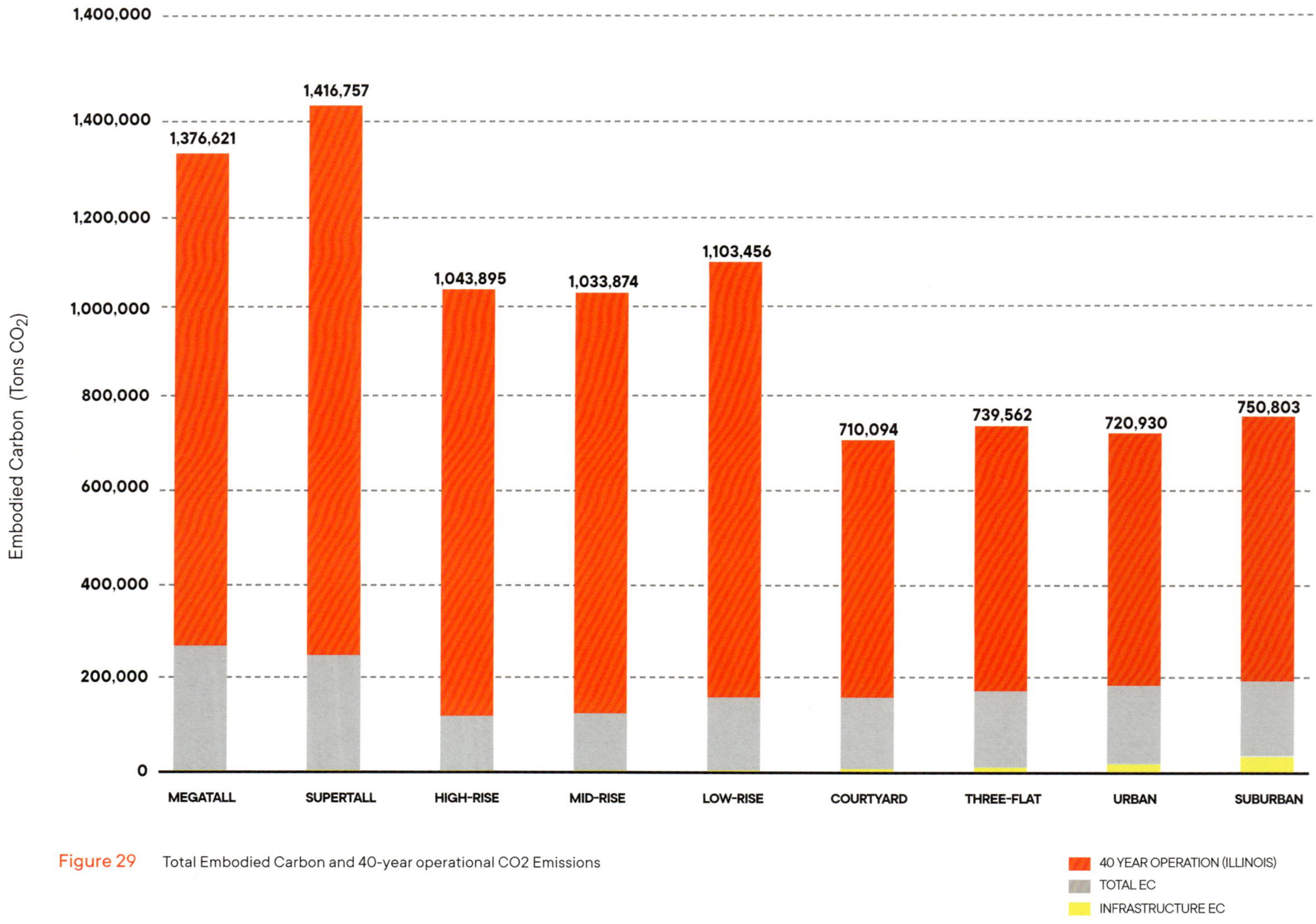

Figure 29 Total Embodied Carbon and 40-year operational CO2 Emissions

Figure 31 shows how the so-called payback period—the length of time taken for operational emissions to exceed embodied carbon—varies for countries having different grid emissions factors. For example, it shows that in the United States a megatall building that operates using energy from the grid, having an emissions factor of 0.453 kgCO2/kWh, would require 10 years to exceed the embodied carbon. The same building built using exactly the same materials and operated in the same climate zcne but with an emissions intensity as low as that of France would take 43 years, which is approximately the time it takes for major components to need replacement. In Quebec, Canada, it would take over 100 years for operational emissions to exceed embodied carbon.

Clearly, if a developer is interested in reporting carbon emissions over a 40-year life cycle, then reducing embodied carbon would be the higher priority. On the other hand, when building a 38 or 65 story building, even in a location where the emissions factor of the grid is relatively low, energy saving will still have the greatest impact on lifecycle emissions.

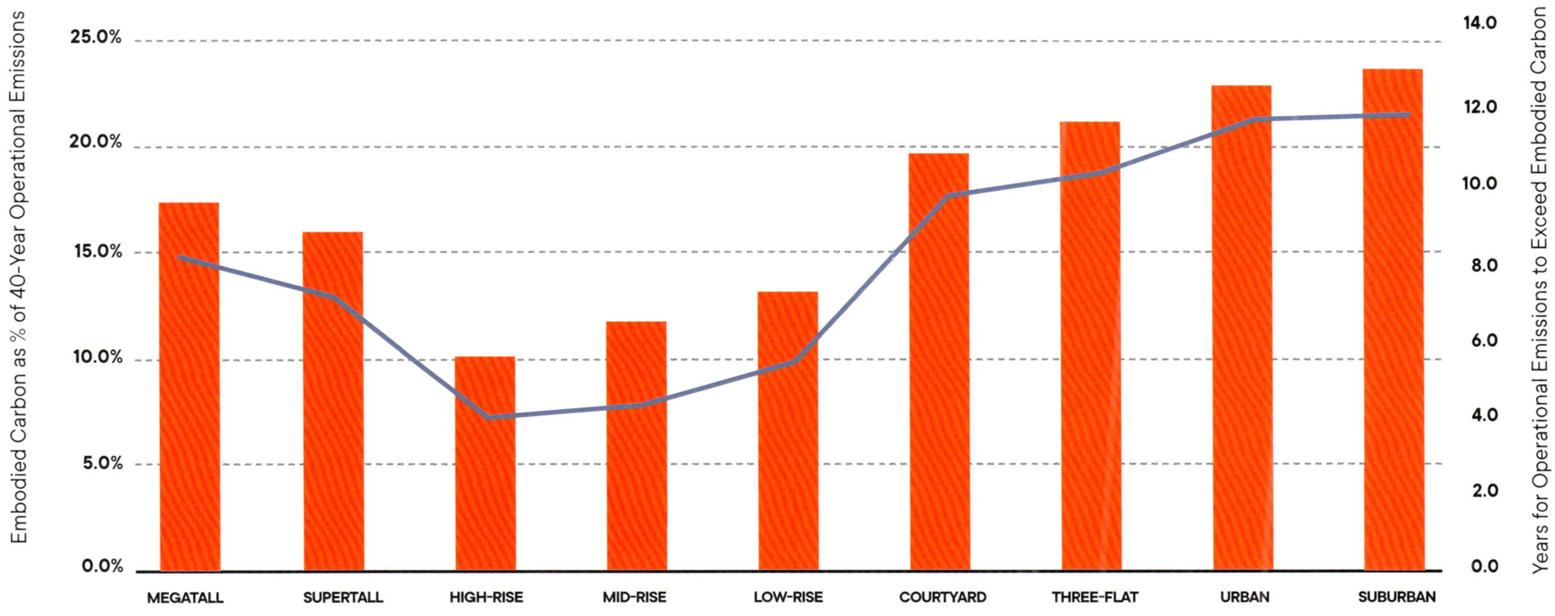

Figure 30 Embodied carbon as a percentage of 40 years operational CO2 emissions and payback period in years for embodied carbon

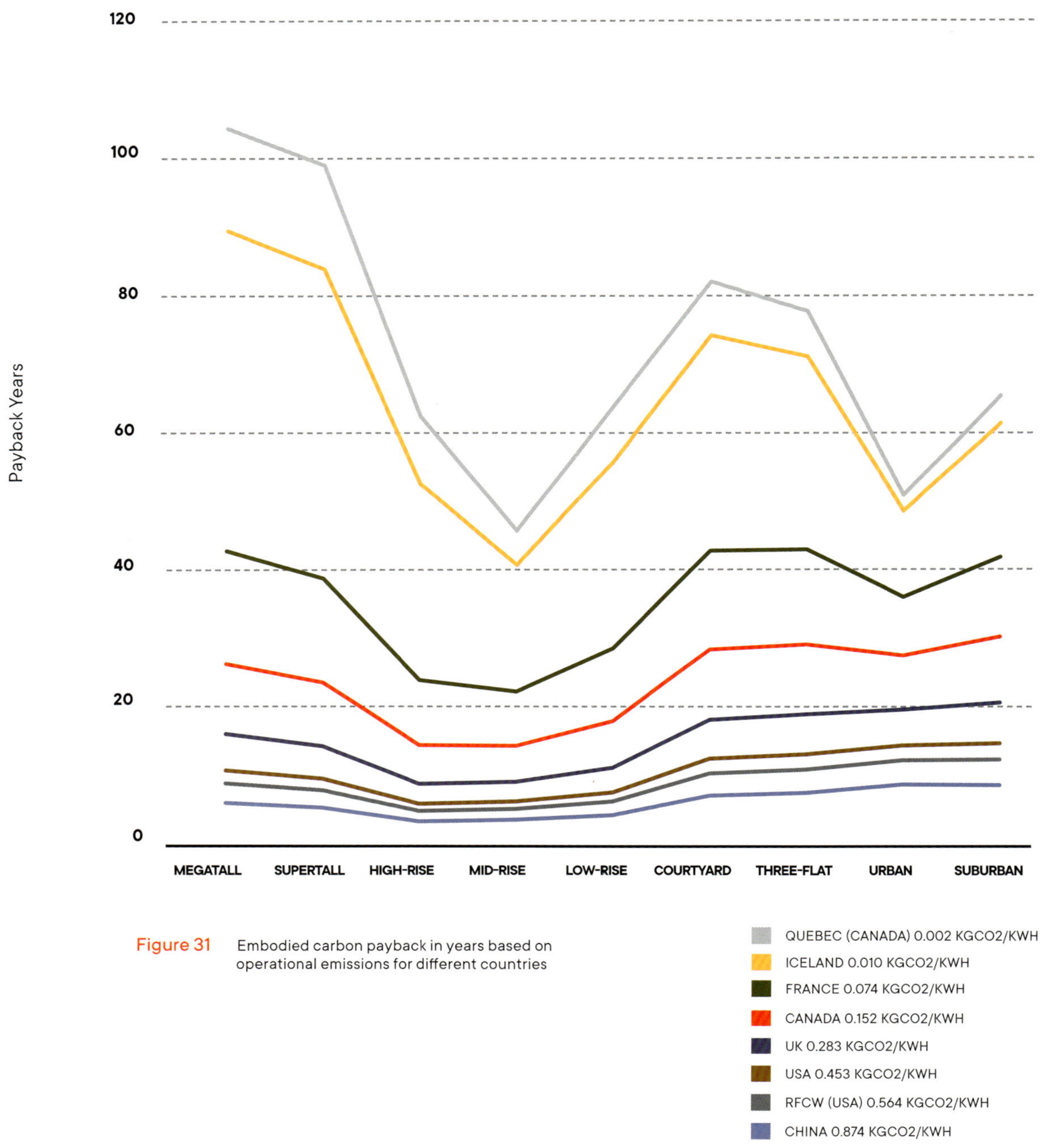

Figure 31 Embodied carbon payback in years based on operational emissions for different countries

CARBON SEQUESTRATION

The sequestration of atmospheric carbon dioxide by grass lawns has become an increasingly discussed, and researched, topic. According to the Lawn Institute, there is a total of 10.1 million hectares (25 million acres) of cultivated lawn in the United States. The vast majority of this area is privately or professionally managed and ranges from required mowing to more intense irrigation, fertilization, and professional management. Each maintenance regime has some associated carbon dioxide emissions, nevertheless, it is estimated that lawns with a minimal maintenance regime of mowing only, sequester an average of 46g of carbon/m^2/year.

Home management, which includes mowing, irrigation, and fertilization, sequesters an average of 124.5g of carbon/m^2/year. A professionally maintained turf sequesters an average of 129 g of carbon/m^2/year (Zirkle et al. 2011). The same study discusses carbon emissions associated with lawn maintenance. Minimal maintenance has an emissions rate of 20.6g of carbon/m^2/year; home management has an emissions rate of 43.9g of carbon/m^2/year; professional management has an emissions rate 77.3 g of carbon/m^2/year.

METHODS

For the comparison, this study assumes that single family homes are maintained by the owner, that the green space associated with multi-tenant buildings is maintained with a more intense professional management regime, and that the open space surrounding the building plots is maintained by mowing only—similar to the way that school fields or public open spaces are managed. The study does not address other greenhouse gas emissions, nor does it address the impact of fertilizer and pesticide applications contaminating ground water or the surrounding environment.

The inter-governmental Panel on Climate Change methodology suggests that 2% of nitrogen added as fertilizer is lost to the atmosphere as N_2O, a greenhouse gas with 310 times the global warming potential of CO_2. It is likely therefore that intensely managed areas sequester less carbon and fertilizer run-off, and the potential for contributing to eutrophication of water bodies could be an issue that requires addressing.

BUILDING PROTOTYPE	GREEN SPACE (M²)	CARBON SEQUESTRATION RATE (G C/M²)	OPEN SPACE AVAILABLE (M²)	CARBON SEQUESTRATION RATE (G C/M²)	NET SEQUESTRATION RATE (G C/M²)	TOTAL ATMOSPHERIC CO2 SEQUESTRATION (KGCO2)
SUBURBAN SINGLE FAMILY	1,956,769	80.6	0	25.4	157,716	578
URBAN SINGLE FAMILY	537,953	80.6	1,689,963	25.4	86,284	316
THREE-FLAT	147,014	51.7	2,481,729	25.4	70,637	259
COURTYARD	88,920	51.7	2,644,137	25.4	71,758	263
LOW-RISE	0	51.7	2,881,002	25.4	73,177	268
MID-RISE	0	51.7	2,921,629	25.4	74,209	272
HIGH-RISE	0	51.7	2,930,607	25.4	74,437	273
SUPERTALL	13,359	51.7	2,930,607	25.4	75,128	276
MEGATALL	11,464	51.7	2,940,241	25.4	75,275	276

Table 19 Carbon sequestration by prototype

GREAT CITY CHENGDU
Chengdu, China
Adrian Smith + Gordon Gill Architecture
Proposed 2012
1.3k^2 | 100,000 people

CONCLUSION

The RESIDENSITY study examines nine building prototypes: Megatall, Supertall, High-Rise, Mid-Rise, Low-Rise, Courtyard, Three-Flat, Urban Single-Family, and Suburban Single-Family. While these typologies do not cover all the possible housing options, they are a strong cross section of the built world and embody a methodology that yields empirical data to help to answer the question:

What is the ideal density for the built environment?

However, this is a complex question, and although there are solid conclusions that result from the study, it would not be accurate, or realistic, to simply end the analysis there. Many factors, beyond the data, also need to be considered.

WHAT THE DATA TELLS US

According to the data gathered, the Courtyard prototype is the most efficient residential building—in terms of its lifecycle carbon emissions—because it has the lowest operational energy usage over 40 years, which, with the grid emissions factor chosen for this study, represents the bulk of lifecycle emissions. There are several explanations for this: The Courtyard prototype is efficient, in terms of its leasable-to-built area, meaning there are less shared or unoccupied spaces needed to be heated or cooled; it has a low window-to-wall ratio; it is largely shaded by its neighbors; it has no elevators; and the Courtyard prototype needs no booster pumps for increasing water pressure. The next most efficient prototypes are the Urban Single-Family, followed by the Three-Flat, followed by the Suburban Single-Family.

This conclusion however, only applies if the prototype is built following ASHRAE 90.1 (2010) as energy code and the electricity supplied has a relatively high grid emissions factor. The trend across all global planning authorities is toward the implementation of more stringent energy codes, driving operational energy demand ever lower. Simultaneously, the energy grids in all developed countries are becoming less carbon intense as renewable energy systems and cleaner fossil fuel derived power replaces older carbon intense electricity generation facilities.

If we reanalyze lifecycle emissions assuming a 10% reduction in heating and cooling demand against ASHRAE 90.1 (2010)—in line with likely code improvements up to 2020—and a grid dominated by renewable energy (for example Canada, at 0.152 kgCO2/kWh), then the High-Rise prototype advances to the third best performer, in terms of lifecycle emissions (Figure 32). The reality is that as energy performance improves, embodied carbon increases due to increased wall thickness—thicker insulation, deeper studs / mullions, double to triple glazing etc. We would therefore expect to see the difference in lifecycle emissions between the Courtyard, the Three-Flat and the High-Rise become even narrower.

The above discussion does not consider the environmental benefits of using less land. One of the fundamental and most obvious benefits of densification is that land no longer needs to be used for housing and can be used for other purposes. In Chapter 3 we see that considerable amounts of land are saved through higher density vertical development. Comparing the High-Rise with the Courtyard, the former uses 89% (28 ha) less land. This land has a real estate value and the capacity to generate power through renewable energy, grow crops, and provide habitat in support of natural biodiversity, among other uses.

Perhaps the question should not be what single typology is best, from an environmental standpoint, but what combination works best, and in this case, the answer is a combination of High-Rise buildings and Courtyard or Three-Flat typologies.

DESIGN CONSIDERATIONS FOR SPECIFIC BUILDINGS

Designers can spearhead solutions to improve the performance of each prototype. This study is based on the mechanical systems, exterior wall systems, infrastructure, and structural elements that are required for each specific building type and, while it is possible to improve the baseline assumptions for a site or design, there may be trade-offs in qualitative elements like the amount of glass used or in energy-related and cost concerns such as initial cost and embodied energy of materials used. In addition, as technology improves and it becomes more practical, designers can start to consider buildings that generate their own clean energy.

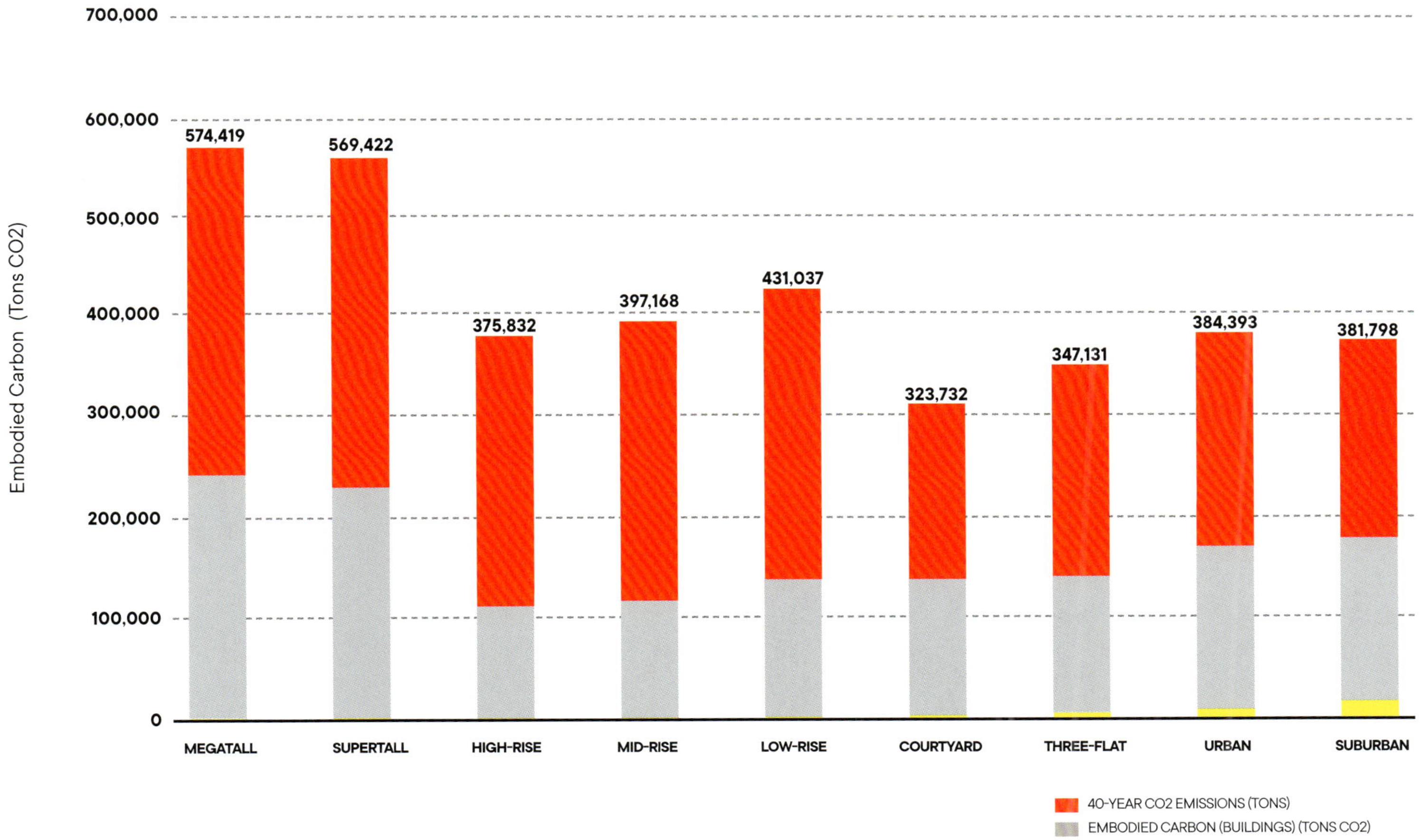

Figure 32 Carbon Emissions: Low EF And Energy Efficient

A well-designed high-rise building can have a lower carbon footprint than a courtyard or three-flat building that is not designed to be efficient or is in an isolated area that requires more infrastructure. In a similar way, a single-family house in the suburbs or a single-family house in the city can perform better than a courtyard building—if it is designed to be high performing.

The study concludes that overall, the Courtyard and the Three-Flat have the smallest carbon footprints, but we attest that it is possible for the other typologies to exceed these prototypes if they are well-designed. In conclusion, some of the typologies are inherently more energy-intensive than others but this can be reduced through designing to more stringent energy standards.

QUALITATIVE FACTORS

When drawing conclusions from this study it is also important to consider qualitative factors like the lifestyle of each prototype. A users' basic needs, such as social and economic status, desires and aspirations, and stages of life, will determine the best residential prototype. The Courtyard or the Three-Flat may be the most ideal typologies, in terms of carbon footprint, but they are not considered preferred or practical for everyone in the population, nor are they available in every location. The building itself depends on the assumption that people are comfortable living close together and in an urban or semi-urban area, without a private yard. Disadvantages such as crowding, noise, or privacy may prevent some people from choosing to share a building with others such.

While it is relatively common for young people to choose to live in an apartment building during a certain stage in their life, it becomes less common as people begin to raise families or become unable to use stairs as they get older. Not everyone wants to live in a medium-density urban neighborhood where courtyard buildings are often located. Some people enjoy the high density and amenities offered by high-rise living; others prefer the open spaces and tranquility of the suburbs. Qualitative factors like traffic, availability of good schools, social factors, cultural demographics, and crime inform choices that are related to density. It would be beneficial if these choices were accounted for when designing new buildings and new cities.

OCCUPANT BEHAVIOR AND UNIT SIZE

It is important to account for the fact that within the nine prototypes studied, the residential units themselves are assumed to be the same size at 150m^2. Additional non-occupied gross area is accounted for, which is attributed to common areas of the building or—in the case of the Suburban Single Family—the garage space. In this way, the typologies are treated as equally occupied. Using the same criteria, the carbon emissions presented are averages in a society where each unit is 150m^2 and has an equal number of people occupying the unit. Although the actual carbon emissions per capita and per building for each typology will vary when based on a variety of factors, the comparison presented in this study is valid.

It is possible that certain prototypes have advantages over others in terms of their typical use by the occupants and their unit size due to factors such as culture or land value of a specific area. For example, the Supertall or Suburban Single-Family prototypes have a higher carbon footprint than other typologies. While this can be examined through the occupant's energy usage, the type and amount of amenities and infrastructure typically found in those buildings and neighborhoods, should also be examined. It would require further study to fully incorporate occupant behavior within each prototype into this density study.

In terms of energy usage, it would be more efficient if the world's population was willing to live in higher-density areas, regardless of which typology they chose as a residence. But in terms of quality of life, luxury is often directly related to having access to a large amount of space—or a comparatively large amount of space, considering the cost of living in a certain residential market.

LAND VALUE, NATURAL GEOGRAPHIC, AND OTHER ECONOMIC FACTORS

Throughout history, urban density has developed organically, based on supply and demand, which increases land value. Developers build the largest, most dense buildings in the areas that have the highest land values, and this is a factor in both the built and natural environment. High-density areas are driven by factors such as existing surrounding density; low availability of buildable land in a desirable area; proximity to certain amenities; proximity to geographic features; and the high cost of building in certain geographic areas, like small islands or mountainous regions. At the less dense end of the spectrum, land value is also created by designing lower-density communities that feature generous open land, large lot sizes, and parks and other amenities, as well as their proximity to a major urban job center.

The prototypes that are the most carbon-efficient—the Courtyard, Low-Rise, and Three-Flat—are more common where land value and incomes are in the medium to low range, unlike with the most carbon-intensive prototypes: the Megatall, Supertall, or Suburban Single Family. While this is not always the case, it is more common for a person with a lower income to occupy an apartment in a low-rise building, than it is for a higher income earner. This is primarily because these typologies are lower-cost to build, offer smaller unit sizes, and have some qualitative disadvantages related to their design. Ideally, developments accommodate users of all social and economic groups but currently it is not practical to assume a city plan that lacks a variety of density satisfies the needs of all of its users, or that it will satisfy the business-driven economic factors related to the local real estate market.

THE VALUE OF VARIETY

Another factor is that there is not one sole building typology that is appropriate for all geographic areas—or for all residents. If every building was a three-flat or lower, it would result in a significant amount of urban sprawl, higher commute times, and a lack of variety in the building environment and in its ability to accommodate a diverse group of users. The city would be so uniform that the quality of the urban environment itself would likely be lower. The distribution of amenities or commercial centers in the city would not have a natural relationship to the density.

When buildings are capped at a certain size throughout a city, density typically begins to evolve organically through higher value properties and smaller unit sizes closer to the areas that are more desirable. Although this model exists in some areas of the world, it is not economically advantageous for owners of property, nor is it the most efficient for planners of commercial centers, open spaces, amenities, or modern urban transportation infrastructure.

Urban environments benefit from a variety of density, which in turn encourages residents from a variety of ages and income levels and thereby a diverse workforce that can support a mixed-use environment. While there are residential building typologies that are less carbon intensive than others, this fact cannot be looked at in a vacuum without considering the overall urban environment that includes transportation infrastructure, amenities, geographic features, and uses. The lowest overall carbon footprints for urban areas, and most qualitatively interesting, varied and desirable urban environments, can and should be created through reasonable allowance for different densities within a city.

GREAT CITY CHENGDU
Chengdu, China
Adrian Smith + Gordon Gill Architecture
Design completed 2012
$1.3k^2$ | 100,000 people

PROTOTYPE CITY

The GREAT City Master Plan was developed by AS+GG as a new city for 100,000 people outside of Chengdu, China. The plan represents best practices for a medium-density city with a calculated mix of prototypes. While the Courtyard and High-Rise prototypes are both represented, a mix of buildings from Three-Flat to Megatall towers ensure the community is energy-efficient. As an ideal mixed-use city, the building design guidelines designate each building's orientation based solar exposure, energy use, and possible energy generation. Taller buildings, which are more energy-intensive to begin with, have stricter energy standards for their construction to reduce their carbon footprint. The city includes a wide variety of functions and places a high importance on walkability. The program includes residential at all densities, as well as commercial and office, retail, elementary and higher education, medical, hospitality, and cultural. Mixed-use buildings are integrated within residential developments and occur at a variety of scales, located throughout the city so that all residential district are within walking distance of jobs, or basic services.

Major streets are designed around geographic features. Residential areas are designed to allow occupants to benefit from the geographic features of the area, which in this case include the natural hills and valleys related to the original landscape and local river network. Major streets are also are zoned to have iconic or cultural buildings that increase the character and sense of place of the city. Public parks increase access to recreational space, with additional natural open areas maintained around the geographic features. The plan calls for city zoning to deny future sprawl of protected areas, so that natural light and views are preserved and so that potential community agriculture areas can be used to grow local produce. The plan also specifies that major streets and the commercial city center should consist of buildings equivalent to the High-Rise prototype, which surround the most valuable commercial areas and are located near the central transit hub that has direct connections to the main regional train line.

In conclusion, we have found that the solution to the question of density is not about identifying one ideal density for the built environment. It is about designing intelligently within a range of densities that are appropriate for the specific place that is being designed. While human behavior is not controlled by building design, intelligent design can help drive human behavior so that it is easier to make choices and live in a way that is more environmentally responsible. Designers throughout the world are striving to create the most ideal city of the future in order to increase sustainability of the building environment, as well as the quality of human life. It is our hope that this study provides data and analysis that can contribute to wider critical thought toward this ultimate goal.

Brownstone D and Golob T. (2009). The impact of residential density on vehicle usage and energy consumption. Journal of urban Economics. 65:1, 91–98.

Buehler r. and Pucher J. (2012) Cycling to work in 90 large American cities: new evidence on the role of bike paths and lanes. Transportation. 39, 409–432.

Carbonbrief (2017). Mapped: The world's largest CO2 importers and exporters. Accessed September 2018 from https://www.carbonbrief.org/mapped-worlds-largest-co2-importers-exporters

CAIT (2015). CAIT Climate Data Explorer. 2015. Washington, DC: World Resources Institute. Accessed September 2018. http://cait.wri.org

Eichholtz P., Kok N. and Quigley J. M. (2013). The Economics of Green Building. Review of Economics and Statistics. Vol. 95 No. 1. 50–63.

Etheridge D., Steele L., Langenfelds R., Francey R., Barnola J. and Morgan V. (1996) Natural and anthropogenic changes in atmospheric CO2 over the last 1000 years from air in Antarctic ice and firn. Journal of Geophysical Research: Atmospheres. 101. D2. 4115–4128.

Farmland Information Center (2018). Farms under threat – acres developed by land cove/use 1992–2012. https://www.farmlandinfo.org/statistics. Accessed August 2018.

Friedman M., Powell K., Hutwagner L., Graham L. and Teague W. (2001) Impact of changes in transportation and commuting behaviors during the 1996 Summer Olympic Games in Atlanta on air quality and childhood asthma. JAMA 2001; 285: 897–905.

Fuerst F. and McAllister P. (2011) Green Noise or Green Value? Measuring the Effects of Environmental Certification on Office Values. Real Estate Economics, 39:1, 45–69.

Hanam B., Finch G. and Hepting C. (2011). Metered calibrated energy simulation of high rise residential buildings: lessons learned, presented at the 13th Canadian conference on buildings science and technology, Winnipeg, MB.

REFERENCES

Holtzclaw J., Clear R., Dittmar H., Goldstein D and Haas P. (2002) Location Efficiency: Neighborhood and Socio-Economic Characteristics Determine Auto Ownership and Use—Studies in Chicago, Los Angeles and San Francisco. Transportation Planning and Technology, Vol. 25(1),pp 1–27.

ICCT, The International Council on Clean Transportation (2017) Impacts of world-class vehicle efficiency and emissions regulations in select G20 countries. Briefing paper. Accessed from www.theict.org.

Illinois Department of Agriculture (2017) Fertilizer tonnage total by County 2017. Accessed from https://www2.illinois.gov/sites/agr/Plants/Fertilizer/Pages/Fertilizer-Reports.aspx.

Illinois Farm bureau (2017). Information Research Center-Farm and Food Facts '17. http://www.ilfb.org/media/1453/2017-farm-and-food-facts-pdf.pdf

International Union of Railways (UIC) (2011) High Speed Rail and sustainability. UIC, Paris.

IRENA (2018). Renewable power generation costs in 2017. International Renewable Energy Agency, Abu Dhabi, United Arab Emirates.

Mohlenbrook, R. (1986) Guide to the vascular flora of Illinois. Southern Illinois university Press. Carbondale, Illinois.

Mumm R., Goldsmith P., Rausch K. and Stein H. (2014). Land usage attributed to corn ethanol production in the United States: sensitivity to technological advances in corn grain yield, ethanol conversion, and co-product utilization. Biotechnology for Biofuels 7: 61. Published online 2014 Apr 12.

NOAA (2018) Recent Monthly Average Mauna Loa CO2, Accessed September 2018. https://www.esrl.noaa.gov/gmd/ccgg/trends/

Papadimitriou G., Ntziachristos L., Wuetrich P., Notter B., Keller M., Fridell E., Winnes H., Styhre L. and Sjodin A. (2013). TRACCS - Transport data collection supporting the quantitative analysis of measures relating to transport and climate change. EMISIA Report No. 13.RE.025.V1, http://traccs.emisia.com, accessed on.

Pew Social Trends (2018). Shrinking share of Americans in rural counties. http://www.pewsocialtrends.org/2018/05/22/demographic-and-economic-trends-in-urban-suburban-and-rural-communities/. Accessed August 2018.

Reichardt A., Fuerst F., Rottke N. B. and Zietz J. (2012). Sustainable Building Certification and the Rent Premium: A Panel Data Approach. Journal of Real Estate Research. Vol. 34 No. 1. pp. 99–126.

U.S. Department of Transport (2010) Public Transportation's Role in Responding to Climate Change 2010.

U.S. Environmental Protection Agency (2018). Inventory of U.S. greenhouse gas emissions and sinks: 1990–2016.

U.S. Postal Service (2010). Audit Report – Delivery Vehicle Replacement Strategy (Report Number DA-AR-10-005). USPS

Warburton, D., Nicol C., and Bredin S. (2006). Health benefits of physical activity: the evidence. CMAJ. Vol. 174, Issue 6.

West J. and Haake D. (2014) Estimation of Carbon Sequestration in a Restored Tallgrass Prairie Ecosystem in Eastern Missouri. Missouri Botanical Garden.

Wiley J., Benefield J. and Johnson K. (2010). Green Design and the Market for Commercial Office Space. The Journal of Real Estate Finance and Economics. Vol. 41 No. 2. pp. 228–243.

Zhou Y., Wu Y., Yang L., Fu L., He K., Wang S., Hao J., Chen J. and Li, C. (2010) The impact of transportation control measures on emission reductions during the 2008 Olympic Games in Beijing, China. Atmos. Environ. 44, 285–293.

PROJECT TEAM

ADRIAN SMITH + GORDON GILL ARCHITECTURE

Sara Beardsley, Technical Director
Christopher Drew, Director of Sustainability
Katrina Fernandez Nova, Senior Designer
Robert Forest, Partner
Gordon Gill, Partner
Jocelyn Moriarty, Lead Communications
Adrian D. Smith, Partner
Richard Wilson, City Design Director
Xi Yi, Architect

FORMER ADRIAN SMITH + GORDON GILL ARCHITECTURE

Craig Burton, Associate Principal, Interface Engineering
Donald W Davies, President, Magnusson Klemencic Associates
Keara Fanning, Central Region Sustainability Practice Lead, Jones Lang LaSalle
Rezvan Farahany, Architectural Designer, Goettsch Partners
Alex Gormley, Project Designer, Drawing Dept Architecture & Design
Kenneth Griffin, Building Scientist at Environmental Systems Design
Peter J. Kindel, Director of Urban Design and Planning, Skidmore, Owings & Merrill
Soeun Lee, Associate Urban Designer, AECOM
Suncica Milosevic, Doctoral Student at University of Massachusetts Amherst
Tashio Martinez, Architectural Designer, Goettsch Partners
Natalia Quintanilla, Building Science Specialist, Arup
Daniel Ramos, Architectural Designer, Goettsch Partners
Dennis Rehill, Associate, Henry J. Lyons Architects

CONSULTING PARTNERS

Arup Chicago, Civil Engineering Consultant
John Viise, Structural Engineering Consultant, DeSimone Consulting Engineers

INTRODUCTION

Photograph by Marchello74 (page 8);

Photograph by HomoCosmicos (page 16);

Photograph of Vorschlag zur Bebauung der Berliner City', Ludwig Hilberseimer, 1929 (page 18);

Photograph by Gizmodo (page 16);

Photograph by unknown, public domain (page 19);

All renderings and drawings ©Adrian Smith + Gordon Gill Architecture.

PROTOTYPES

Photograph by Tim Griffith (page 28);

Photograph by James Steinkamp (page 31);

Photograph by HG Esch (page 31);

Photograph by Hedrich Blessing Photographers (page 34);

Photograph by Fougeron Architecture (page 45);

Photograph by Jocelyn Moriarty (page 48, 49, 52, 53);

Photograph by Jodie Johnson (page 56);

Photograph by Adrian Smith (page 57);

All renderings and drawings ©Adrian Smith + Gordon Gill Architecture.

LAND USE

Photograph by Tianjin 4k (page 60–61);

Photograph by Dan Prat (page 62);

Photograph by Getty Images (page 87);

Photograph by Project Eden (page 90);

Photograph by Earth Observatory (page 92–93)

All renderings and drawings ©Adrian Smith + Gordon Gill Architecture.

IMAGERY

ENERGY

Photograph by Hedrich Blessing Photographers (page 94);

Photograph by ThyssenKrup (page 103)

All renderings and drawings ©Adrian Smith + Gordon Gill Architecture.

TRANSPORT

Steve Geer (page 126–127)

All renderings and drawings ©Adrian Smith + Gordon Gill Architecture.

CARBON

Rudmer Zwerver (pages 132–133); David Dods (page 142)

All renderings and drawings ©Adrian Smith + Gordon Gill Architecture.

CONCLUSION

All renderings and drawings ©Adrian Smith + Gordon Gill Architecture.